ROUTLEDGE LIBR
CHINESE LITERAT

MW00785759

Volume 7

CHINESE FAIRY TALES
AND FOLK TALES

CHINESE FAIRY TALES AND FOLK TALES

WOLFRAM EBERHARD

Routledge
Taylor & Francis Group

LONDON AND NEW YORK

First published in 1937 by Kegan Paul, Trench, Trubner & Co. Ltd.

This edition first published in 2022
by Routledge
4 Park Square, Milton Park, Abingdon, Oxon OX14 4RN

and by Routledge
605 Third Avenue, New York, NY 10158

Routledge is an imprint of the Taylor & Francis Group, an informa business

© 1937

British Library Cataloguing in Publication Data
A catalogue record for this book is available from the British Library

ISBN: 978-0-367-11183-0 (Set)
ISBN: 978-1-032-24447-1 (Volume 7) (hbk)
ISBN: 978-1-032-24449-5 (Volume 7) (pbk)
ISBN: 978-1-003-27863-4 (Volume 7) (ebk)

DOI: 10.4324/9781003278634

Publisher's Note
The publisher has gone to great lengths to ensure the quality of this reprint but points out that some imperfections in the original copies may be apparent.

Disclaimer
The publisher has made every effort to trace copyright holders and would welcome correspondence from those they have been unable to trace.

CHINESE FAIRY TALES
AND FOLK TALES

Collected and Translated by

WOLFRAM EBERHARD

LONDON

KEGAN PAUL, TRENCH, TRUBNER & CO. LTD.

BROADWAY HOUSE: 68–74 CARTER LANE, E.C.

1937

Translated from the German
By Desmond Parsons

First published . . . 1937

Printed in Great Britain by T. and A. Constable Ltd
at the University Press, Edinburgh

CONTENTS

Contents

vi

Contents

INTRODUCTION

THE fairy tale lives. It lives on the tables of men, as they sit sipping their wine. It lives with children, as they play in the streets; and with women in the court-yards. It even lives in the newspapers. Formerly it was said: 'There are no fairy tales in China! The Chinese are far too sober a race.' Then appeared the first books to aim at translating fairy tales—for the most part they were extracts from novels, plays, or even from classical literature—and a strange world of demons and foxes, of wise emperors and virtuous women, was revealed. But it was much later that the real fairy tale appeared through the missionaries, and then the Chinese produced their old tales, which were revealed as something well known, so to speak sister to our own fairy tale. Almost all our most charming characters appear, in another dress it is true, and with other forms and customs, but they are none the less related. There is no division between them and us. We find the same naïve atmo-sphere, where the Emperor is depicted as a rich peasant, where the fool carries off the prize, the step-mother ill-treats the daughter, and the wanderer departs for the other end of the world. Men and gods, animals and flowers, are all one, they are brothers. One helps the other. They speak—they live. The whole of nature is alive.

To-day the fairy tale is as alive as thousands of years ago. Not painfully in books, as with us, but openly in the streets, where one meets it every day. A short time ago there was a report in the paper about a police official in the West City of Peking. He suddenly fell ill and

had to go to the hospital. While there he had a dream:
an emissary of the God of Heaven appeared to him and
told him that he had been appointed City God of a
Temple outside the West gate. The official begged to
be excused from taking up the post at present, because
he still had his parents to look after, but the emissary
informed him that the appointment could not be re-
scinded, but that he would be allowed a few more days
to arrange his affairs. The official regained his health,
but a year later he fell ill again and died without any
apparent reason. At the same time a man, who lived
near the aforesaid temple, had a dream, in which he
learnt that the new City God would arrive the next day
and that in his former life he had been such and such a
man with such and such a name. Without ever having
known the dead policeman, he suddenly knew his name,
and all about his appointment. This account appeared
in the newspapers a year ago. And if you look through
old books you see that the same thing occurred a hundred
years ago. In every district you find this legend current
and every day a new legend or fairy tale is created.
Really they are not even composed, for the necessary
spiritual background is still there and the fairy-tale
mind still exists. And anything strange or inexplicable
that occurs is transposed, transformed into a fairy tale,
a legend, a saga, a joke, or an anecdote. It is not an
invention. It is fanciful thought, creative thought.

Fanciful thought is all-embracing thought. It does
not halt before daily life, nor before beast, man, nor god.
Fairy tales, sagas, legends, fables, jokes, anecdotes, all
mingle. They are imbued with the same spirit. They
take birth from the same impetus. We cannot separate
them and must not separate them, and so we include
every tale in which their simple, conclusive mode of
thought has found expression.

The tales which follow differ from all other collections
in this way; they are perhaps not always so beautiful

xii

in outward form as others, but they are ' Chinese,' they have the characteristics of the Chinese people. Former collections contained tales heard by Europeans in China and retold by them. The European unwittingly told as 'Chinese' a tale half European in thought and often entirely European in form. For his own thoughts and ideas fuse with the story. This will be made quite clear by a comparison of the tales that follow with others. The difference is plainest in the case of the humorous tales. I had a collection of about eight hundred of these, from which to choose, but I only selected twenty-four. I know that in translation hardly one of the remaining seven hundred and seventy could make the reader laugh. By considerable transposition and alteration even they could be made ' European,' they could be made to appeal to our reader—and then the Chinese element in them would have disappeared. So they have remained un-chosen, in company with many other things which could only have been made effective by falsifying their original values. I am bringing out shortly a survey of the whole mass of Chinese fairy and folk tales of all kinds, in a scientific work of over three thousand tales.

Further, many of the previous collections of tales do not contain fairy and folk tales at all, but, to a great extent, the retold stories of plays, short stories, novels. Others introduce translations from short stories and novels as folk tales. The difference between the true tale and the 'art' tale or the novel is tremendous. I have made comparisons over a wide field. Many of the art tales or short stories contain no fairy- or folk-tale motif at all, in spite of outward similarity. Thus, most of the fox stories so popular in Chinese literature are pure art products. There are only a few fox stories among the folk tales, which usually turn out very differently. Other art tales or short stories contain fairy-tale motifs, as, for example, many of the short stories in the collection Liao-chai chih-i by P'u Sung-ling (translated by L. Giles: *Strange Stories from a Chinese Studio*), or the Tse-pu-yü collections by Yüan Mei or the Hsiao-tou-p'eng by Tseng Yen-tung. But in them the fairy-tale motif is almost always transposed in a way characteristic of them. At the least, a moral is added to the end of them. So these art tales and short tales—and still less the novels and plays—cannot be counted as fairy tales, and form a group of their own side by side with our fairy and folk tales.

The present collection of tales is not diluted fare. In them it is the peasant, the child, the old woman, or even the student, who is speaking. I have taken them down as they were related to me, as nearly word for word as possible, and I have only altered enough to be sure that a fairy tale appears and not a scientific treatise. Many of them have been published in Chinese by my friends and colleagues, in small books or minor periodicals, most of which are out of print. Many have never appeared, and for these I am indebted to my friend Ts'ao Sung-yeh, a native of Chekiang and a notable folk-lorist. To him I want to express my heartfelt thanks. I am also very deeply indebted to Mr. Desmond Parsons, who as translator has so very kindly given me great help.

WOLFRAM EBERHARD.

May 3rd, 1937.

PART I
FAIRY TALES

1. *The Great Flood*

IN a mountain village lived a woman and her son. She was more than fifty years old, and her son, Chou Ch'eng, exactly nineteen. They were very poor and earned their living by collecting firewood.

Every morning Chou Ch'eng hung his axe on his carrying pole and went into the mountains. By midday he had collected a large load of firewood, which he took into the town to sell. With the money he received he bought rice and went home, where his mother had dinner ready for him. He put down his stick, and while he ate the meal he told his mother all that had happened during the day. By the time he had finished it was nightfall and time to go to bed. The next morning he would go out for firewood as usual, and his mother cooked the rice bought the day before, ate some of it, and kept the rest for her son. In this manner the days went by.

One day Chou went to the hills as usual. His mother had finished dinner and was mending his clothes, when she heard the loud clang of a gong ceaselessly beating outside. Putting down the clothes, she went to the door to see what it was, and there she found an old beggar monk. She said to him: 'We are poor people and have no spare rice. You must go elsewhere.' 'Lord Buddha! I am so hungry!' said the monk. 'Please give me the remains of the rice in the pot.' The woman was frightened when she heard this, because the rice-pot was standing in the house and he could not know what was in it. Fearing he might be a saint, she said to him: 'The rice in the pot is really for my son. But if you are very hungry I will give you half of it. Please wait a moment.' She went back into the house, put half the rice into a bowl, and brought it out to the monk. While

3

he was eating he said to her: 'I still have something important to say to you. When your son Chou Ch'eng comes home, tell him to return to the town and buy some sheets of paper and some flour, prepare some paste, and then stick some straw and the paper together and make a boat. When the eyes of the two lions in front of the big temple in the village become red, you must both get into the boat, because the land here will disappear and the town will be covered by a large lake. But remember this: if you see sparrows, ants, or snakes swimming in the water, you may save them; men or wolves, however, you must on no account assist. Do you understand?' Then he went away.

The woman looked up at the sun, and calculating from its place in the sky that her son would soon return, she went into the house, poured the rest of the rice into a bowl, and then went out again to watch for his coming. As there was no sign of him, she went in again and tidied up the clothes that she had mended, and then when he still did not come, she went and stood at the door.

The sun was slowly sinking behind the hills in the west. The birds, who had already retired to their nests, were singing their bedtime songs. She became quite tired from standing by the door, and was worried and anxious about her son. Only when it was almost dark did she see him coming, and she felt as if a load had been lifted off her heart. She saw that he had a bag on his stick and was pleased that he was bringing the rice. 'Hurry up!' she called out. 'Why are you so late to-day? After dinner I have some news for you.' 'I have already eaten,' answered the son. 'As I was coming home from the hills to-day, I met an old man who wanted to buy all my wood. He didn't ask the price, but wanted me to carry it back to his house, which was over thirty li away. As I put down the load, I saw a delicious-looking meal standing on the table, which the old man invited me to partake of. At first I refused, but he insisted on

4

my eating, and being very hungry, I did take some. Afterwards, I was afraid he would give me no money, but in the end he gave me twice as much as I ordinarily receive, and when I told him that I had to go into the town to buy rice, he suggested that I should buy a bushel from him, and gave me much more than usual,' and Chou Ch'eng pointed to his bag. While they were talking, they went into the house, and after putting down the bag, he asked his mother what had happened to her.

She told him all about the beggar monk who had urged them to make a boat of straw and paper, but her son was sceptical and asked her: 'How can a paper ship carry people?' 'That's not our business,' replied the mother. 'This monk was really a saint, because otherwise how could he know you were called Chou Ch'eng and that there was still some rice in the pot?' Usually Chou agreed with his mother, but this evening he thought she was wrong.

Next morning, Chou went into the town to buy the things and then came home to stick the ship together. Meanwhile, his mother washed the rice and cooked one pot full, and then another to serve as provisions on the boat. By midday the boat was ready and Chou ran off to the temple to look at the lions' eyes, but seeing them as white as usual he went home. Then he went again, but still there was nothing to see. He returned again and again, until his mother said to him: 'It is now too late to-day for them to become red. Wait until to-morrow.'

During the night, neither could sleep long and they got up before the sun. Chou rubbed his eyes and ran off to the temple, while his mother packed the clothes and put them into the boat together with the rice, a pot, a bowl, a basin, and a sieve, not forgetting even the old bed.

Again and again the son went to the temple, but the eyes were still not red. In the evening, as he was running there again, people asked him why he continually went

5

there, and Chou called out to them, as he hurried by, that he was going to see if the lions' eyes were red. Two young wags heard him say this, and thought to themselves: 'What a fool Chou is! How can the lions' eyes become red? Let us, though, paint them ourselves and see what he does then.'

When Chou Ch'eng came once more and saw that the eyes were red, he rushed home to tell his mother the news, helped her into the ship, and then went on board himself. Scarcely were they inside, when they heard an appalling crash, and on opening their eyes again, they saw nothing but water all round. Their craft, however, was floating on the water just like a real ship, perhaps even quieter. Only it had no rudder and went wherever it wished.

Chou was so horrified that he could barely utter a word. But his mother kept on murmuring: 'So many people have met their death! What a disaster! The saint told me that if we saw a sparrow, a snake or an ant swimming about, we could save them, but not a man nor a wolf.' Just as she spoke, a swarm of ants came by, and when they were near enough, she fished them out with the sieve. Then a snake appeared and Chou rescued it and put it in the boat. It was nearly evening, but although it was near autumn, it was not at all cold. So they sat in the boat and looked into the water and up at the sky. Then they saw a sparrow fly up and prepare to settle on the boat, but seeing people on board, it became frightened and flew up and down without daring to descend. Chou called out: 'Sparrow! come down and I will save you!' But the sparrow only flew up higher, on and on, until it became exhausted and fell into the sea. But it fell not far away, and Chou was able to reach it with his hand and fish it out.

Suddenly the ship began to shake, and Chou, looking round, saw a white wolf clutching on to the side and preparing to jump over. Chou wanted to knock it off and began to beat it, but the wolf kept on jumping up,

6

till at last his mother called out: 'Let it come in, my son. Poor wolf; after all, it is also a living thing.' Chou ceased to hit the wolf and it sprang into the boat. After a while, a man came swimming by, quite exhausted, and Chou asked his mother what he should do. 'Of course save him,' she said. 'As we have saved a wolf, we can't very well let a man drown.' The ship moved in the direction of the man, and Chou put out his arms and pulled him into the boat. He soon recovered enough to thank Chou for saving his life, and he asked his name and the name of his mother, saying at the same time that he was called Wu Yi, and that out of his family of five people, all except he, who could swim, had been drowned. 'Don't talk so much, Chou,' his mother called out. 'Give him an old coat to change into and then come and eat.' While they were eating, Wu Yi continued: 'I cannot thank you enough for rescuing me, and as a small recognition, I should like to call you "Elder brother," but I don't know if this idea would please you.' Before Chou had time to answer, his mother said: 'That is a good idea. As Chou is much younger than you, he must call you "Elder Brother."' So Wu Yi knelt down before the mother and Chou accepted him as his blood brother, and they found so many things to talk about that they quite forgot their desperate plight.

It had become dark, and on all sides the sea stretched out to the horizon. There was no wind, but the ship sailed along without the three people feeling any danger. Chou fed the animals they had saved, and then they went to bed. Next morning, when they woke up, the sun was high in the sky and the boat was lying on the shore. Chou jumped ashore and looked around, but there was no sign of men, nothing but mountains and hills. He fetched his mother, and Wu Yi helped him to take off their belongings. The animals ran off, but the wolf ran backwards and forwards, as if he wanted to remain with his rescuers.

7

They chose a nice spot on the island and built themselves a house of straw and stone to live in. They still had a little rice, so they did not suffer from hunger, and then Chou discovered that there was a town thirty miles away. He and Wu collected firewood, which they took into the town and sold, thereby gaining enough for their livelihood.

One day, when Chou had just felled a large tree, a thick black cloud came up from the north-west. Chou thought to himself: 'In fairy tales such black clouds are always evil spirits. I will give it a blow with my axe,' and as the cloud came roaring and blustering by, with all his might he hurled his axe into the air, and when it fell down again, it was covered with blood. The cloud sped away towards the south-east and Chou pursued it with his weapon. After chasing it for about five miles, he saw it disappear under a stone, which, he found on going nearer, was concealing something. With a great effort, he managed to lift it up, and underneath he saw a dark hole stretching into the earth. He carefully replaced the cover, and after marking the spot, took up his axe and returned to where he had left Wu Yi. 'I have been searching everywhere for you,' said Wu. 'Where have you been?' 'I was right about the dark wind cloud,' answered Chou. 'There was a spirit in it whom I wounded with my axe. Look! There is still some blood on it.' 'Oh, don't bother about that,' said Wu Yi. 'It is almost dark and we must be getting home. Mother will be waiting at the door.' Noticing that his brother was in an ill-humour, Chou said no more, but stuck his axe in his belt and took the load of wood. As it was already so late, they went straight home without going into the town. When they got near, Chou was surprised not to see his mother standing at the door, and when he looked closer he saw the wolf eating something. Yes, the wolf he had rescued from the water had killed and eaten his mother. With a roar, he raised

8

his axe and dashed out the wolf's brains, but his mother was dead. They both wept. Wu Yi was the first to recover himself and say: 'Don't weep, brother. She is dead and all our tears won't bring her to life again. Let us carry her into the house, and to-morrow we can sell our wood and buy a coffin with the proceeds to bury her.' Chou wiped his eyes and they both carried the body into the house. They began to weep again, and went to bed without eating anything.

The next day, Chou stayed with the body, while Wu Yi went into the town, sold the wood, and bought a miserable cheap coffin. They placed the body in it and buried it in a beautiful spot. Then they began to collect firewood again.

One day Chou went to town to sell wood. At the town gate he put down his load and rested a while. A crowd of people were standing in front of a red notice on the gate, and being unable to read, Chou asked an old man what it was all about. The old man answered: 'On such and such a day, the daughter of His Excellency Wang was carried off from the garden by an evil cloud spirit. The man who finds her will receive 10,000 ounces of gold, and if he is over twenty and under thirty, she will become his wife.' When he heard this, Chou remembered his experience a few days before, but before saying anything, he wanted to go home to ask his brother's advice. He took his load, went into the town, found a purchaser for the wood, and then went home. He told Wu Yi the contents of the red notice, and asked him if he would accompany him and climb down into the spirit's cave. 'Of course I will go with you,' Wu said. 'If we don't find her, we are no worse off: If we do find her, we shall become rich and have a wife.' Next morning, Chou went into the town, and when he had found the house of Excellency Wang, he said to the door-keepers, 'Please tell His Excellency that I am here. I know where his daughter is hidden. I want to fetch her.'

9

The doorkeepers informed their master that a man had come who claimed to know where his daughter was hidden, and Excellency Wang sent for him at once, and asked him his name, where he came from, and what he knew about his daughter. Chou told him his name and said: 'One day while I was collecting wood in the Eastern Hill, a dark storm cloud came up from the north-west. As I had always heard that dark clouds were evil spirits, I decided to try and wound it with my axe, and when the axe fell down again, it was all bloody. I pursued the cloud to a hole in the hills that was covered by a stone. All this occurred on the same day that your daughter was stolen away.' 'Then she is lost beyond hope, if you are telling the truth,' said Excellency Wang in despair; but he became more cheerful when Chou said he would climb down the hole and look for her. 'Go there at once. Do you need soldiers or weapons?' he asked. 'No!' said Chou, 'only a basket and a long chain and a few bearers with a chair to bring your daughter back.' Excellency Wang ordered everything to be prepared, and Chou sent a messenger to his house to tell Wu Yi all that had happened. Then he thrust his axe into his belt and set forth. Outside were gathered fifty or sixty people sent by Wang, and a large crowd of sightseers. Chou and Wu led the way, followed by the whole crowd. Spurred on by their excitement, they soon arrived at the spot. Chou said to Wu: 'Brother! Fasten the chain to the basket, and tie the bell to the other end. I will then get into the basket and you must let me down. If I pull the chain, the bell will ring and you must pull the basket up again at once.' Then Chou tightened his belt, grasped his axe, took off the stone cover, got into the basket, and was let down into the hole. The farther down he went, the broader the hole became, until, about thirty or forty feet down, he touched ground. As he was coming down, everything was dark below and bright above; now everything was bright below and dark above. He sprang out of the basket, and looked around. The place was just like a garden; beautiful trees and flowers such as he had never seen before were growing everywhere. The ground was covered with such perfectly mown grass that he hardly dared to walk on it. To the west, he could see an artificial mountain. Although it was light, there was no sun in the sky. Chou did not waste time looking at all these wonders, but grasping his axe, he set off in the direction of the artificial mountain. From there he would be able to see everything, but before he reached it he heard a terrible noise, and turning round, he saw a stone house among the trees. With great care, he peeped through the door, and there he saw a spirit asleep in a chair. He had a grey-blue face, red hair and a red beard, and huge lips, through which two great tusks protruded from his mouth. He was wearing a long, old-fashioned black robe and black trousers, beneath which could be seen a black foot covered with golden hair with a great bleeding ulcer. A bowl of hot water stood on the ground beside him, and on his left sat a beautiful young maiden, with a pale and tragic face, who was continually wiping the ulcer with a sponge of hot water.

Chou coughed slightly, until the maiden heard him. She motioned him to go a little to the side so that the spirit should not see him, and then she went out to him. Chou asked her: 'Are you not the daughter of Excellency Wang?' 'Yes,' she said, 'but why have you come here?' 'I am looking for you,' he replied. 'Oh!' she sighed, 'the spirit is so dangerous. He has seven heads, and if one is cut off another grows at once. A few days ago he was wounded in the foot by a woodcutter, and I have to wash the wound. At the moment he is sleeping,' but just then, there was a rumbling sound and the spirit awoke. She signed to Chou to hide in the wood, and returning to the spirit, she continued to wash his wound with the sponge. The spirit rolled his eyes and roared: 'I smell human flesh.' 'But, Master,' replied the maiden, 'I have not been here long. Perhaps I still smell of human flesh.' Satisfied by this the spirit went to sleep again. Chou silently ran back to the entrance, tugged the chain to have the basket let down, and then got into it and was rapidly pulled up. 'The maiden is there,' he told the excited people, 'but the spirit is very dangerous. He has seven heads, but I will find a way to dispose of him.' Then he said to Wu: 'If I have killed the spirit I shall send the maiden up first, and come up myself.' Wu nodded, but already an evil plan was forming in his mind. Chou, however, suspected nothing and let himself down once more. Having arrived at the bottom, he grasped his axe, crept through the wood to the door, and listened until he was sure the spirit was asleep. Miss Wang was still washing his leg with hot water. When she glanced up, he showed her the axe and she nodded assent. He crept up behind the spirit and cut off one head, but immediately a new one grew, which he also cut off, but only after the last head had fallen was there any blood. 'Now he is dead,' said the maiden, 'but why did you take such risks for me?' Chou told her everything, and she said to him: 'As one never knows what may happen to one, I will give you a token,' and taking a golden clasp from her hair, she broke it in half and gave Chou one of the pieces. 'This is your token,' she continued, 'and three years is the appointed time, after which it is no more good.' Chou hid the clasp in his clothes, and leading the maiden to the basket, he shook the chain. Wu knew that the maiden would come up now and quickly pulled up the chain. Yes, she was very beautiful. The maid-servants that Wang had sent led her to the litter and stood round her.

Then Wu called out: 'Quickly, shut the hole. The spirit is coming.' The people had turned to look at the

12

maiden, and did not remember that someone was still in the hole. Now they all ran up and helped Wu to fill up the hole, and then, amidst rejoicing, they returned to Wang's house. But Wang had no sooner seen Wu than he said: 'This is not Chou Ch'eng. He was at most twenty years old, and you are over thirty. How dare you pretend to be Chou?' Then Wu answered: 'Chou asked me to come instead of him, but I will fetch him,' and he went out, wondering to himself what he could do, and whether he would have to go out and collect firewood again.

Chou was waiting for the basket to descend again, when suddenly a shower of sand and stones poured down and nearly killed him. The shower stopped, but there was no sign of the chain, and he saw that the hole had been shut. Sighing, he thought to himself that his end was near, because nowhere could he find another exit from the cavern. 'Whether the hole has been shut or not does not matter, because I cannot get out without a basket and chain. I can only await my death.' He wandered aimlessly about, until suddenly he saw a little white dragon sitting on a pedestal, swishing its tail. Seeing it fastened with a nail, he went up and pulled the nail out to let the dragon get down, saying: 'We are companions in sorrow.' Meanwhile, he had become very hungry, because he had eaten nothing the whole day, so he sat down on a stone to see what the dragon would do. It came to the stone he was sitting on, licked it with its tongue, then wriggled back to the grass, curled up, and went to sleep. Chou was very hungry, but there was nothing to do except lie down and try to sleep; though when he woke he was still hungrier. Day and night were the same, and therefore he did not know how long he had slept. The little dragon wriggled up again, licked the stone, and then went back to sleep. Wondering why it did this, Chou decided to try himself, and the moment his tongue touched the stone, his hunger

13

and thirst left him. He was delighted with this discovery, because now his most pressing need was solved,
and he no longer had anything to worry him; he licked
the stone, slept, and admired the flowers and trees. In
this manner, the time passed without his knowing. One
day, when he was fast asleep, he heard someone call his
name. He was very surprised, for he could see no living
thing except the dragon, which was lying at his feet.
'Did you call me?' Chou asked the dragon. 'I wanted
to repay your kindness,' it replied. 'To-morrow is the
day on which I fly up to earth.' 'What is to-morrow?'
asked Chou. 'To-morrow is the second day of the second
month,' said the dragon, 'and punctually at midday I
fly up and can take you with me.' 'How can you know
that to-morrow is the second day of the second month?'
asked Chou, 'and how do you know when it is noon?
You cannot see the sun here.' 'I can feel it,' replied the
dragon, and without saying another word, it slithered
off. Chou, naturally, was quite overjoyed. He decided
to take up to earth a bit of the stone that allayed hunger
and thirst, but although he banged it with his axe until
his arms ached, he could not break off the tiniest piece.
Seeing it was hopeless, he went for a walk in the garden,
and then licked the stone for the last time, and went to
sleep. When he woke, the dragon was lying by his
side. 'Is it time to go?' he asked. 'Yes,' said the
dragon, curling itself up. 'You must get on to my back
and shut your eyes, and not open them again until I tell
you. Hold my horns tightly.' Then Chou heard a clap
of thunder and the wind whistled in his ears. 'Open
your eyes,' said the dragon a moment later, and Chou
found himself falling gently into a heap of grass, which
was outside the town of Excellency Wang. When he
learnt in the town that Wang's daughter was not yet
married, he went to the house and announced his arrival.
But he had been so long in the hole where there was no
sun that his skin had turned a dirty yellow colour, and

his clothes were hanging in rags. Believing him to be an impostor, Wang greeted him in a distant manner, but he did not venture to send him away. Instead, he thought of a difficult test and said to Chou: 'Although you say you are Chou Ch'eng, I do not recognize you. Perhaps my daughter could do so, but first I shall set you a task. If you can do it, you can see my daughter.' Chou asked hesitatingly what the task was. 'I have two bushels of beans,' said Wang, 'one is yellow, the other is black. The two kinds are mixed, and you must separate them in half a day.' Then he called the servants, and ordered them to lock Chou up in an empty room and give him the beans. Chou did not dare refuse, but he was very depressed, and thought: 'That is a clear refusal of the wedding. But why does he set me such a hard task if he does not want it to take place?' After looking at the beans, he lay down to sleep, since it was impossible to separate them. Then a swarm of sparrows appeared; some picked out the yellow beans, others the black, and soon they were all divided. At dusk the servant returned, and when he saw the beans already separated and Chou sleeping peacefully on the ground, he called out: 'Mr. Chou! How did you complete the task so quickly?' Chou woke up to see the servant standing in front of him and the beans nicely divided into two piles, but he was careful not to utter a word, because he had no idea who had divided them. The servant, however, thought he was in a bad temper, and went off laughing to inform his master of what had happened.

When Mr. Wang heard it, he mixed a bushel of rice with a bushel of corn and ordered Chou to separate them during the night. Chou, however, was furious and merely lay down to sleep. Then many, many ants came and divided the seeds for him, so that when he woke up he saw that the task was done. He could scarcely believe his eyes and wondered to himself what spirit was helping him.

15

In a short while the servant arrived, saw the rice and corn divided, and went to tell his master. Mr. Wang did not believe it and went in person to see the two heaps, but not a single seed was in the wrong heap. However, he set him one more task. In the west room of the treasure chamber there were ten bars of gold. If Chou could carry them into the east room he would take him at once to his daughter, but if he failed he would have him executed. While Chou was being led to the treasure chamber, he was quite happy, because he thought it would be easy to take ten bars of gold from one room to another; but to his horror he found them more like pillars than bars, one-tenth of which he could not move. He thought to himself: 'Well, I shall certainly have to die this time, but at least I shall sleep first.' And while he was sleeping, snakes came and rolled the beams, one after another, into the east room, so that when Chou woke up he saw with delight that all the gold was already moved. 'Certainly some god is helping me,' he thought, and then he asked to be brought before Mr. Wang. 'I have fulfilled all the tasks that you set me,' he said, 'now you must fulfil your promise without setting me any more.' Mr. Wang first went to the treasure chamber to see if the beams had really been moved, and when he saw them all in the east room, he thought, 'He certainly must be Chou Ch'eng. If he had not been so able, he would never have managed to kill the evil spirit,' but to Chou Ch'eng he said, 'It is possible that you are the real Chou Ch'eng, but I have no means of deciding. First, my daughter must see you.' Then a maid-servant led him to the door of the ladies' apartments, and told him to wait. Through pearl door-hangings, marvellous perfumes were wafted towards him, making his senses reel. From inside he heard a voice ask: 'Have you got the token?' He took the half of the golden clasp out of his breast-pocket and gave it to the maid. The daughter compared it with her own, and then ordered the maids to take Chou to the guest-rooms and inform her father. But Mr. Wang led him to the bath, and when he was washed, he gave him a beautiful gown. He sent for the calendar, and seeing that the next day was favourable for weddings, he decided that they should be married at once. There is no need to tell what a sumptuous room Chou was given and what a marvellous bed he slept on.

Next day, all the relations, friends, and guests were there; great trumpets blared and everyone was very happy. The bride and bridegroom made their obeisance to heaven and to earth and then went into the bridal chamber. When they both had drunk many cups of wine, and all the servants and other people had left them, his wife asked him softly: 'Beloved, why did you come so late?' Then Chou Ch'eng told her everything that had happened since their separation. How incalculable is the course of life! They went on talking for a long time, till suddenly they heard shouting and screaming in the court. 'Autumn Scent! What is the matter?' the young wife called out. 'A thief fell down from the chimney and was killed,' replied the maid. Chou went out to see, and the maid led the way with a candle. Outside in the courtyard the torches shone as bright as day, and Chou saw that the dead man was his blood brother Wu Yi.

Chou now no longer had to collect firewood, but lived happily ever after.

2. *Cinderella*

THERE were once two sisters; the eldest was very beautiful and everyone called her 'Beauty'; but the younger had a face covered with pock marks, and everyone called her 'Pock Face.' She was the daughter of the second wife, and was very spoilt, and had a bad character. Beauty's mother had died when her daughter was very small, and after her death she had turned into a yellow cow, which lived in the garden. Beauty adored the yellow cow, but it had a miserable existence, because the step-mother treated it so badly.

One day, the step-mother took the ugly daughter to the theatre and left the elder one at home. She wanted to accompany them, but her step-mother said: 'I will take you to-morrow, if you tidy the hemp in my room.'

Beauty went off and sat down in front of the stack of hemp, but after a long time she had only divided half. Bursting into tears, she took it off to the yellow cow, who swallowed the whole mass and then spat it out again all clearly arranged bit by bit. Beauty dried her tears, and gave the hemp to her mother on her return home: 'Mother, here is the hemp. I can go to the theatre to-morrow, can't I?'

But when the next day came, her step-mother again refused to take her, saying: 'You can go when you have separated the sesame seeds from the beans.' The poor girl had to divide them seed by seed, until the exhausting task made her eyes ache. Again she went to the yellow cow, who said to her: 'You stupid girl, you must separate them with a fan.' Now she understood, and the sesame and beans were soon divided. When she brought the seeds all nicely separated, her step-mother knew that she could no longer prevent her going to the theatre, but she asked her: 'How can a servant girl be so clever? Who helped you?' And Beauty had to admit that the yellow cow had advised her, which made the step-mother very angry. Without, therefore, saying a word, she killed and ate the cow, but Beauty had loved the cow so dearly that she could not eat its flesh. Instead, she put the bones in an earthenware pot and hid them in her bedroom.

Day after day, the step-mother did not take her to the theatre, and one evening, when she had gone there herself with Pock Face, Beauty was so cross that she smashed everything in the house, including the earthenware pot. Whereupon there was a crack, and a white horse, a new dress, and a pair of embroidered shoes came out. The sudden appearance of these things gave her a terrible fright, but she soon saw that they were real objects and, quickly pulling on the new dress and the shoes, she jumped on to the horse and rode out of the gate.

While riding along, one of her shoes slipped off into the ditch. She wanted to dismount and fetch it, but could not do so; at the same time she did not want to leave it lying there. She was in a real quandary, when a fishmonger appeared. 'Brother fishmonger! Please pick up my shoe,' she said to him. He answered with a grin: 'With great pleasure, if you will marry me.' 'Who could marry you?' she said crossly. 'Fishmongers always stink.' And seeing that he had no chance, the fishmonger went on his way. Next, an assistant of a rice shop went by, and she said to him: 'Brother rice broker, please give me my shoe.' 'Certainly, if you will marry me,' said the young man. 'Marry a rice broker! Their bodies are all covered with dust.' The rice broker departed, and soon an oil merchant came by, whom she also asked to pick up her shoe. 'I will pick it up if you consent to marry me,' he replied. 'Who could want to marry you?' Beauty said with a sigh. 'Oil merchants are always so greasy.' Shortly after a scholar came by, whom she also asked to pick up her shoe. The scholar turned to look at her, and then said: 'I will do so at once if you promise to marry me.' The scholar was very handsome, so she nodded her head in agreement, and he picked up the shoe and put it on her foot. Then he took her back to his house and made her his wife.

Three days later, Beauty went with her husband to pay the necessary respects to her parents. Her step-mother and sister had quite changed their manner and treated them both in the most friendly and attentive fashion. In the evening, they wanted to keep Beauty

at home, and she, thinking they meant it kindly, agreed
to stay and to follow her husband in a few days. The
next morning her sister took her by the hand and said
to her with a laugh: 'Sister, come and look into the well.
We will see which of us is the more beautiful.' Suspect-
ing nothing, Beauty went to the well and leant over to
look down, but at this moment her sister gave her a
shove and pushed her into the well, which she quickly
covered up with a basket. Poor Beauty lost consciousness
and was drowned.

After ten days, the scholar began to wonder why his
wife had still not returned. He sent a messenger to
enquire, and the step-mother sent back a message that
his wife was suffering from a bad attack of smallpox
and was not well enough to return for the moment.
The scholar believed this, and every day he sent over
salted eggs and other sickbed delicacies, all of which
found their way into the stomach of the ugly sister.

After two months, the step-mother was irritated by the
continual messages from the scholar and made up her
mind to practise a deception, and to send back her own
daughter as his wife. The scholar was horrified when
he saw her and said: 'Goodness! How changed you
are! Surely you are not Beauty. My wife was never
such a monster. Good Heavens!' Pock Face replied
seriously: 'If I am not Beauty, whom do you think I
am then? You know perfectly well I was very ill with
smallpox, and now you want to disown me. I shall die!
I shall die!' And she began to howl. The tender-
hearted scholar could not bear to see her weeping, and
although he still had some doubts, he begged her for-
giveness and tried to console her, so that gradually she
stopped weeping.

Beauty, however, had been transformed into a sparrow,
and she used to come and call out when Pock Face was
combing her hair: 'Comb once, peep; comb twice,
peep; comb thrice, up to the spine of Pock Face.' And

the wicked wife answered: 'Comb once, comb twice, comb thrice, to the spine of Beauty.' The scholar was very mystified by this conversation, and he said to the sparrow: 'Why do you sing like that? Are you by any chance my wife? If you are, call three times, and I will put you in a golden cage and keep you as a pet.' The sparrow called out three times, and the scholar bought a golden cage to keep it in. The ugly sister was very angry when she saw that her husband kept the sparrow in a cage, and she secretly killed it and threw it into the garden, where it was once more transformed into a bamboo with many shoots. When Pock Face ate them, an ulcer formed on her tongue, but the scholar found them excellent. The wicked woman became suspicious again and had the bamboo cut down and made into a bed, but when she lay on it, innumerable needles pricked her, while the scholar found it extremely comfortable. Again she became very cross and threw the bed away.

Next door to the scholar lived an old woman who sold money-bags. One day, on her way home, she saw the bed and thought to herself: 'No one has died here, why have they thrown the bed away? I shall take it,' and she took the bed into her house and passed a very comfortable night. The next day, she saw that the food in the kitchen was ready cooked. She ate it up, but naturally she felt a little nervous, not having any idea who could have prepared it. Thus for several days she found she could have dinner the moment she came home, but finally, being no longer able to contain her anxiety, she came back early one afternoon and went into the kitchen, where she saw a dark shadow washing rice. She ran up quickly and clasped the shadow round the waist. 'Who are you?' she asked, 'and why do you cook food for me?' The shadow replied: 'I will tell you everything. I am the wife of your neighbour the scholar and am called "Beauty." My sister threw me into the well and I was drowned, but my soul was not dispersed. Please give me a rice-pot as head, a stick as hand, a dish-cloth as entrails, firehooks as feet, and then I can assume my former shape again.' The old woman gave her what she asked for, and in a moment a beautiful girl appeared, and the old woman was so delighted at seeing such a charming girl, that she questioned her very closely. She told the old woman everything, and then said: 'Old woman, I have got a bag, which you must offer for sale outside the scholar's house. If he comes out, you must sell it to him.' And she gave her an embroidered bag.

The next day the old woman stood outside the scholar's house and shouted that she had a bag for sale. Maddened by the noise, he came out to ask what kind of bags she sold, and she showed him Beauty's embroidered bag. 'Where did you get this bag?' he asked. 'I gave it to my wife.' The old woman then told the whole story to the scholar, who was overjoyed to hear that his wife was still alive. He arranged everything with the old woman, laid down a red cloth on the ground, and brought Beauty back to his house.

When Pock Face saw her sister return, she gave her no peace. She began to grumble and say that the woman was only pretending to be Beauty, and that in point of fact she was a spirit. She wanted to have a trial to see which was the genuine wife. Beauty, also, would not admit herself in the wrong, and said: 'Good. We will have a test.' Pock Face suggested that they should walk on eggs, and whoever broke the shells would be the loser, but although she broke all the eggs, and Beauty none, she refused to admit her loss and insisted on another trial. This time they were to walk up a ladder made of knives. Beauty went up and down first without receiving the tiniest scratch, but before Pock Face had gone two steps her feet were cut to the bone. Although she had lost again, she insisted on another test, that of jumping into a cauldron of hot oil. She hoped that Beauty, who would have to jump in first, would be burnt. Beauty, however, was quite unharmed by the boiling oil, but the wicked sister fell into it and did not appear again.

Beauty put the roasted bones of the wicked sister into a box and sent them over to her step-mother by a stuttering old servant woman, who was told to say: 'Your daughter's flesh.' But the step-mother loved carp and understood 'carp flesh' instead of 'your daughter's flesh.' She thought her daughter had sent her over some carp and opened the box in a state of great excitement; but when she saw the charred bones of her daughter lying inside, she let out a piercing scream and fell down dead.

3. *The Tale of Nungguama*

A WOMAN was once taking some cakes to her parents. On the way she met a man-eating Nungguama with a body like a bull, a head like a measure of rice, and sharp teeth and claws. His eyes gleamed and his coat was shaggy and thick. The monster roared with laughter and said: 'Give me all your cakes to eat.' The woman said timidly: 'I can't do that, they are for my parents.' 'Good,' said Nungguama. 'I will come back this evening and tear your flesh and crunch your bones and eat you up.' The woman began to scream with terror and, fearing lest men might come and catch him, the monster fled into the hills like an arrow from a bow.

The woman was frightened to death. She did not go to her parents, for her heart was beating like a hunted deer's. She sat in the doorway and wept. To everyone that passed she told her story and begged for their help, but everyone blenched at the word Nungguama and remained speechless for a time. Naturally, no one could help her, and she began to cry harder.

Finally, a mixed-goods tradesman came by with two

bamboo baskets on his carrying pole and a little clapper in his hand. He was surprised to see a woman weeping bitterly, surrounded by a gaping crowd, and asked: 'Woman, what are your troubles that you cry so bitterly?' Between her sobs the woman replied: 'The Nungguama is coming . . . to . . . eat . . . me . . . this evening.' 'My dear woman, don't weep,' said the old man. 'I will give you twenty needles to stick in the door, and when the Nungguama arrives, he will prick himself,' and the mixed-goods man gave her twenty needles and then continued on his way beating his clapper as before. But the woman considered that twenty needles would do little harm to the monster, and continued to sit weeping in the doorway.

Then a man arrived who collected swine's dung, dog's dung and cattle dung, as manure for the fields. Seeing a woman sobbing, he asked what was the reason: 'Don't worry,' he said when she told him, 'I will give you some dung, which you must stick on the door. When the Nungguama arrives, he will soil himself and run away.' The woman accepted the gift, but she was still not comforted and continued to weep.

A little later, a snake-catcher came by with a basketful of snakes. He walked slowly, crying: 'Snakes for sale,' but at the sound of weeping, he also asked for the reason and was told the whole story. Then he said to the woman: 'You needn't be anxious. Nothing will happen.' But she begged him to help her, till he said: 'I will give you two big snakes, which can climb trees and are terribly poisonous. You must put them in the water-pot, because, when the Nungguama comes in with dirty hands, he will certainly want to wash them, and then the snakes will bite him to death. You see you needn't worry.' Then he put the two enormous green bamboo snakes into the pot, but after his departure the timorous woman began to weep again.

Next a fishmonger arrived, who saw that the woman's

face was swollen with tears. He did not dare to question her himself, but he soon learnt from other people what the trouble was. He was sorry for her, and putting three pounds of round fish into the cooking-pot, he said: 'Don't weep, my woman, pay attention to me and you need have no fear. Take this pot with the round fish, but don't put any water in, or they won't bite. If the Nungguama is bitten by the snakes he will go and wash in the cooking-pot. The fish will bite him, which ought to frighten him away at least, if it doesn't finish him off.' But when the fishmonger had gone, the poor woman cried again.

Next an egg-seller appeared, calling: 'Eggs! Good fresh eggs! Eight for ten cents.' He also saw the weeping woman and asked: 'Good woman, why are you weeping? It breaks my heart to hear you. Have you quarrelled with your husband, or with your mother-in-law, or your sister-in-law?' The woman told him her sad story, though she never imagined that such a man would be able to help her. At any rate, it could do no harm, she thought. However, the egg-seller said: 'Don't worry! Don't weep! I will give you ten eggs to hide in the ashes on the hearth. When the Nungguama is bitten by the snakes and the fishes, he will try and stop the bleeding with ashes. Then the eggs will burst in his eyes and blind him.' But the woman was still a little nervous and did not cease weeping.

Finally, there came a man who sold millstones and iron goods. When the weeping woman confided in him, he also promised to help her. 'I will give you a one hundred and twenty pound millstone,' he said, 'which you must hang on the framework of the mosquito netting round your bed. Prop it up from beneath and fasten it to the bar with a wire, and when you hear the Nungguama coming, cut through the wire and he will be crushed by the stone.' Then he added: 'I will also give you an iron tool. If he is still not dead, you can finish him off with that. Now there is nothing more to be done. Just follow the instructions carefully.' Now the woman was really consoled, and she went into the house to prepare everything before the evening.

She lay quite alone in the pitch darkness, with the iron tool clasped in her hands in case the monster arrived. The first and second night-watches went by, but although she strained her ears listening she could hear nothing. The third watch began at midnight. The sky was blue, with scarcely a star to be seen, for the bright moon shone into her room and lit up the floor. A cool refreshing wind sprang up. She was so tired that she soon fell asleep. Suddenly she heard a noise. 'Du, du, du . . .' it was footsteps, and she knew the Nungguama had arrived. Hardly daring to breathe, she listened carefully and clasped her iron tool more securely.

'Open the door!' shouted the beast, 'if you don't open it, I will eat your bones,' and with three kicks, he broke down the door. A scream and a curse followed, as he tore himself on the needles and dirtied himself with the dung. 'What's all this?' he roared. 'One gets dirty hands here, you filthy brute.' The door was now open, but he said: 'I must first wash my hands. There is time enough afterwards,' and he went across to the water-jar. But as soon as he dipped in his hands, the green bamboo snakes bit him in the finger, and he screamed with pain as the red blood flowed out. With all his strength, he shook off the snakes and then went across to the cooking-pot, thinking to himself that the water in it must be safe and clean, but the moment he touched it, something else bit him in the finger, which made him cry out more loudly: 'Another of this hag's tricks. I will crunch up all her bones. But first I must quench the blood at the hearth.' But while he was burrowing in the ashes, all the eggs exploded, and bits of shell flew into his eyes and blinded him. 'Oh, dear,' he groaned, 'things are going from bad to worse. I

26

have never met such a woman. I really cannot stand it.' Now he no longer cared about the pain, but burst crying into the bedroom in such a hurry, that he tore off his eyebrows on the door beams, though with his mind full of revenge he did not feel the pain. He bellowed and threatened: 'You hag! All your tricks can't kill me. Now I am in your room. In a little while, a little while, I shall have eaten you up, bones and all. Only then will I have exacted full revenge.' With these words, he grasped the mosquito netting, but the woman cut through the wire with a knife, and bang, the heavy millstone dropped on his head. His bones were all broken and the blood flowed out in a stream. He began to weep as if he had to die; whereupon the woman gave him a few blows with the iron tool till he was quite dead.

In this way she avoided being eaten up. Instead, she killed the monster, and sold it for much money, with which she bought everything she wanted.

4. *The Pig that warms the Ocean*

IN a small hut on a field near by the road lived young Baldhead. His parents were no more. Every day he cut grass for sale in his two-acre meadow, and bit by bit he saved enough to buy a little pig. Whenever he had time, he played with the little animal, just as if it had been a child. Every day he said how big and heavy his piglet was growing, but strange to relate, after three months, not only had the pig not grown, but its skin had shrivelled up like that of an old, yellow-haired mouse. The longer he watched it, the worse it became, till finally he said to himself: 'Even pigs won't grow for an unlucky fellow like me.'

One day a Muslim treasure-seeker came by. At the sight of the little pig he said to Baldhead: 'Sell me your pig for one hundred silver pieces.' Baldhead was very

The Pig that warms the Ocean

surprised at the large price offered and, stroking his head, he said to the stranger: 'Why do you want to buy my pig? I won't sell it, unless you tell me.' The stranger answered: 'Your pig is a so-called ocean-warming pig. If you place it in a cauldron on the seashore, the sea will become as hot as the water in the pot. If the water boils in the pot, the sea will also boil, and when the water has all boiled away, the sea will also be dry. You can imagine what treasures there are at the bottom of the sea.' At this news, Baldhead quickly seized the pig and dashed off, calling out behind him: 'No, I won't sell it. If you can do such things, so can I,' and the Mohammedan had to continue his journey without the treasure.

The next morning before crack of dawn, Baldhead put the pig in a cauldron, took a few bundles of wood, and went down to the shore. He did everything the Mohammedan had told him, till the water fell several fathoms and the sea became full of steam. Suddenly an envoy of the Dragon-King shot through the waves: 'Stop boiling,' it said, 'or the Palace of the Dragon-King will collapse.' But Baldhead answered: 'I am merely cooking my pig. I know nothing about your palace.' While the envoy was vainly imploring his pity, suddenly the Dragon-King appeared in person. 'Stop boiling, please,' he cried, 'and I will give you anything you want.' The vision of the King majestically swaying upon the waves in his ceremonial red dress was too much for Baldhead, and he quickly removed the wood from under the pot, just in time to prevent the pig being completely cooked. The Dragon-King then invited him to visit his dominions, and the envoy raised his banner and lashed the waves, which separated, forming a broad road. The three advanced down it to the bottom of the sea, but despite the roaring waves that dashed by on both sides like millions of white eagles, their persons were not even moistened, and on their arrival they found a delicious meal all ready prepared for them.

28

During the four or five days that Baldhead spent in the palace, he struck up a friendship with a water-carrier in the kitchen. One day this man said to him: 'On your departure the Dragon-King will offer you gold and silver. Don't accept it; demand instead the third flower-vase on the table.' Baldhead made a note of this, and soon after asked for permission to depart. Lung Wang, the Dragon-King, said to him: 'I have no particular treasures to give you, but take that little gourd if you like.' 'I don't want the gourd,' answered Baldhead. 'Give me the third flower-vase on the table.' For a moment the King remained undecided, but then he said: 'All right, take it if you want it,' and he ordered a crab-General to escort him back to the shore, on which there was no longer any sign of the pig or the cauldron.

At home he placed the vase on the dinner-table, and then went out to mow grass. Just before sunset, he went home to cook his evening meal, but when he opened the dishes one was already filled with pork and the other with rice. 'Who has done that?' he wondered, and called out to ask if anyone was there. However, since no one answered, he sat down and ate his fill. The next evening, when he returned home, the meat and rice were again cooked, but again no one answered his call. He decided, therefore, to stay at home and watch the next day. He turned an old water-container upside down, bored two holes in the bottom, and hid himself inside to watch what would happen. In a short time the flower-vase turned into a beautiful maiden, who began to tidy up the house with a smile on her face, and then began to prepare the food. Baldhead waited for his chance and then sprang out and seized hold of her. 'Who are you?' he asked, 'and why do you cook my food every day?' Blushing as red as a peony, the young lady replied: 'I am the third princess of the Dragon-King. I had turned into a vase and was carried off by you.' Suddenly Baldhead felt a tap on his head, a silver plate

29

fell down and beautiful shining coal-black hair appeared all over his head. Then the princess drew a line across the field with her silver hairpin and immediately a hall and a bedroom arose, more beautiful than you can imagine, in which they lived happily together.

Next door to Baldhead lived Mr. Chang. One day as he was coming past with his followers in his litter, he saw a beautiful, big, tall house, where formerly there had only been a field. Baldhead led him into the guest-hall and begged him to take a seat. It was just midday, and Mr. Chang ordered his cook, who had accompanied him, to go into the kitchen and roast a thrush. In the kitchen the cook saw the princess, and the more he looked at her, the more beautiful he found her. He continued to watch her and paid no attention to the bird, with the result that it was burnt to a cinder and could not be eaten. 'Oh, dear!' he groaned. 'My master will beat me for this,' and he ran around in a terrible state, till eventually the princess asked him what was the matter. 'My master never eats anything except thrushes,' he explained, 'and now I have let it burn.' The princess took a lump of flour, rolled it to the left and rolled it to the right and fashioned a thrush, which she gave to the cook. 'Take this and roast it for your master,' she said. When it was cooked, he carried it into the dining-room, and at the first mouthful Chang knew that it tasted much better than ever before. He seized his tobacco pouch and began to belabour the cook, shouting: 'To-day it is really good. You were too lazy to cook it well before.' Then the cook knelt down and confessed everything, and as Baldhead was not in the room, he also said how beautiful the wife was. Chang was excited by this news, and said: 'This evening, take off your clothes and give them to me. I want to see her myself.' And that evening, he pulled on the cook's filthy, greasy clothes, and by doing as the cook did, he managed to see the princess.

30

The next day, before dawn, old Chang sent his cook across to call Baldhead. 'You have such a beautiful wife,' he said to him. 'How can you live on the roadside without a moat? If you don't make a moat round your house within three days, your wife belongs to me.' Then he got into his litter and rode away.

Baldhead was so upset that he could no longer eat, and tears rolled down his cheeks. The princess asked him what the matter was. 'Mr. Chang has said that if I have not dug a ditch round the house in three days, you must go to him,' he explained. The princess knew of a way at once. 'Go and buy one hundred garments made of cocoanut, one hundred hats and one hundred stakes,' she said. 'This evening, place the stakes in the field behind the house, and on every stake hang a dress and a hat. Then let the old fool come and see his moat in three days' time.' Baldhead carried out her instructions exactly.

Three days later, Chang came gaily by, but he was horrified to see a six-foot-wide moat all round Baldhead's house. Anxiously he ran over the little bridge, called for Baldhead and said to him: 'You now have a moat, but there is no water in it. Your wife is still not protected. If, within three days, there is not five feet of water and a dragon in it, your wife belongs to me,' and shaking his long sleeves, he took himself off.

Weeping, Baldhead again went to his wife for advice. 'That's quite easy,' she said. 'Ask my mother to give you a dragon. Here is a water-dividing pearl. Hold it in your mouth and you can go through the sea as easily as along a street.' Baldhead took the pearl in his mouth and went to the Dragon-Palace, but there he discovered that all the dragons, great and small, had gone off to Heaven on a pleasure trip with the Dragon-King and the third prince. There was only one lazy reptile sleeping in the garden. He took this one and put it in the moat, and each time it yawned, it squirted out so much water, that the moat was soon filled to the depth of five feet.

Three days later, before dawn, old Chang went past and saw the whole place covered with water, and as he came nearer, it looked as though the house was swaying on the waves. The dragon blew up the waves, and shooting out its tail, covered Chang with water. For a moment he remained quite speechless, but then he shouted out to Baldhead: 'Now the moat has enough water, but you still lack a hedge of green trees. If, within three days, you have no wood, your wife belongs to me.' And he went off scratching his head.

When the princess heard of Chang's new demand, she said to her husband: 'Cut down a couple of trees in the wood and stick them at the side of the moat. In three days you will have a wood.' Baldhead fetched his axe, which had become quite rusty through lack of use, and going into the hills, he cut down a couple of trees and planted them at the edge of the moat.

At the end of three days, Old Chang entered Baldhead's courtyard after dinner. There he saw a green wood, already as high as a man, thick and dense. In crossing the bridge, he knocked against a big tree and got a great lump on his head, and as he stepped back, he ran a thorn deep into his skin. But when Baldhead came out, he hid the pain and merely said: 'Now there is a wood, but there are no birds in it. That is too lonely. If, within three days, the wood is not filled with twittering birds, your wife belongs to me.' Then he placed a clod of wet earth on his aching head and went home.

This time, Baldhead had no fears. He went and told his wife at once, who said to him: 'Buy a few sheets of paper in the street. I will do the rest.'

He went off to buy the paper, and the princess cut out thousands of birds, blew them into the air, and they flew off with a chirrup into the trees.

On the third day, Mr. Chang, whose head was still

bleeding and aching from his last visit, found Baldhead
seated beaming in the shade of the trees, in the branches
of which thousands of little birds were perched singing.
As he was going to sit down, he noticed that his head
was moist and damp, and, when he put up his hand, he
realized what had happened. Baldhead scolded the
birds: 'Silly things! Silly things! How can you
behave so badly to an old man?' He really intended to
say 'stupid birds' but had mixed the words up. But
old Chang seized his chance and said at once: 'You
spoke of silly things. Find me some silly things. If
you can't bring me "silly things" within three days,
your wife belongs to me.' Then he went to the moat,
washed his head like a water-fowl and returned home.

This time, little Baldhead was very depressed, and
going sadly to his wife, he said: 'You will have to go to
old Chang. This time he wants "silly things." Where
on earth can they be found?' But the princess only
laughed. 'I can arrange that,' she said. 'Go down to
the sea and call three times towards the east "silly
things," and they will arrive. They are hidden in a pot,
and you must tell the old man to remove the cover and
they will then come out.' Baldhead went to the sea
and called 'silly things' three times, and a pot came
floating up on the waves. He picked it up and carried
it home, and three days later he got into his litter and
visited old Chang. He was in the best of tempers and
said to Baldhead: 'Well! my friend, be quick and show
me your "silly things."' 'Here they are,' said Baldhead.
But when Chang saw that he had only brought a pot,
he said angrily: 'You call that "silly things"? Hurry
up and bring your wife here.' But Baldhead said:
'Just take the cover off and the silly things will come
out.' But when Chang did so, a bright flame of fire
shot out so swiftly, that he was unable to jump back,
and all his hair, eyelashes, and eyebrows were singed.
At the same time a voice called out of the pot: 'Silly

c

thing! Silly thing! Why do you always want the wife of another?' And quickly covering his head, Chang dashed back to the house and never spoke of 'silly things' again.

5. *The Big Girl*

A PEASANT had married two wives; the first had died on the birth of a daughter, and the second wife had also borne a girl. Soon after, the peasant died and left a large property to his wife and two children.

The wife, though, was a wicked woman. Seeing that the eldest daughter was beautiful, while her own had a face covered with pock marks, she was very jealous and maltreated her step-daughter. One day, before setting off with her own daughter to visit her parents, she handed a pot filled with white feathers, wheat, and green beans to the eldest, with these words: 'Look after the house, and separate the feathers, wheat, and beans. Don't be lazy. If they are not ready by this evening, I will give you a beating.' The girl knew it was impossible to finish the task and sat weeping in the courtyard. 'Oh, Mother,' she said. 'How can I divide feathers, beans, and wheat? Oh, Mother!' A black raven flew down on to the roof and said to her: 'My daughter, you must not weep. Bring it out here.' The daughter carried everything out into the courtyard, and quantities of ravens, magpies, and other birds flew down, and long before evening the feathers, beans, and wheat were lying in three separate piles.

When the step-mother saw that her daughter had easily performed this difficult task, she ordered her to go into the hills with a cow. 'You must not return until the cow produces golden droppings,' she said. The big girl went off into the hills, but by sunset the cow had produced no gold. She sat down on a grave and

34

began to weep: 'Oh, Mother! I must keep the cow grazing until it produces gold. Help me, Mother.' The raven flew down to a tree and said: 'Don't weep, daughter. Draw it out of the cow. Draw it out.' The daughter spread out her coat beneath the animal, and it produced heaps of gold. The next day the wicked step-mother did not let the girl take out the cow; she and her daughter put on fine new clothes and then she sent her daughter into the hills with the cow, telling her to do exactly as her step-sister had done. Towards evening, the second daughter also sat down on the grave and began to weep: 'Oh, Mother, I must graze the beast until it produces gold. Help me, Mother.' Thereupon a dark raven really did call out of a tree: 'Don't weep, second daughter. Draw it out of the cow. Draw it out.' The second daughter quickly spread out her new dress beneath the cow, which lifted up its tail; but this time it was a stream of dung that descended.

6. *The Magic Box*

HUNDREDS, maybe thousands, of years ago there lived a rich man with four sons. The eldest son had married a daughter of the Emperor, the second the daughter of a famous general, and the third the daughter of a minister; but the fourth son had no wife, for he had sworn to marry no one but a fairy.

There were great celebrations on the marriage of the three brothers. The halls and courtyards were over-flowing with guests come to congratulate the happy couples. The fourth son, though, was bored at having no wife and went out for a stroll in the fields. On the way he met a maiden dressed in simple clothes, which, though common, were quite powerless to conceal her incomparable beauty. She was more delicate than a fairy, and even the maiden in the Moon would have

35

looked ugly beside her. The fourth son asked her to be his wife, and when she gave her consent he rushed home to fetch a litter. 'I have a wife! I have a wife! A wonderful, beautiful wife,' he kept on shouting, and ordered the men to take a litter to fetch her, but instead of paying attention, everyone laughingly enquired where he had found his wife. He dashed about in a terrible state, and at last he forced the chair-bearers to bring back the maiden in the common clothes. Then the marriage was celebrated in the presence of the three brothers.

The next day the wives all came home, and each brought her relatives some tea. The eldest, being a princess, brought Korean ginseng tea. The second also brought ginseng tea, being the daughter of a general. The third was the daughter of a minister and also brought wonderful tea. But the fourth merely brought ordinary green tea; everyone despised her, and her sisters-in-law looked down on her. 'He was to marry a fairy,' they jeered. 'Instead he has found a beggar woman without a copper cash.' At New Year all the sons went to congratulate their parents-in-law, but the fourth son remained at home, pacing up and down. At length his wife said: 'Don't you want to pay a New Year visit to my parents?' 'Where can I go?' he asked. 'I will tell you,' she said, and she made a horse of straw and told her husband to ride down to the seashore. Then she unwound a bit of the bandage on her foot and told him to lay it in the sea, whereupon a broad road would appear before him, along which he should go. A few days later he came back with a great quantity of ginseng from Korea, which he divided among the family. The sisters-in-law now no longer dared to give the fourth wife the cold shoulder.

The fourteenth day of the first month is the day for presents, and all the daughters brought a large supply. The wife of the fourth son said to her husband: 'Go

36

down to the sea and fetch me the drifting box. Don't throw it away!' The fourth son went down to the seashore, where he saw an old chest bobbing about on the waves, but when he finally dragged it ashore, he saw it was quite rotten. He thought to himself: 'This bit of junk can't be of any use,' and he threw it back into the water. On his return he said to his wife: 'What is the use of an old box like that? I threw it back into the sea.' 'Go back and fetch it quickly,' she said in a serious tone, and he returned to the beach and brought the box to his wife. On the evening of the fourteenth his wife opened the chest, and inside were countless large houses and halls, in which strange plays were being performed. The shops, filled with goods from the metropolis and foreign lands, were large prosperous establishments, which drove a thriving trade. The restaurants sold swallows' nests, sharks' fins, sea-slugs, and every kind of rare and costly delicacy that the gourmet could desire. The wife invited her brothers and sisters-in-law to watch the plays and wander through the parks, which were stocked with all the birds and flowers in the world, lions, stags, tigers, panthers, elephants, dragons, five-coloured birds and flowers, such as are only known in the home of the Immortals, and many other things that had never been seen before. After the walk she invited them to dinner, and served the most delicious food you can imagine, so that it was very late before they went to bed. The next morning the three wives told their fathers all about it, and naturally they wanted to see it themselves. The Emperor said to himself: 'That is the rarest treasure in the world and belongs to me as Emperor. I will take it away.' And the general said: 'That is a marvellous object. When I am in difficulties on the field of battle, I can use this treasure to save myself.' And naturally the minister also wanted to have it, and he thought out a plan to seize it and live the rest of his life in luxury. The next day the Emperor, the general and the minister came on a visit, and the daughters-in-law received them respectfully and were attentive to their slightest wish. The day of their departure, each had prepared a plan. The Emperor decided to punish them all with death, because they lived in greater splendour than he; the general decided to send for his troops and murder them all; and the minister thought of slandering them and banishing them to the frontier. But as each of them had a daughter in the house, they were unable to carry out their plans. Eventually, the Emperor, hearing that the two others wanted to steal the chest, ordered the general to be strangled and the minister killed. He thought that now no one could gainsay him, but as he was seated in the palace quaffing wine, water suddenly welled up, and more and more came until all the halls vanished beneath the flood. The Emperor continued to drink wine in the palace, although the water soon had reached his beard. He remained sitting there, and before long the water swept him away and he was drowned. The halls and houses were at once transformed into nothing, and only the old chest remained.

7. *The Witch's Daughter*

IN the midst of wild mountains lay a small straw hut, where lived an old man with his three sons. Every day the father went out to look for fuel, and once he met in the wood an aged widow in white clothes, who was seated on a square stone playing chess. As the old man was a keen player himself, he stopped to watch the game. 'Will you play with me?' asked the widow. 'Certainly,' said the old man, and when the widow asked for what stakes they should play he suggested playing for his wood. But the old woman said: 'No, we can't play for wood, because I don't own any. How many children have you, though?' When she heard that the old man had three sons she was very pleased and said: 'That is perfect. I have three daughters. If you win, I will send them as brides for your three sons; but if I win, you must send me your sons as sons-in-law.' The old man stroked his beard for a while, but finally gave his assent. He lost each of the games they played, and when the widow got up to leave, she said, pointing into a dark valley: 'There is my house. To-morrow send me your eldest son, three days later the second, and again after three days, the youngest.' She then departed, and the old man went home without collecting any more wood, to tell his sons what had happened. How pleased they were when they heard it.

The next day he sent the eldest son. Three days later, the second, and on the sixth day he sent the youngest.

As the third son was wandering along, he met an old hermit with a white beard who asked him where he was going. 'I am going to be the son-in-law of the widow in the valley. My two brothers are there already,' said the youngest son. The hermit sighed and said: 'This widow is an old witch. She has only one daughter, with whom she has decoyed many young men and killed them. Your elder brother was eaten by the lion that waits by the outer gate, and your second brother by the tiger that waits by the inner door. You have had the good luck to meet me,' and taking an iron pearl from his breast, he continued: 'Throw this to the lion by the outer gate.' Then he gave him an iron rod, saying: 'Give this to the tiger by the inner gate. Then cut off a stick from the cherry tree by the stream, and when you reach the third door, push the door open with it, and you can enter safely.'

The young man took the pearl and the rod, went into the cherry wood to cut off a branch, and after thanking the hermit, entered the valley. Soon he came

39

upon a large high house, and at the outer door he threw the iron pearl to the lion, who began to play with it. At the second door he threw the iron rod to the tiger, who also began to play. The third door was fast shut, but he gave it a push with his cherry stick, and 'bum,' a thousand-pound block of iron fell down and the door opened. If he had opened it with his hand he would certainly have been crushed.

The witch was seated sewing in her room when she heard a noise at the door. She looked out and saw a young man come in, who she knew must be the third son of the old man. She wondered how he had passed safely through all three doors, but as he entered she pretended to be very pleased, and said: 'You have arrived just at the right time. I have got a bushel of linseed that I want you to sow in the field before it rains. When you come back we will have the wedding.' The young man looked out, and sure enough the sky was full of dark clouds, which looked like rain. He took the bushel of linseed and went out into the field; but the ground was so covered with weeds that he said to himself: 'How can one sow this field without a bullock and a plough?' He tried to pull up a few weeds, but then lay down and went to sleep. When he woke up towards evening he saw that a herd of swine had turned up the soil and pulled up all the weeds; so he sowed the linseed, thanked the swine for their help, and went back to the old woman.

When she saw him coming, she asked: 'Have you finished the sowing?' 'Yes,' said the young man. But the widow frowned. 'You don't trouble to look at the sky,' she grumbled. 'How could you sow the linseed? All the clouds are gone, the moon is shining brightly and no rain will fall, and the seeds won't sprout. You must collect them all again and not one must be missing. When you come back we will have the wedding.' The youngest son bit his lip, took the empty measure, and

40

went out into the field to search for the seeds. Long he searched, little he found, though his back ached from bending. As he was sadly regarding the moon he looked round and saw thousands and thousands of ants appear, each of which dropped a seed into the measure. In no time it was full and the son returned to the widow after thanking the ants. When she saw him she asked: 'Have you got the seeds?' 'Yes,' said the son. 'Good,' she nodded. 'I am going to sleep now. To-morrow I have a new task for you.'

Next morning the old witch told him: 'I am going to hide. If you can find me, we will have the wedding.' And no sooner had she spoken than she was gone. The son searched high and low but could find no trace of her. While he was looking he heard a voice call out from the top of the house: 'My mother has hidden in the garden. She has turned herself into a half-red, half-green peach that is hanging on a tree against the wall. The green part is her back, the red her cheek. Bite her in the cheek and she will turn back again.' The son looked up and saw a maiden in a sea-green dress, with rose-pink cheeks like the half-opened flower of a lotus. He knew she must be the witch's daughter, and, blushing with confusion, he went quickly into the garden. Sure enough, there on the wall was a peach tree, and hanging on it was a half-green, half-red peach. He plucked it, bit the red side, and flung it on to a stone, whereupon the old woman stood before him, with a stream of blood running down her cheek: 'Son-in-law! Son-in-law! you nearly crushed me to death,' she said. But the son answered: 'How could I know you had turned into a peach?' The old woman turned to go, saying as she was leaving: 'Bring me a bed of white jade from the palace of the Dragon King, and we will have the wedding.'

While he was standing in the garden with a drooping head, the daughter came to him and asked what was on his mind. 'Your mother told me to bring her a bed of white jade from the palace of the Dragon King,' he said. 'But no mortal can pass through the sea to his kingdom.' But the daughter consoled him: 'That is quite simple. I have got a golden fork. If you draw a line across the sea with this, a way will form and you can go wherever you want.' The young man took the fork, went to the seashore and drew a line; and in a flash a way was formed in the waves that led straight to the palace of the Dragon King. When he arrived he saw the King and told him that he had come to borrow a bed of white jade. 'Certainly,' the King said. 'In the back palace there are many beds of white jade, just choose one of them.' The young man was very pleased and, having selected a bed of white jade, he returned to the widow.

When she saw that he had brought back the bed, she said to him: 'In the west, on the mountain of the Monkey King, there is a big drum. Bring it back and we will beat it at the wedding.' Just as the son was going away, the daughter appeared and asked: 'What task has mother given you now?' 'I must steal the big drum from the mountain of the Monkey King,' he said. 'I have heard,' the daughter told him, 'that the Monkey King has gone in the Western Heaven and not yet returned. Below the mountain there is a lake of mud. If you roll about in the mud like the Monkey King, the little apes will think you are their ancestor and will bring you to their homes. I will give you a needle, some lime, and some bean-oil. These you must take with you, and when danger threatens, throw first the needle, then the lime, and lastly the oil behind you.'

The son took the three things, went to the lake of mud below the mountain, and rolled about until his whole body except his eyes were caked with mud. He went quickly up the hill, and all the little apes came down from the trees and cried: 'Grandfather, you have arrived!' Then they gathered round him and bore him off in a big chest. The son clapped his hands and said: 'Your grandfather has come a long way and is very hungry. Quickly, go into the peach orchard and bring me some peaches.' Off they ran, as quickly as they could, into the peach orchard with baskets of all sizes. But the young man jumped down from the chest, seized the big drum that he saw hanging in a shelter, and ran away. He had not got far from the hill of the monkeys when he heard them pursuing him, screaming: 'Big black thief! You pretend to be our grandfather and steal our big drum! Wait till we catch you!' The son quickly took the needle out of his pocket and threw it behind him, where it turned into a needle mountain. The little apes pricked their skin and scratched their eyes on it, but they followed him farther. Then he took out the lime and threw it behind him, where it turned into a mountain of lime. The little apes with their torn skin and bleeding eyes stuck to the lime and suffered such terrible tortures that some died, but still they followed him farther. Then he threw behind him the bottle of bean-oil, out of which the oil poured and turned into a slippery mountain. Whenever the little apes wanted to climb up they slipped down again, and the son escaped and returned to the old woman before the sun had set.

When the widow saw he had brought the big drum, she said to him: 'It is still early in the day. Go into the garden and cut down two hair-bamboo sticks, so that we can make a mosquito frame for you.' But the son thought to himself: 'What sorcery is there in the garden?' He plucked up his courage and asked the daughter. 'The gardener is a hairy man,' she said. 'He likes to flay men and eat their fingers. If you must cut down the bamboos, it is certainly very dangerous.' She took out a coat of cocoanut and put it on his shoulders, placed ten small bamboo reeds on his fingers and gave him a two-edged hatchet. 'Be quick,' she said, 'and nothing can happen to you.' The son hurried into the garden, found the bamboo, and cut it down, but a dark hairy man came out of the thicket, seized the cocoanut coat with one hand and pulled off the bamboo reeds with the other. Thinking the coat was the skin, and the bamboo were the fingers, he began to eat them, and in the meantime the son ran away.

When the old woman saw him coming, she asked: 'Have you brought the bamboo?' 'Yes,' said the son. 'Good,' said the widow, 'but you have not eaten anything all day. Here are some noodles of wheaten flour you can have.' The son was really very hungry, and going into the kitchen, he took the cover off the pot. He seized the delicious white noodles in his hands and began to eat them, but soon after he felt pains, terrible pains. The door opened and in came a servant-girl with a lamp, who said: 'My mistress asked you to join her.' He went up to the beautiful maiden, who told the servant to hang the young man on a beam, pull off his shoes, and beat his body with them. After a few blows, ten small snakes fell out of his mouth and crawled about on the floor. The maiden untied the young man and said: 'My mother always wants to harm you. She gave you snakes instead of noodles to eat. Now ask her to have the wedding quickly.'

The next evening, the wedding really took place. In front of the hall the drum of the Monkey King was beaten, in the room stood the bed of white jade from the palace of the Dragon King, and a beautiful mosquito net had been made with the bamboo; everything was very fine and beautiful. But when they went to bed, there was a broad river flowing down the bed between him and the maiden. His wife said: 'This is another trick of my mother's.' And she looked everywhere until under the dressing-table she found a pitcher of water with a bit of wood floating in it. She took out the wood, threw the water away, and the river vanished at once.

But she said to her husband: 'We must flee quickly; my mother will certainly try to do us more harm,' and taking a torn umbrella and a cock, she gave them both to her husband, and they fled away in the middle of the night.

The moon was half-full and lit up the road in the hills. They had gone but a few miles, when suddenly they heard a whirring sound over their heads. The wife took the umbrella and said: 'My mother has sent a flying knife after us. If the knife sees blood it falls, but throw out the cock and the knife will kill it.' He did as he was told and the knife vanished at once. A little later, the wife said: 'The knife will certainly return. Chicken blood is sweet, human blood is salt. My mother will know that she did not kill us last time. What are we to do?' The son listened carefully, and he soon heard again the whirring of the flying knife. Then he began to cry and said: 'I will die.' But the maiden refused: 'No, I must die, because I can come to life again. After my death you must carry my body home, and buy a large lotus pail to put it in. In seven times seven days I will come to life again.' When she had finished speaking, she stepped out and the noise of the knife ceased. The young man saw his bride lying on the ground, her eyes closed, and her face white as a pear-blossom, with the knife sticking in her heart and blood pouring out. He wept bitterly and carried her to his home.

It was not yet light in the east when he arrived. He told his father all that had happened, and the father began to weep when he heard how his eldest sons had been killed by the witch. But the son bought a pail, covered up the maiden's body and watched.

After forty-eight days, he heard loud groans coming from the pail, as if someone was in great pain. Then he thought: 'If I don't let her out now, but wait another day, she will perhaps die again.' So he took the lid off the pail. The maiden slowly lifted up her head, and

45

said softly: 'Why did you uncover me a day too soon? Obviously fate had not intended us for each other.' Then her head slowly sank down and her eyes closed fast. She was dead for ever.

8. *The Pretty Little Calf*

THERE was once a man who had three wives, but none of them had borne him a son. He did so long for one. One day he had to go away to take up a new post, and as he was leaving, his eldest wife said: 'When you return, I will offer you gold.' The second wife said: 'I will offer you silver.' But the third wife said: 'I will offer you a son.' The husband was delighted, but the two other wives were very jealous.

When the third wife really bore a son, the eldest wife tied up her head in a red cloth and bandaged her eyes, and the second wife banged a drum so loud that the third wife swooned. When she woke up and asked for her child, the two other wives deceived her: 'You did not bear a child,' they said, 'it was only a horrible lump of flesh.' Actually she had borne a beautiful strong son, but while she was unconscious the eldest wife had thrown it into the lotus pond to drown; but do what they might, the child floated on top of the water and refused to sink. Then the second wife thought of another plan. They collected some straw and grass, wrapped the child up in it, and gave the whole bundle to an old water-buffalo, which swallowed it down at once, much to the satisfaction and relief of the two women.

When the official returned, the eldest wife gave him the gold, the second the silver, but the third wife was ashamed to appear before him. He asked why she did not produce her son, and the two other wives explained that she had only borne a lump of flesh and did not dare to appear. When the disappointed official heard this,

46

he stamped his feet with rage and ordered her in future to grind rice in the mill as a punishment for the disaster. There she stood and ground rice, and tears ran down her cheeks.

Shortly after, the old water-buffalo gave birth to a beautiful, round, glossy calf with golden skin as smooth as satin. Everyone that saw it fell in love with it, and the whole day it ran round with its master, rubbed against his clothes, stroked him with its horns, and was very, very affectionate. The official always gave it some of his food, and the calf bowed its thanks just as if it was a transformed human being. One day, when the official was eating dumplings, he put a couple into the calf's plate and said to it: 'If you truly understand the human voice and human speech, take these dumplings and carry them to your mother.' The calf slowly pushed the plate along with its two fore-feet, and everyone thought it would push it into the old cow's stall. Instead, it went towards the mill where the repudiated wife was working and dropped it at her feet. Both the official and the wife were very surprised, but the other two wives said to each other: 'This pretty little calf is obviously the transformed child.' The eldest wife pretended to be ill and declared that she could eat nothing except the liver of the little calf. The second also retired to bed and declared that she must have the skin of the little calf to cover her. The official wanted to spare his beloved pet, but the eldest wife screamed: 'I am going to die, only the liver of the calf can cure me.' The second cried: 'I am going to die, only the skin of the calf can save me.' But the official was determined to spare the calf at all costs, and he let it loose in the hills and bought another similar calf, which he had killed instead. The moment the eldest wife had eaten the liver, and the second wife had pulled on the skin, they jumped up cured. But the official was always pining for his lost calf.

47

The Pretty Little Calf

A Miss Huang was looking for a suitor and had announced that on a certain day, at a certain time, she would throw a coloured ball down from her house, and whoever caught it would become her husband. But strangely enough the ball did not touch this man or that man, but fell straight on to the horn of the little calf. The young lady sighed: 'Even a beggar is a man, but to have an animal!' But as she had made the announcement beforehand, she could not break her word. She hung the wedding dress on the horns of the calf and let it run on in front. But no one can run as fast as a cow, and before long the young lady was half a mile behind. She saw it take off the wedding dress beside a large pool of water and then jump in, and when she herself arrived at the pool there was no sign of the calf, but only a handsome young man in a wedding dress. The young man signed to her to follow him, but Miss Huang said: 'I can't go with you! I must look for my calf!' Then the young man told her he was the transformed calf, and that, if she did not believe him, she could see the skin lying in the water. The skin was really there, and the young lady was quite delighted.

The young man led Miss Huang to his parents' house, but when they arrived, it was already dark and the doors were fast shut. He knocked and called out: 'Father, open the door, your son has arrived.' But the father cried from inside: 'Who is calling me father? I have no son. You must have made a mistake.' 'No,' answered the young man. 'I have not mistaken the house. I am the child that my mother formerly said she would present to you when you returned home. I was turned into a calf, but now I am a man again.' He related everything that had happened to him, and his father was happier than ever before in his life, but at the same time he flew into a terrible passion. He sent his son to fetch his mother, but ordered the two other wives to be slain at

48

once, and it was only at the request of his son that he consented to pardon them. Now the mill ceased to work and the youngest wife returned to her husband.

9. *Brother Ghost*

THERE was once a man, whose name I have forgotten, who went fishing in the river to provide food for his mother and his wife. On one occasion he caught no fish for two whole days, and on the third day it began to rain. Now, with the fish that he caught on one day he was able to buy two measures of rice, which was enough for the next day; and therefore he was very worried when he caught nothing for three days. While he was brooding on his troubles, there was a movement in the net, and he quickly pulled it out of the water, hoping he had caught a large fish. He saw something dark wildly thrashing about in the net, and he bravely shouted out: 'A ghost! A ghost! Wife, hurry up and bring me a rope to bind him with. He is the cause of my catching no fish for three days.' His wife was terrified when she heard that he had caught a ghost, but she brought him the rope that she used to tie up crab. Before the man had time to use it, the ghost cried out from the net: 'Please don't bind me. Please don't. I will help you to catch fish.' The fisherman replied: 'You are a ghost. How can you be of any assistance to me?' 'It is true that I am the ghost of a drowned man,' it replied, 'but I can collect the fishes together in the water and drive them into your net.' 'All right! I won't keep you,' said the fisherman, and he let his net down into the water again. After a while he pulled it up again, to find it full of large fish, gaily jumping about. This continued for two or three days, and the fisherman and the ghost became such close friends that they swore brotherhood, with the ghost as elder brother, since death takes pre-

D

cedence of life. From time to time, the fisherman bought some wine and some food, which he took down to the river to eat in the company of the water spirit. Three years passed in this manner, till one evening, when the moon was shining on the river bank, the spirit came out of the water and said to the fisherman: 'Brother, I must now depart.' The fisherman asked him where he was going to, and the ghost added: 'Now that three years have gone by, my time is up; I must go away and be born again. To-morrow a woman is coming down to the river with her daughter-in-law to fetch water, and I will choose one of them as a substitute. If you happen to meet them, for God's sake don't breathe a word.'

The next morning, two women did come down to the river to fetch water. The daughter-in-law wanted to go into the stream in place of her mother-in-law, but the fisherman rushed out and pulled her back. That evening the water spirit came ashore and said angrily to his brother: 'Why do you harm me? Now I have missed my chance, and must wait another three years.' The fisherman replied: 'Brother, the two women were closely related. If one had been drowned, the other would have jumped into the water out of despair.' The water spirit answered sadly: 'I forgive you. You have such a good heart,' and he continued to drive the fish into the net every day.

Another three years went by, and they got on better together than two human brothers. But one evening the ghost said: 'Brother, I must leave you.' The fisherman asked: 'Brother, do you still have to find a substitute in order to be born again?' 'No,' said the ghost, 'the King of the Underworld has appointed me city god in such and such a place.' 'I cannot be separated from you,' said the fisherman. But there was no way out, and they both began to weep. Before leaving, the ghost added: 'If ever you are in a bad way, come and visit me.'

After the departure of the spirit, the fish became

scarcer and scarcer, until again he caught nothing for two whole days. At last, on the evening of the third day, he caught a red fish more than six feet long. The head of some family wanted to eat it and ordered his cook to pay twenty-five ounces of silver for it. The two cooks in the house prepared the fish and put it in the frying-pan, but the smell was so delicious that first one cook and then the other had a taste. 'Thank the Lord it is such a large fish,' they both said, 'no one will know if we eat a little.' But after one mouthful they wanted to have another, until finally they had laid bare the bones on the head. Then they suddenly found that they had become quite light, and with outspread arms they flew up into the air. Meanwhile, the master of the house and his guests grew impatient at the delay, and at last the host sent a servant into the kitchen to see what had happened to the big fish. The servant found the kitchen quite empty, but the smell of the fish in the pan was so exquisite that his mouth began to water. 'After all,' he thought, 'so much of the fish has been eaten already that no one will notice if I have a bite.' But he was as greedy as the two cooks, and went on eating, till the fish was finished. Then he, too, found himself very light, and stretching out his arms he rose into the air. The master waited for the servant, but when he did not return, he went into the kitchen himself in a terrible temper. There was no sign of anyone, and the frying-pan was empty except for a little fish soup. He nearly died of rage and began to curse loudly, but suddenly he heard a voice cry out above him: 'Master, drink the fish soup'; and when he looked up, he saw his two cooks and his servant standing on a white cloud. Then he knew that they had become immortal through eating the fish, and hastily drinking down the soup, he spread out his arms and tried to fly, but not being fated to become an Immortal, he did not succeed.

Meanwhile, I have been forgetting the fisherman,

who no longer worked after the sale of the red fish, but lived with his family on the twenty-five ounces of silver and even bought clothes. Money, however, does not last for ever, and half a year later, being reduced to the verge of starvation, the fisherman decided to visit his brother the spirit.

He went along the town and found the temple of the city god; but his brother was not at home, only his sister-in-law. He bought some incense and paper money and burnt it before the statue while he prayed, and then went out to wander through the streets. Towards evening, the god returned and noticed the ashes before his statue. 'Who burnt these?' he asked his wife. 'I don't know the man,' she replied. 'But while he was burning the paper, he called out "brother" several times.' 'He is obviously my brother,' said the god, and he sent out some spirit servants to look for him and bring him back. When the fisherman arrived, he said to the god: 'Brother, please help me, I have become poor again.' The god replied: 'Quickly return home. Your wife is dying.' The fisherman's eyes nearly started out of his head at the news. 'Can't you save her?' he asked the god. 'The registers of the living and the dead have never passed through my hands, so how can I save her?' replied the god. But when the fisherman had beseeched him three or four times, he took out ten strings of cash and said: 'Take this as journey money. When you reach home, don't say a word to your wife, but fill the house full of firewood, cover up all the bright places with paper, buy three bushels of rice, which you must grind together with your wife, and tell her to cook it for three days and three nights. If you carry out my instructions, she will not die.'

The fisherman hurried back home with the ten strings of cash, and did everything that the god had told him without saying a word to his wife. His wife had cooked some food for him, but instead of eating it, he rushed out and bought three bushels of rice with the remains of the money. He helped his wife to grind it and then, when it was ready, he told her she was to bake cakes with it and not to sleep until they were finished. The woman had begun by understanding what he wanted, but now she asked him, quite at a loss: 'When must the cakes be ready?' But instead of making a reply the fisherman told her to hold her tongue and reserve her energies for the baking. His wife was very angry, but she had to do as she was told, and the old mother ate two of the cakes, because she was very hungry. The fisherman and his mother soon fell asleep, but his wife went on baking for two days and two nights, until her eyes were red with fatigue. She could not understand, but she went on taking the dish off the fire and putting it on again, till during the third day all the wood had been consumed. She tried to wake up her husband and tell him to fetch some more, but do what she would, he and her mother-in-law went on sleeping like the dead. She put the last two bundles of wood under the stove, and not bothering whether the cakes were burnt or not, she went out to fetch some more wood. But as soon as she opened the door she saw innumerable little ghosts, who produced iron chains, and proceeded to fasten them round her neck. As she fell down she let out a scream, which woke the fisherman, who began to beat his breast in despair and curse himself, when he saw his wife lying dead in the doorway. 'Why did you fall asleep, you silly fellow? Oh, why did I sleep so soundly?' he cried.

For the next ten days he and his mother became daily poorer, until at last he decided to return to his spirit brother. On his arrival at the city temple he told the god the sad news of his wife's death, but the spirit scolded him: 'You ought not to have fallen asleep. She is now the wife of the spirit servant in the Southern Temple.' 'I have such a longing for her. Can't you let me see her?' begged the fisherman. 'You can visit her if you like, but she won't recognize you,' said the god, but as the fisherman refused to give up his plan, the god accompanied him to the Southern Temple. She was sitting in a little room doing needlework, but she made no reply to all his questions. The god said to him: 'You two are no longer for each other. Go home now.' When they got back to the temple of the city god the fisherman said: 'Can't you find me some work to do here, brother?' 'All the work here is performed by spirits,' answered the god, but when the fisherman swore that he had no work and would certainly die of starvation, he added: 'There is soon to be a performance in honour of the god of the Western Temple. I can recommend you as drummer.' 'Good,' said the fisherman. 'I might earn a little money.' During the night the city god went over to the Western Temple and appeared to the leader of the orchestra in a dream: 'To-morrow a man is coming here,' he said. 'You must employ him as drummer. Don't send him away,' and, therefore, when the fisherman came next morning and asked to be engaged as a drummer, the leader obeyed the dream and engaged him. But when he played he did not bother to beat the drum in the correct way, and banged away anyhow, with the result that after four or five days the membrane was full of holes.

He threw away his drumsticks and went back to the city god. 'I'm no drummer,' he said. 'Can't you find some other job for me?' 'Yes,' said the god. 'One hundred miles from here to the north-west there is a high mountain, inhabited by hairy men. Many of the people in that district have been devoured by them. They never leave their home by day, so you must go to the caves and build a wall of lime and pour oil on it. The hairy men are very excitable, and will never dare come out for fear of beating themselves to death against the wall. The pumpkin wind-caps and the red jackets they wear are both treasures. If you put the cap on your head and the jacket on your body you become invisible to men. I have here a magic sword, which you can take with you to kill the little hairy men in the cave. If you succeed in freeing the district of these ogres, the people will certainly give you heaps of gold and silver.' The fisherman took the sword and went towards the north-west.

Just as the sun was beginning to set he arrived in the district of the hairy men. Weeping men and women were shutting their doors; the inns were already closed. He implored a shopkeeper to open the door again, and soon after the man had let him in, there came a tapping and snuffing at the door, and a knocking on the walls and the windows, and the fisherman knew that the hairy men had arrived. They remained all night and only went away at cockcrow.

As soon as it was light the fisherman girded on his sword, bought the lime and oil, and went into the hills. He soon found the cave of the hairy men, in front of which he built a wall of lime and poured the oil on it. At dusk the hairy men pulled on their caps and jackets and came singing out of the cave, but when the leader arrived at the opening and saw the wall, he cried: 'Who has obstructed our path? We will eat him up if he doesn't quickly pull it down.' But the fisherman had hidden behind the wall and did not utter a sound. Then the old hairy man clambered on to the wall, but as the oil was slippery he fell down again. Trembling with rage, he charged it with his head, which split in two, and he fell down dead. Their leader gone, the little hairy men fled screaming back into the cave, but the fisherman tore down the wall and, pulling on the cap and jacket, which were lying beside the dead ogre, he grasped his sword and sprang through the opening. He hit blindly in all directions, and the little hairy men saw their heads rolling about on the floor without being able to see who had struck them. Soon they were all dead and, after hiding the cap and the jacket, the fisherman took the corpse of the old ogre and went back to the village. The news of his deed ran through the village like wildfire, and everyone began to jump with joy when they heard that the hairy men were dead, and they vied with each other in loading their saviour with gold and silver.

But I have heard that later, with the cap and red jacket of invisibility, he committed many evil deeds; but the story never went any further, and we must go on to something else.

10. *The Bank of the Celestial Stream*

THERE was once a poor young man with only one cow; and because he was always tending his cow, people called him the cowherd.

One day the old cow said to her master: 'In the stream, south of the meadow, seven heavenly fairies are bathing. If you go there and steal one of the fairy dresses, you can gain one of them as bride.' The young man did as he was told, and the other fairies quickly seized their dresses and flew up to Heaven, leaving one behind, who was called the weaver. She was unable to flee without her dress, and having nothing else to do she followed the cowherd and became his wife.

Shortly after, the old cow fell ill, and feeling its end drawing nigh, it said to its master: 'When I am dead, cut off my skin and fill it with golden sand; then take the ring from my nose and make it up into a packet. Carry this always with you on your shoulder, for one day, when you are in trouble, it will help you.' This time also the man obeyed the cow's words.

During the next two or three years the weaver bore the cowherd a son and a daughter. She often asked him where he had hidden her fairy dress, but he would never tell her, till one day she asked so often and so caressingly, that he eventually betrayed his secret. Then she seized the dress, jumped on to a cloud, and flew away.

The cowherd seized his son and his daughter, and flew up to Heaven by means of the magic cowhide on his back. The weaver took a golden hairpin and drew a long line to cut off the pursuit, which turned into a broad raging river. Then the cowherd shook the sand out of the hide into the river, and it formed a big sand-bank. But the weaver, seeing herself in danger, took her hairpin and drew a long, celestial river, which successfully impeded the cowherd, who had used up all his sand. Instead, he took the ring out of his packet and flung it at his wife, who flung her weaving-shuttle in return. But suddenly a white-bearded god appeared, bearing with him an order from the Ruler of Heaven that they should make peace. From then on each of them must stand on one side of the celestial river, meeting only once in the year on the east bank of the stream on the seventh day of the seventh month.

The two stars that are now visible beside the cowherd and the weaver are the ring and the shuttle.

11. *The Strange Picture*

LI TZU CH'ANG was a very good painter. One day he met one of the Immortals, whom he seized with both hands. But the Immortal immediately flew into a blazing furnace, and although only Li's hands were pulled into the fire, he was very frightened. The Immortal thereupon disappeared and Li Tzu Ch'ang remained a mortal man, only his hands had become immortal and the pictures he painted were able to come to life.

He once painted a moon on the fifteenth day of the month according to the old calendar, when the moon was full, and he pawned it in a pawnshop. The shop-keeper knew that it had been painted by immortal hands, and that it waned from the fifteenth of the month, and waxed from the first, and therefore advanced five hundred pieces of money on it. But ten days later Li Tzu Ch'ang redeemed it, and when he saw there was a large piece of moon missing, he demanded one thousand pieces of gold from the pawnbroker as compensation. But the man said: 'The moon was pawned on the fifteenth day of the month, and you cannot redeem it until the following fifteenth day,' and on the fifteenth the moon was full again.

Later he used his paintings to do all the housework: he painted pictures of grinding corn, of drying it, of threshing, watering, woodcutting, fetching water, plough-ing, tailoring, and of everything that can be done by man, and the work was done much better and quicker than otherwise.

Before his daughter's marriage, Li Tzu Ch'ang painted any number of pictures for her wedding trousseau; clothes, shoes, stocking, coverlets, and everything that is needed in a house, in order that she might have a happy married life. But directly after her marriage her husband's family looked through her trousseau to see how much she had brought, and when they opened the chests and saw nothing but paintings on paper by Li Tzu Ch'ang, they nearly died of rage, and threw all the pictures on to a bonfire. The daughter, of course, knew how useful her father's paintings could be when they came to life, and, therefore, when she saw them in the fire, in spite of being a young bride, she rushed out in a terrible state and just managed to save two pictures, one of a corn-grinder and the other of a corn-pounder.

When the daughter's turn came to grind corn she merely hung up the picture, which did the work for her; and when she had to pound it, she hung up the picture of the corn-pounder, and it did the pounding for her.

Then the whole family regretted their hasty action, but it was too late.

12. *The Wishing Stone*

THERE was once an old man with three sons, but the sons had never learnt anything and sat around all day doing nothing.

One day the old man called his sons to him and said: 'Year by year I grow older. You are more than twelve years old, but you never went to school to learn a trade, and after my death you won't be able to feed your family.' Then the boys answered: 'We will go to work tomorrow,' and they made a plan that they would meet again in three years' time. Their mother cooked a great bowl of rice, which they all ate together, and the remains she gave to her sons for the journey. Then they went to sleep.

At midnight the eldest son got up, rubbed his eyes, went to the bowl, ate some mouthfuls of rice, and set off along the broad highway.

When the second son awoke he saw that his brother had already left, and quickly jumping up, he ran to the fire, gobbled up some food, and followed his brother along the road.

The sun was already shining on the straw roof of the cottage before the third son awoke. 'The others have already gone,' he said. 'I had better be off.' He hurried across to get some food, but not fancying the rice-water left in the pot, he did not eat it, but ran out of the back door and went along the by-way.

The third son wandered along for two days and two nights, till he came upon a troop of men with small gongs and drums. He went nearer and saw that it was a theatre company. He stood quite still watching, until the audience had gone away and the drums and gongs had ceased to beat. After a time one of the players said to him: 'What are you waiting for here?' 'Nothing,' answered the third son; 'I would like to learn to be an actor.' 'You can remain, if you like,' said the man. 'We will teach you to play the second clown.'

In this way the third son joined the troop, wore theatrical costumes, twanged the guitar, and jumped around, until his clothes were worn to tatters. Everyone that heard his songs and his playing said: 'How beautifully he plays.' He travelled all over the land, and like a flash the three years went by. One day, at the thought of his old mother, he threw himself down on the ground and wept. Then he thought of his brothers, who were waiting for him at the meeting-place, and he wondered why he had not returned. He took his guitar, pulled on his tattered old trousers, and travelled day and night towards his home. But after two days he arrived at the shores of a great sea and could not go any farther. On all sides were high waves and clouds, and there was not a single ship to be seen. The rollers were breaking continuously over the sandy beach, and he felt so sad that he wanted to cast himself into the sea. First, though, he took out his guitar, plucked the strings, and began to play such a sad melody that the tears coursed down his cheeks. He was thinking of his parents, and with these thoughts in his mind, he strode singing into the sea.

Suddenly, he heard a call like a human voice, and looking up, he saw before him a messenger of the Dragon-King with his wave-dividing banner. The envoy said to him: 'My master, the Dragon-King, is enchanted by your song. He begs you to go down to his kingdom and sing something before him,' and when the third son agreed to follow him, he raised his banner and beat the waves, which parted before them, leaving a broad road for them to proceed down. The Dragon-King was delighted to see the singer and asked him: 'Was it you who were singing so exquisitely on the beach?

You must be very hungry, though, so drink a little wine and have something to eat.' In a flash crab-servants appeared and placed delicious-smelling dishes before him, and being very hungry, the young man ate everything without even noticing what it was. After the meal he began to sing so wonderfully that the Dragon-King never ceased to stroke his beard in pleasure, and at the end, the Dragon-Prince ordered him to appear before him.

The third son remained three days in the Dragon kingdom, but then he thought of his parents and wanted to return home. The Dragon-Prince asked him anxiously: 'Are you not happy here?' 'Of course, I am happy,' said the third son, 'but when I think of my mother I become sad.' 'I understand,' replied the Prince. 'To-morrow you can return home. If my father wants to give you gold and silver, don't accept it, but ask for the precious stone that I wear on my breast. If later you are in difficulties, you only need to ask the stone for something, and it will appear.'

The next morning, as the third son was taking his leave, the Dragon-King said: 'I will give you silver.' 'I do not want silver,' said the third son. 'Then I will give you gold.' 'I do not want gold,' said the young man. 'If you do not want gold or silver, what can I give you then?' said the King. 'I want the jewel that the prince is wearing on his breast,' said the third son. For a long time the Dragon-King remained wrapped in thought, but eventually he turned to his son and asked: 'Are you willing for him to have it?' The prince gave his assent at once, and removing the stone, he put it in his friend's hand. Then two messengers of the Dragon-King escorted the third son back to the beach, from where he rushed off to the meeting-place at which his brothers had been awaiting him many days.

A few days later, they arrived home. Their mother had almost wept her eyes out in longing for her sons.

But when she heard of their return, her sight was restored, and she soon saw her sons standing before her. Then they went in to their father, who had become much more wrinkled in the meantime, and he said to them: 'Eldest son, what trade have you learnt?' 'I became a coppersmith,' answered the young man. 'Good. And you, second son? What did you learn?' 'I am a silversmith,' answered the second son. 'Good. Last-born, what did you become?' 'Father, I became an actor.' But when the parents heard that their son had merely become an actor, they were so angry that they lost control of themselves, and died of mingled rage and sorrow.

In the next three years, the three brothers married one after the other. One day, the eldest wife said to the second: 'Our youngest brother-in-law does nothing the live-long day and never earns a farthing. Since his brothers burnt his guitar, he only bangs on a bench and makes a frightful din, with the result that our children can't sleep. We ought to divide the inheritance; otherwise the third son will eat up all we have.' 'Yes, we must do that,' said the second wife.

When the third son heard of the division, he took a couple of poles, a few bundles of straw, a big cauldron and two broken plates, and calling his wife, he went over to a small uncultivated piece of ground, not more than an acre in extent, where he knocked in the poles, laid the straw on top, and in this manner built a house, in which he lived with his wife. Every morning he went into the hills to gather wood, and they lived from hand to mouth.

Later, the cold north-west wind came and blew against the straw hut, and the autumn rain beat against the doors. The third son could no longer go out and collect wood; he lay on his bed the whole day and looked into the cooking-pan, which contained only water. From time to time, he drank a little to warm himself, and then rubbed his hands. Suddenly he remembered the wishing stone of the Dragon-King, and he called to his wife: 'What would you like to eat? What about some fish and some roast? Choose whichever you like.' His wife was still in bed, but now she turned over and re-settled the straw on her legs. 'Don't make such silly jokes,' she grumbled. 'If only we had a bowl of bean-curd to eat!' But her husband asked her again: 'Don't you want any fish or meat?' But she paid no more attention, and after cursing him for being a fool, turned over and went to sleep.

He, though, secretly rubbed the stone and said: 'Dear stone, we do so want a bowl of bean-curd and some fish and some meat.' In a flash, a spirit appeared, with a dish of bean-curd in his left hand and a dish of meat and fish in his right, and laying them down on the ground, he said: 'Poor devil, I hope it tastes good,' and disappeared. The third son woke his wife and gave her the bean-curd, which she gobbled up in a moment, and then he offered her the fish and the meat. She was still suspicious, but, when she looked at the plates, they were piled high with delicious fish and fat pork. She seized them and ate as much as she could, till the fat ran down her clothes.

Afterwards, she asked her husband: 'When did you buy this food? Or did you steal it?' Slowly and carefully he pulled the wishing stone out of his pocket. 'I didn't buy it,' he said, 'I got it from the stone. Anything I ask for I can get.' Then the woman cried: 'If you possess such a treasure, why don't you ask it to build us a beautiful house? Our old hovel is soon going to fall down.' So he grasped the stone firmly and said: 'Dear stone, build me a beautiful big house.' Immediately a spirit appeared, and said: 'Poor devil, enjoy living in it!' And from then on, the man and his wife lived in a wonderful, tiled house.

One day, the eldest brother had to climb on to the roof to mend the tiles, and from there he saw his youngest

63

brother, clad like a prince, riding through the village on a stallion. He quickly ran down and said to the second brother: 'Come and look. Our brother has turned robber, he has stolen a horse, and obviously means to attack us.' And, therefore, when the brother arrived at the house, dismounted, and knocked at the door, no one opened it. Finally, he heard his elder brothers shouting: 'You wretch! You villain! You never do any work, and now you have become a thief.' But the youngest son explained: 'I have a wishing stone, why should I rob others? Look at the large house over there among the trees, that belongs to me.' Filled with curiosity, the brothers looked in the direction indicated, and sure enough, there was a beautiful house in the wood, gleaming like silver in the sun. The sight of this persuaded them to open the door and let their brother in. 'What is your wishing stone?' they asked eagerly. 'I only need to ask for something and it is there,' explained the brother. 'Can't you lend it to us for two days?' begged the two elder brothers. The third son took the stone out of his pocket and put it on the table, where it fell in two pieces, one of which he gave to his eldest brother, putting the other back in his pocket. They talked a little longer, and then he went home.

The elder brother shut the doors and began to stroke the stone: 'Stone, stone, I want great riches,' he said, and immediately the spirit appeared with a heap of gold. 'Poor devil, I hope you enjoy it!' it said, but the brother frowned and said angrily: 'I own fields and have enough to eat. Next time, don't call me poor devil,' but while he was speaking there came a great gust of wind through the house, the money disappeared off the table, and the spirit sprang into the air and vanished. The half stone flew away out of the window.

The third son meanwhile was seated at his meal, when the half stone came in through the window, and, after circling round a few times, joined the other half, which had flown out of his pocket. Then both halves fluttered off, like two butterflies, and slowly sank beneath the sea.

13. *The King of the Bees*

THERE was once a man who, when he became Imperial Censor, had to live in the capital many months' journey from his blue hills and green waters. He was a faithful official, and every morning, while the dew was still on the ground, he went to the audience in the palace. But, besides his love of duty, he had another love; and every night he returned to his wife and spent the night with her. His mother, however, knew nothing of this. One day the wife found that she was going to have a child, and her mother-in-law also noticed it and said: 'You faithless woman! You shameless thing! You adulteress! How can you have a child when your husband is not at home? Who comes and visits you? If other people hear about this we shall no longer be able to live here. We shall completely lose face if there is a scandal. What have you to say? Tell me everything.'

'Dear mother,' said the young wife, blushing, 'how could I dare do such a thing? My husband comes to visit me every night.'

'Don't tell me such stories! How can he make such a long journey? Does he bring anyone with him? You can't deceive me,' cried the mother angrily.

'But it is quite true, he does come to me. How could I deceive you? Really I have no . . .' and her words were choked by sobs.

'He is not a spirit, so it is impossible. You are lying. It is no good crying, because I will never believe you,' said the mother.

E

'Dear mother,' said the young wife, 'I can explain. It is true that he is not a spirit, but he has a pair of magic shoes. When he puts them on, he can cross over the sea like a bird.'

'I don't believe it! How can there be shoes like that?' retorted the mother.

'It is true,' replied the daughter, 'and if you don't believe . . .'

'All right,' interrupted the mother; 'if you can show me one of the shoes, I will forgive you.'

When the daughter found there was no other means of convincing her mother-in-law, she decided to steal one of her husband's shoes; but little did she know what unhappiness this would cause.

That evening, when her husband came as usual, she stole one of his shoes and showed it to her mother-in-law. But in the morning when the husband was ready to leave and wanted to put on his shoes, he could only find one of them. He had to run down to the seashore and make a shoe of mud and slime so as to go to the audience. While he was making the shoe, the sun came shining over the horizon. This made him so angry that he pointed his finger at the sun, which went down again at once.

When the shoe was ready, he set off for the audience. That morning, as usual, all the ministers and notables were present, but everyone wondered why the Censor had not yet arrived. Suddenly someone said to the Emperor: 'To-day a miracle has occurred. Just after the sun had risen, it disappeared again. I don't know what that betokens.' While the Emperor and his ministers were discussing in an agitated manner what was the meaning of the prodigy, the Censor came absent-mindedly into the Audience Chamber. Everyone crowded round him, and soon they noticed something very strange: one of his shoes was wet and slippery and the other dry. The Emperor asked him: 'Why have you arrived so late to-day in such a hurry that you did not even put on your shoes?'

Overwhelmed with confusion, the Censor did not know what reply to make. His face became pale as ashes, and when he was known to have meddled with the sun, he was accused of treason and sentenced to death.

After he was beheaded, his body stood up again, took up its head, and went home. On his way, he met a woman mowing grass, whom he asked: 'Can grass go on living when it is cut down?' The woman replied: 'It soon grows up again.' He went on his way and soon came upon a maid cutting garlic. 'Young lady,' he said, 'does the garlic go on living?' She answered: 'It comes up stronger than before.'

When he heard this, he did not ask anyone else, but went home and asked his mother: 'Mother, when a man's head is cut off, can he go on living?' His mother answered in horror: 'My son! That is not possible. How can someone come to life again?' At this he fell down on the floor and blood poured out of his body in a ceaseless stream. He had hoped to be able to go on living, and when he heard the replies of the woman and the maid, he was full of hope, but when he heard his mother's words, he collapsed.

After his death, his soul could find no peace, because he had been unjustly condemned. His first attempt having failed, he appeared to his wife in a dream and said: 'Since I ought not to have died, I am able to live again. On no account must you bury my head, but place it in a pot and wait until the worms appear. If you feed them every day, I can come to life again.'

When the wife heard that, she was comforted a little in spite of her sorrow and mourning, and she did as her husband had told her. She hoped that when the worms had appeared she would live with him as before.

One day, when she had to return to her parents'

house, she asked her mother-in-law to feed the worms. But to her it seemed a useless task, so she poured boiling rice into the pot and killed all the worms that the wife had reared with such care, and threw them into the garden. But in the place where she threw them a lovely tender bamboo soon shot up.

When the wife came home and saw that all the worms had gone, she nearly wept herself to death, and wanted to end her life, but her husband appeared to her again and said: 'There is still a third chance. The bamboo outside the window is my transformed soul. Tend it carefully for one hundred days, and then, if someone wants to buy it, ask exactly one hundred cash, no more and no less, and wait till the following day.' This consoled the wife a little.

The time swept by like a stream and the last day drew near. One morning a high official on a tour of inspection was passing through the village, when one of the supports of his litter broke and could not be mended. He ordered his servants to find another pole, but though they searched high and low they could not find a good bamboo, until they came to the house of the wife. They went in and asked her to sell it. First they offered ninety pieces of money, then they went up to ninety-nine, but more they refused to give. The mother-in-law lost patience and sold it for ninety-nine pieces.

The wife, meanwhile, was sitting in the house listening to the hum of voices. Looking out, she saw that they were talking about the bamboo.

'How much are they giving?' she asked. 'I must have one hundred cash, no more, no less. In any case it is not old enough yet, so I cannot sell it.'

'But your mother-in-law has already sold it for ninety-nine pieces, you cannot bargain any more. We are going to cut it down now,' answered the servants.

'No! No! I must have one hundred pieces; on no account more nor less! If you cut it down, then . . .'

68

'Be quiet, don't make so much fuss about one copper piece. What are you talking about?' said the mother-in-law, and she told the servants to cut it down and not listen to the wife.

The servants quickly drew their knives, but they had not yet cut the bamboo half through, when it split in half from top to bottom. And, strange to relate, in each knot they found a little man on a little horse. Some of them had already opened their eyes, others not yet. In the last knot, however, was a large bee, which flew away with a loud hum. The people could only talk about the strange occurrence; with the bamboo there was nothing to be done.

But the bee flew away to the Imperial palace, into the Audience Hall, where it stung the Emperor. No one could drive it away, until the Emperor questioned his ministers and learnt that the bee was the ghost of the Censor that he had wrongly condemned to death. Since the Emperor found no peace, he decided to let the bee sit on his throne for three days and to make him King of the Bees.

The men and the horses in the bamboo were meant to come forth after one hundred days, take their swords, and press into the capital to kill the Emperor out of revenge. But as the hundred days were not finished the husband only became King of the Bees.

14. *The Sacrifice of the Maiden*

IN former times in a village in the Chu district lived forty or fifty families of brick-bakers, all of whom were quite rich. Living as they did from the manufacture of bricks, they were all very respectful to the god of brick-ovens. Before building a new furnace they used to sacrifice and ask permission of the god, and when it was ready they used to sacrifice a whole pig and a whole sheep in front of it. In that case, everything was in order, but if it was not done the bricks came out yellow or soft, and sometimes even the whole furnace collapsed.

In the village lived a rich Mr. Ts'ai, who spared neither time nor money to get the whole brick-making business into his hands. He built a large new furnace three miles outside the town, but everything did not go according to his wishes, because the first time he baked bricks they remained yellow without being properly fired. He angrily sent for the builders and the workmen to question them, but none of them could find any explanation, till finally an old man suggested consulting a fortune-teller. All agreed to this suggestion, and the owner sent for one.

The next day the magician gave the following answer to the questions of the old workman: 'It is true that Mr. Ts'ai offered sacrifices during the building of the furnace, but he has an evil heart. As a punishment he must offer his daughter alive, and the furnace will be all right.'

The old workman reported to Mr. Ts'ai what had been said, but Ts'ai straightway bought a thirteen-year-old girl for the sacrifice in a village one hundred miles away. At the time of a sacrifice there is also a large festival, and as well as the officiants, many friends and relatives like to take part.

The rich man had a daughter of his own, who while a small child had gone to another family as their future daughter-in-law. Her father now brought her home to be present at the ceremony. She was the same age and hardly distinguishable from the girl he had bought, in fact it was very easy to mix them up if you didn't look carefully.

Not wanting the slave-girl to be aware of her fate, Mr. Ts'ai arranged for her on the day before the sacrifice to eat with his daughter, just like a relation, and to sleep in the same bed. Now nobody in the village, except some tile-workers, knew anything about the proposed human sacrifice; they thought the young girl was merely a personal attendant of the master. Mr. Ts'ai had told the workmen that when the girl arrived with their food they were to seize her and throw her into the furnace, afterwards sacrificing a sheep and a pig. The same evening he told the girl to go early to bed, because the next morning she must rise early to go and call the workmen to breakfast and tell them to bring the sacrifices. The two girls went off to sleep, but Miss Ts'ai was so excited at the idea of a sacrifice that she discussed it all through the night and never slept a wink.

As it became light, everyone was sleeping except Miss Ts'ai. She quietly opened the door and, in place of the slave-girl, called the workmen to breakfast. The workmen were all ready waiting for her arrival, and when she reached the furnace, they seized her and flung her inside. Shortly after, when Mr. Ts'ai ordered the slave-girl to go to the furnace, he was horrified to find no sign of his daughter. He dashed out to the furnace, but when the workmen saw him, they shouted: 'Everything is done as you said, Mr. Ts'ai.' Overcome by his grief, tears poured out of his eyes.

15. *The Spirit*

IN former times a poor kind-hearted man, by trade a fisherman, lived with his family of three in a straw hut on the banks of a river in the middle of a thick forest. Unfortunately the fish had been nearly exterminated by the cormorants, and for several days he carried an empty basket home, and there was nothing to eat in the cooking-pot. His children cried, his wife scolded, but all he could do was to knit his brows. One night, when the moon had just disappeared behind the mountains, he was restlessly tossing about in their joint bed. His wife and children were sleeping soundly. Suddenly he seemed to hear a knock at the door, but thinking that no one could be about at such a late hour, he paid no attention, till finally the knocking became very insistent. Having no fear of ghosts, he pulled on a covering and glanced out of the window near the bed. The silvery-green disc of the moon was shining through the pines on the Western Hills, and an icy wind blew in through the window. Going to the door, he called out: 'Who is there?' 'It is I,' answered the voice. 'I am bringing you fish. Open the door quickly.' 'Oh, are you Little Number Three?' asked the fisherman, because he had once heard that 'Little Three' caught fish for other people, and as the voice answered his question in the affirmative, he opened the door.

A dwarf, clad in a raincoat and a large straw hat, came smiling into the room with a basket full of fish on his back. He told the fisherman to take out half of the fish, and to cook and eat the other; on no account, though, must he talk to other people about him. Number Three did the cooking himself in the simplest fashion. He used no herbs, only salt and oil, but in spite of that the food tasted delicious. When they had finished eating, he made an appointment with the fisherman for the following night at a certain place to catch fish. The next morning the fisherman sold the fish, and bought some rice, and told his wife that a friend had lent him some money. He sat at home all day and pondered over his experience, and when his wife urged him to go out, he merely replied that there were no fish and that it was a waste of time to go down to the river.

It was soon time to go; his wife and children were asleep; silently he took a large fishing-basket and went off to meet Little Three. He met him by the wild rocks near the river, and the spirit impressed on him the need of following closely and not saying a word, and of breathing as softly as possible. The fish could not recognize the clothes of Little Three, but if they made any noise, the fish would swim away at once. The strangest thing was that the dwarf was able to walk on the water, and he only needed to spit on the soles of the fisherman's shoes to enable him to do the same. Naturally the fish could not see them.

The fisherman did exactly as he was told; he took great care not to breathe too loudly, and when Little Three caught a fish, he took it from him and threw it into the basket. He was kept very busy and soon became quite out of breath. Before they had gone a quarter of the way the basket was full, and he merely threw the fish back into the water again, because the spirit caught fish without bothering whether there was room for them or not. A little later they both stepped on to the bank, and shivers ran down the fisherman's spine at the appalling sight of the deep water they had crossed over. They returned home, cooked and ate half the fish, and put the other half aside according to the rule of the spirit.

Every night, except at the time of full moon, they went out fishing, but the fisherman said nothing to his wife, and so as to avoid all suspicion, from time to time even went fishing during the day. But he earned so much money that his wife became suspicious, and eventually she discovered everything. One night she pretended to be asleep and watched to see what her husband would do. She saw him eating fish with another man, and then he came into the bedroom and went to sleep. She made no sign, but when he had fallen asleep she got up and saw what had been happening.

The next day she bored a small hole in the plaster wall and watched the two men cooking the fish. She saw how they only cooked half, and she thought to herself that if only they could keep the other half they would have food for several days. She made a plan, and the

73

following night, when Little Three came again and placed the pot on the fire, it suddenly went up in flames. The spirit saw at once that something was wrong and ran away. The fisherman was very angry, but not till his wife came into the room with a smile on her face did he know that the pot had been made of paper. From then on the spirit never came to cook and eat fish.

16. *The Bridge of Ascension*

JUST near the East Gate of Ch'üan-chou there is a small stone bridge called the Bridge of Ascension. It is related that in olden times every man, woman or child that wanted to ascend to Heaven and become an Immortal only needed to go to the bridge on a bright moonlight night when no one was about, and an Immortal would appear and guide them to the gardens of Paradise. The next morning there was not even a corpse to be seen, and for this reason the bridge was very celebrated. At the time when the bridge still enjoyed this magic power, one of the Immortals called Pei, who had heard of its fame, came by to investigate the truth of the report. He soon discovered that in reality a giant serpent, which had perfected itself for a thousand years in the Ch'ing-yüan mountains, was deluding the people into the belief that the bridge led to Heaven, and really eating them up himself. Now Pei was a moral Immortal. If he had not known about the ogre, he could not have done anything; but knowing it as he did, he considered it his duty to assist mankind and destroy the monster that was injuring them.

Towards midnight, he went into the mountain, where, after a short search, he came face to face with the serpent. The moment they saw each other, they began to fight with swords, with magic weapons, with charms and prayers to the spirits, and they fought till heaven and earth began to shake, but at last good was stronger than evil, and having exhausted all its magic tricks, the snake fled to an old well. Despite all the insults Pei hurled at it, it refused to come out, and Pei was at a loss, because he could not enter the water; on the other hand, he did not want to leave it free to harm mankind. At last, he decided to sacrifice himself, and, placing himself over the mouth of the well, he transformed himself and died. With his body covering the opening, the serpent could not escape, and with its death the magic of the bridge was at an end.

Later on, an altar was built at the well in honour of Pei, who had given his life to save the district; and a statue was made out of his body, which was coated with plaster. It remains there to this day.

17. *The Tale of the Serpent*

IT is so long ago that I have forgotten in what district the lotus pond was, in which every year the lotuses bloomed red in May and June, bigger than the head of a man. The strangest thing was that they rose up above the water at night and sank down in the morning. No one knew what the explanation was, but anything that was laid on them went under with the flower.

At that time, a monk heard about this lake and spread the report: 'This lotus flower has a connection with the Western Paradise. It is a lotus throne such as the Buddhas of the Three Ages have. If virtuous people sit on this seat, they can go straight to Heaven.' A few days later, all the men and women in the town had heard this report, and every one over sixty years old placed themselves on the lotus flower and went to the Western Paradise.

75

Three or four years passed, and no one knows how many old men and women had travelled to Heaven on the lotus. The mother of the district governor became sixty years old at this time, and having heard these tales from her maids, she decided to go to Paradise herself. She said to her son: 'My son, I am just the same as other women. They can all ascend to Heaven, and being now sixty years old, I have decided to go there to-morrow and not waste any more time on earth. I hope that you will lead a virtuous life and prepare for the world to come. If I see that from the Western Paradise, it will be a great comfort to me.' The official was horrified at his mother's decision, and when he heard the reports of the maid-servants about the lotus pond, he said to her: 'You cannot believe such stories, mother. Don't think any more about it, I want to keep you with me for a long time yet, and I won't let you go.' His mother was very angry when she heard this: 'You want to be District Administrator, but you don't yet know how to look after your mother. All sons, daughters, and wives rejoice when their old parents attain to Paradise, but you want to hinder me. You are the most undutiful son.' Quickly the official answered: 'Forgive me, mother. Do as you will. I will prepare some food for you and order all the things that you will need in the Western Paradise.' But his mother cut him short: 'I don't need anything,' she said. 'In the Western Paradise one is in the realm of the Buddha and needs nothing to eat. I will only take some incense and a staff, nothing else. Order the litter, I want to leave to-morrow at dawn.'

The official withdrew, but after thinking the matter over for a long time, he formed a plan. He ordered his servants and employees to fill a great number of sacks with gunpowder and quicklime, and during the night he loaded them on to two ships and sailed off to the lotus lake. The lotus flower was standing several feet above the water, and he poured sack after sack into it.

The flower opened and shut and transported the two cargoes of sacks into the Western Paradise.

The next morning the official arrived with his sons, his daughters, and all his relations, to escort his mother to the Western Paradise. But on their arrival at the lotus lake the people collected round and said: 'The lake has been turned into a big river by an enormous serpent.' The official at once ordered his servants to catch the snake and cut it open, and after they had cut for three days and three nights, they brought out bushels of heads and innumerable buttons off the clothes of the old people. The gunpowder and the quicklime were still burning. Everyone now knew that this enormous lotus flower was the tongue of a giant serpent.

18. *The Gratitude of the Snake*

THERE was once a child belonging to a well-to-do family, whose father unfortunately died soon after his birth. His mother, however, carefully looked after the inheritance and they lived quite comfortably. She sent the child to a school where there was a good teacher, and he was very happy, going there early and coming home late. But, excepting her natural love for her son, the mother was deserted and lonely.

The boy was very kind-hearted and friendly towards all living things. He studied industriously, and nearly every day earned his teacher's praise. The teacher commended his work and his kind-heartedness; for, whenever he found an animal on the point of being killed by another, he always took the trouble to save it and bring it out of danger. He was fond of keeping animals as pets, and he put wounded birds into cages, and fed them and looked after them carefully until they were well, when he set them free again.

77

The Gratitude of the Snake

One day, when he was coming back from school with his books on his back, he found a tiny snake, not more than three inches long, lying half-dead and covered with blood in the middle of the road. His kind heart was touched, and he quickly went up and saw that it was not quite dead. He knew that the little snake must have been attacked by some big animal, and pitying the poor thing he picked it up to look at it. Then he made up his mind, took his ink-box out of the packet of books, placed the little snake inside, and went home.

His mother was standing by the door and asked him why he was so late returning. He told her the truth, and his mother did not reprove him, but fetched some ointment to put on the wound, and hoped that the snake would soon be well again. From then on, when the boy went to school, he always took the snake with him and was never separated from it. After a month the wounds were healed, and the snake began to know him. He kept on thinking he ought to let it go now that it was cured, but he could never make up his mind to do so.

Time passes quickly. Several years went by. The little snake gradually became bigger, but it never left the boy. The ink-box had become too small for it, and he put it in a large pot. But that also became too small, and then it just fitted into a drawer in his study. Every day, when he left for the school, he first opened the drawer and fed his pet, and the snake raised its head to receive the food he put in its mouth. He did this every day and the snake never harmed him. Only when he had brought too little, or had forgotten to bring it anything, did it stretch its head right out of the drawer as if it were asking for its dinner.

One year it was again the time for the triennial examinations in the capital. The boy was already twenty years old, and, although he was still in the school, his knowledge was very great. When he heard of the examination, he begged his mother to give him leave to compete, and having received her permission, he chose a favourable day to set out. By this time the snake had become very big, but he still kept it, and on his travels he took it with him in his luggage. He packed up all his things, took enough money for the journey, and when the favourable day arrived, he took leave of his mother and departed.

In those times travelling was not so convenient, and from his home there was no ship or carriage to be hired for the journey. He had, instead, to go on foot over hills and through rivers for more than a month, and he was quite alone, without a single companion. He felt very lonely, because he had never left his village before, and he was terrified at the idea of the long journey. One day he arrived at a mountain, where he lay down to rest. He looked at the thick forest and the range of mountains, which stretched away as far as the eye could see, and he became very uneasy at the thought that he would need at least ten days to cross them. While he was sitting on a stone, wrapped in these gloomy meditations, the snake suddenly shot its head out of the basket and stared at him without making a sound. The boy sighed and said: 'Dear snake. I have cared for you since the time you were three inches long. Many years have passed, and you have grown big. I am going to the capital to take my examination, and perhaps I shall never return. I must now cross these high mountains and sharp crags quite alone, and if I meet a wild beast I shall be lost. My life is hanging by a thread, and were I to die, you would be shut up in the bundle and would starve to death. I will therefore set you free to hunt for your own food. If Heaven permits me to live, you can wait for me, and I will pick you up on my way home. Now you can go,' and he placed it on the ground. The snake seemed to understand, for it nodded its head and disappeared into the undergrowth.

The Gratitude of the Snake

The student was now quite alone, and he journeyed on for ten days before reaching a small village on the other side of the forest. There he decided to spend the night, because it was already dark, and there was still a long time before the examination took place. But it was too stupid, wherever he went all the inns were full up. He asked a servant the reason, and the man said to him: 'Perhaps you don't know that the examination takes place this year, and that all the candidates lodge here on their way to the capital.' 'Is that the reason?' said the boy; 'but what can I do?' 'I am very sorry, sir,' said the servant. 'But really there is no room here. Have you tried the other inns?' 'Yes, I have tried everywhere, but I always received the same answer. Can't you help me?' begged the boy. 'It is very difficult,' said the servant. 'We have actually one small room, but we never offer it to our guests, because it is haunted. There is nothing else though.' 'I am not afraid of ghosts,' said the boy. 'I will sleep there,' thinking that, after spending so many nights in the open, nothing could frighten him. The servant agreed to give him the room, but refused to take any responsibility. 'That is all right,' said the boy, 'you needn't bother about me.' And the servant brought his luggage and prepared the bed.

There was not a sound to be heard when he retired to his room, but thoughts of ghosts filled his mind and he began to feel a little frightened, since, if anything happened, his life would have been sacrificed in vain. He thought of his home, and of his old mother who was waiting for him. She would weep her eyes out if he never came back. But it was too late for regrets. The wind whistled outside, and the night was as dark as black lacquer. Sitting by his candle, his past rose up before him like a great flood. He felt depressed and sad, but he was also very sleepy and went to bed, because after all everything is decided in heaven, and one cannot

80

avoid one's fate. But his mother—— No, he must not think of her any more, and soon after he fell asleep.

About midnight he woke up; indoors everything was quiet, but the wind was whistling outside. In the room the candle, dimmed by the dark shadows, was guttering as low as a green bean, and he thought to himself it would not be of much use in an emergency. About two o'clock the wind grew stronger. The glass in the window was making a terrible din, shaking and clattering about, and then the window flew open of its own accord. The boy woke up in a fright and ran to look out of the window, from which he saw a dark patch, like a large animal, flying on the wind, closely pursued by another thing. They flew in through the window and stopped by the bed, where they began to fight, one on top of the other in a terrible mess. The boy sat on the bed and screamed for help, but the noise of battle gradually became softer and then ceased altogether. When he raised enough courage to look down, he saw the two combatants lying tangled together on the floor.

It was not yet light, but sleep was out of the question, and he got up hurriedly to investigate. He found a millipede and a snake lying at the foot of his bed, with their teeth locked on each other's throat, and when he looked carefully, he saw that the snake was the one he had set free a few days before. He was very sad and shed many tears, but he had the snake buried by the servant and then continued his journey.

Later he passed the examination in the capital and was made an official in his home town. On his way back he fetched the body of the snake from the inn and took it with him. At home he built a grave for it and made a sacrifice there himself. His mother was overjoyed at his return and chose him a wife. And their life passed in peace and contentment.

19. *The Pearl of the Millipede*

THERE was once a temple to the God of War, Kuan Ti, where sacrifices were offered every spring and autumn. But the chickens, fish, and fruits that were left there had always disappeared by the next morning, and it looked as if someone had eaten them, because only the bones of the meat and fish remained, and the kernels of the fruit, and the dishes were scattered all over the altar. Many people believed that the God of War ate them himself, and therefore the worshippers at this temple were very numerous.

One of the temple servants, however, was suspicious, and next time there were sacrifices in the temple, he hung up a bamboo screen, and hid behind it to see if the god would come. About midnight a huge millipede, more than twelve feet long, appeared from behind the statue of Kuan Ti. The servant turned pale with terror and tried to flee, but his legs refused to obey him and he stayed rooted to the spot, watching what the millipede did. Fortunately it did not see him, but slowly ate up all the offerings on the altar, and then climbed down and wandered up and down the hall. Finally it went outside, and facing the moon, spat out a pearl as big as the mouth of a cup, which effused a dim red glow. After playing with it for a while, it seemed to grow tired, and then it stood quite still, as if it was sleeping. The pearl was only lying about three or four feet away from the man, but, although he knew that it was a treasure, he did not dare to take it. At the fifth watch, about dawn, the millipede awoke, swallowed the pearl again, and vanished slowly behind the statue of Kuan Ti. Next morning, when the servant looked behind the figure, he found a large hole, which seemed to lead into the hill behind the temple.

The servant waited until just before the next sacrifice and then ordered a big strong box from the carpenter.

When the time came he put the box in the hall of the temple and hid inside it. About midnight the millipede appeared from behind the statue, ate the offerings, and went down into the hall, where it spat out the pearl and went to sleep. The servant crept out of the box, snatched up the jewel, and then quickly locked himself in again. When the millipede awoke soon after and found the pearl had vanished, it became wildly excited and rushed about the hall searching everywhere, until eventually it came upon the box. It tried every means of opening it, but finding it was impossible, it whirled round and round, fastened its feet into the box, and died. The servant meanwhile had fainted with terror, and only regained consciousness the next morning, when the temple monks removed the millipede and opened the box.

20. *The Butcher and the Vegetarian*

IN P'u-chiang there is a proverb: 'The butcher gets to Paradise, the vegetarian falls into a ditch.' If one takes it literally it has little meaning; but, if one knows the story connected, one will certainly say that it has one.

In former times there was a long copper bridge on Earth, leading to the Western Paradise. All good men could cross over on it and become Buddhas and Immortals. But later, when Lü Tung-pin was fleeing with Miss White Peony, and they were pursued by her brother with an iron club, he overtook them just as they were crossing the copper bridge. Lü Tung-pin was terrified when he saw the young lady's brother coming, and smashed the bridge with his magic sword, thereby swearing an oath that no one might cross over it to Paradise, which remains true to this day.

Before the bridge was broken there was a butcher on Earth. He had a debtor, who was unable to repay his money, and this annoyed the butcher so much that he threatened to skin the man in pursuance of his trade. A passer-by, who heard this remark, asked the butcher how much he was owed? 'A hundred cash,' the man replied furiously. 'Only one hundred cash?' said the stranger. 'Stop! I will pay it for him.'

Very astonished, the butcher asked the stranger, 'Is he a relative of yours?' 'No.' 'Is he your friend, then?' 'No.' 'Do you know him?' 'No. I have never seen him before,' said the man. 'Why do you want to pay his debt?' questioned the butcher. 'I pity him,' said the man, 'because if you cut off his skin he will die of cold.' Touched by his charity, the butcher thought he also should have pity on his debtor, and without either flaying him or asking for money, he went home, burnt the receipt, and never mentioned the debt again. From then on he gave up his profession and performed so many good works that he acquired the right of entering Paradise.

On his way there he met an old vegetarian, who told him that he had also gained the right to Paradise, through denying himself all meats for forty years. He, also, was on his way there, and as they were going to the same place, they continued their journey together. At dark they arrived at an isolated farmhouse, where they asked leave to spend the night. As they entered they were very surprised to see silver tables and golden chairs, red jade teapots and cups of white jade, which completely dazzled their eyes. They thought it must be a travelling palace of the Emperor, or at least the country house of a chancellor, but they learnt that there was no one in the house except two young widows and four pretty servant-girls. The two widows begged them to remain as stewards, and the vegetarian was charmed to comply with their wishes; but the butcher refused, because he did not consider it proper to spend the night alone with the women. He slept on the stone staircase in front of the house. But as it was summer, beyond providing a hearty meal for the mosquitoes, he came to no harm.

The next morning he was woken by the singing of the birds in the hills, with the warm sun shining on his body. He rubbed his eyes, but the house was no longer there, and he was lying in the grass by the roadside. As he stood up he heard a crunching sound, and his hair stood up on end at the sight that met his eyes; for the vegetarian that had travelled with him the day before had fallen into a ditch and been eaten by two huge snakes. He did not dare to dally any longer, but went into the Western Paradise as quickly as he could.

21. *Kung Yeh-ch'ang understands the Bird Language*

KUNG YEH-CH'ANG was a poor man who lived by collecting firewood. With him lived his old mother. One day, on his way to the phoenix mountain, he saw a number of snakes, both large and small, coming out of a cave and moving about in the most orderly fashion. The last to appear was an enormous golden serpent, which Kung, who had a knowledge of snakes, knew was a snake princess. The princess and her followers advanced into the midst of the mountains, where she shook her head several times as a sign to the soldiers and all the other snakes to move away. A black snake minister alone remained, and the two glided off into the grass, where they were soon entwined. Kung Yeh-ch'ang was horrified at a mere minister daring to embrace a princess, and, seizing his axe, he flung it at the black snake, thus cutting it in two. The sky became dark at once, and he saw a dark mist rise up and fly away.

85

The princess had only been lightly wounded by the axe, and now, calling for her companions, she slid back to the cave, where she dashed into the presence of the ruling snake to complain of the murder of the minister. The ruler was enraged by the news: 'I demand vengeance for the death of my minister,' he hissed, and immediately ordered the snake warriors to go to Kung Yeh-ch'ang's house and bite him to death.

Soon after the snakes were settled in the bedroom, Kung Yeh-ch'ang and his mother arrived. Kung sat down on the bed with a sigh, and his mother asked: 'What's the matter? Did something go wrong to-day? If you tell me, perhaps I can help you.' Kung replied: 'I was cutting wood on the phoenix mountain to-day, when a snake princess appeared with her followers. A shameless snake minister began to fondle her, which is such an unprecedented relation between ruler and subject, that I killed the minister with my axe. The princess was also wounded and fled back to her hole. Don't you think I was quite right, mother?' Meanwhile, the two snakes had listened to every word of this conversation, and when they heard that Kung had killed the minister on very good grounds, they hurried home to make a report. The ruler realised at once that Kung had performed a good deed, and sending for the princess, he swallowed her.

One day, Kung again found himself on the phoenix mountain. As he was passing the snake cavern, he saw a huge golden serpent lying in the entrance, holding in its mouth a thing like a duck's egg. Kung saw that it was really a snake's liver, and said: 'If you want to give me the liver, please go back into the cave.' The snake did as he was asked, and Kung seized the liver and swallowed it.

As a result of eating the liver, he was able to understand the language of birds. One day, at the end of spring or the beginning of summer, a bird—the soul of

86

the murdered snake minister—perched on a tree in front of Kung's house and sang:

> 'Kung Yeh-ch'ang, Kung Yeh-ch'ang,
> A tiger has killed a sheep in the hills.
> You eat the flesh
> And I the guts.'

Kung understood everything, and going into the hills, he found the sheep's carcase and took it home. But he ate up the whole thing and the bird received nothing.

A few days later, a child that had gone into the hills to collect wood was bitten to death by a tiger. The time for the bird's revenge had arrived. He flew to the tree in front of Kung's house and sang:

> 'Kung Yeh-ch'ang, Kung Yeh-ch'ang,
> A tiger has killed a sheep in the hills.
> You eat the flesh
> And I the guts.'

Kung hurried off in search, but instead of a sheep, he only found a dead child, and as he was standing by the corpse wondering what to do, it began to snow. He looked for somewhere to shelter, but there being no hope of the snow stopping he ran home. The villagers had wondered why the child did not return and went to look for it. They soon found it lying dead, but they did not see that it had been killed by a tiger. They saw the footsteps in the snow, which led to Kung Yeh-ch'ang's house, and although he related exactly what had happened they did not believe him, but accused him of the murder and led him off to the District Magistrate.

No amount of questioning could induce Kung, who kept on repeating the same story, to admit his guilt. Needless to say, the Magistrate did not believe that he understood the bird language: 'I have never heard of anyone speaking with birds,' he said, 'and I don't believe it now.' Then Kung replied: 'If you don't believe me, make five heaps of corn and mix in each heap a salt, or sour, or bitter, or sharp, or sweet substance, and place one heap in the middle and one in each of the four corners. When the birds come to eat, I will translate what they say, and you can see whether I am speaking the truth or not.'

The Magistrate agreed to his suggestion, and a bird came and pecked at the heaps in the East and the West, and said: 'The east one is sweet, the west one salty.' Kung translated these words, and, very surprised, the Magistrate set him free.

About seven years later, a foreign land sent a strange bird without head or legs. With it came a letter, which said: 'If you can feed this bird, our country will send tribute to yours every year; if you fail, we will invade your land and kill you.'

The Emperor announced at once: 'Which ever of my ministers can feed the bird will be appointed Earl with an appanage of ten thousand families.' But none of the ministers at the court could discover the solution. After a long time, one minister, who had formerly been District Magistrate, said: 'Six or seven years ago, I was Magistrate in such and such a place. There was a Mr. Kung Yeh-ch'ang who understood the language of birds. If you send for him, perhaps he will advise something.' The Emperor sent an order for Kung to come to court, and a few days later he arrived. After he had made his obeisance, the Emperor sent for the bird. Kung listened to what it said, and discovered that it must be fed on red-hot nails and washed in boiling oil. The bird flourished under this treatment, and Kung was appointed Earl with ten thousand families, and his mother was also rewarded. The bird, too, lived happily in its cage.

88

22. *The Origin of the Two-eyed Fish*

IN former times there were no fish with opposing eyes. It is related that there was once a land so distant and inaccessible that the people were very conservative and the classes were very strictly separated.

On a certain day in the year a theatrical performance took place in honour of the god. The festival occurred one year in March or April, at the beginning of spring, when the cherry trees were covered with pink flowers and the meadows were carpeted with green. The village people were very hospitable and they all used to invite their friends and relations from other villages to enjoy such a happy occasion. Some came to see the performance for which they were invited, and others could visit and gossip with their relatives, whom they had not seen for a year.

Among the well-to-do people in the village, there was one family which consisted of a father, who was forty years old, and his wife and his daughter. The daughter was so beautiful and so cultivated, and at the same time so dutiful, that everyone fell in love with her at first sight. She had arrived at the age when a husband should be found for her, but her father loved her so dearly that he did not want to lose her too soon, and although several people had come to make proposals, he had paid little attention to them. Matters had gone on in this fashion, till finally the young lady discovered that she was not like other people and that she would rather remain single all her life than choose the wrong man. At least she said this, but her heart was rather saddened, for she was no longer so young and the demands of nature were daily becoming stronger.

When the time for the festival arrived, her father was busy, but he agreed at once to her request to visit the performance and persuaded her cousin to accompany her. In great delight, she hurriedly changed her clothes, pinned her jewels in her hair, and stepped into the boat in front of the house with her cousin. The boat set off as soon as her mother joined them, and they chattered gaily until they arrived at the temple, where the boatman tied up the boat alongside the stage.

As it was still very early, she first played a game of chess with her cousin, and then they had dinner. On all sides were boats filled with people who had come to see the performance, and on the land in front of the stage there was not a free place. Finally gongs were sounded, and the play began. The first pieces the young girl saw consisted of pretty scenes and exquisite music, so that she was delighted by the theatre, but the next play was the story of a scholar, who first was in great difficulties, which he overcame by hard work, finally passing the Chuang Yuan examination and gaining great renown and honour. As she followed him through all his trials and difficulties and watched him struggling with his studies till in the end he gained great honours, she was completely carried away and soon began to regard the performer as a real man. Unbeknown to her she was overcome by admiration and love, and finally she was seized by desire. The actor was the only suitable man for her to marry.

During the play the actor noticed how the girl stared at him without moving, and when he saw a slight smile playing over her face he quietly smiled back at her. And when he nodded at her, he thought he saw her nod back. And in this way he also fell in love.

The girl had little knowledge of men. She thought there was no one on earth who could be as intelligent, or lovable, as the actor. During her waking hours she saw him standing before her at her studies, and when she shut her eyes she heard him speak. In this way she had his portrait ever before her eyes, and his voice in her ears, and she was no longer interested in her food and refused to do her work, but sat silent the whole day

90

long. Her parents were most distressed by her condition, but though they asked her several times for the reason, she always refused to tell them. It was only when her mother continued to press her that she related her experience. Her mother was very upset by her avowal, but, loving her daughter as she did, she did not want to destroy all her hopes, and so she promised to help her to persuade her father, and did her best to cheer her up. The daughter was much encouraged by her mother's promise, and outwardly she appeared as before.

The next night her mother confessed everything to her husband. But he wanted to protect his rank, and although he dearly loved his daughter, he considered it would be a terrible disgrace to his family to allow his daughter to marry someone of such a low class, and he was forced to refuse his consent. But he told his wife to tell their daughter that he was looking round for a suitable man. But the girl was in despair when she heard her father's decision.

One evening she was seated at her window, sad and filled with despair, gazing into the distance over the meadows on the farther bank of the river, when suddenly she saw the figure of a man behind the garden wall on the near side of the river, whose two eyes were staring in her direction. When she looked carefully, she recognized her lover, whom she had been thinking of day and night. She was filled with joy, and, seeing no one around, she signed to him, ran down into the garden, and opened the gate to let him in. Then she locked it behind her and led him up to her bedroom.

The young actor was originally a poor child from the neighbourhood. He had entered the troupe a few years before, and being very clever he soon gained a great reputation. But on the day he fell in love with the girl he lost all desire to act, and after enquiring about the girl's home he left the troupe and spent the days creeping around the house, seeking for an opportunity to see her again. To-day luck had smiled on him and he had been fortunate, but he never expected to be taken up to her room, and he became almost mad with joy. And after they had expressed their love and longing for each other, they became man and wife.

In a few days the facts became known, and her father was told of them. In his anger he decided to burn down the house in the coming night, so that they should expiate their crime in the flames, and the family disgrace be wiped out. But the two lovers could not bear to be separated, and after long discussions they decided to seek death together, in the hope of being lucky enough to be born together in the next life. In the evening they stole into the garden, crept along the path to the river bank, and jumped into the water. From that time a strange fish was seen in the water. It has two heads, two bodies and two tails, but only one pair of eyes. And many people say that this fish with the opposing eyes is formed out of the girl and her lover.

23. *The Tiger General*

THERE was once a man whose name was neither Five nor Tiger General, but whom everyone called by these names, for the following amusing reason.

One day a man went into the hills to collect firewood. As he was chopping wood he heard the painful sound of whimpering and crying. Not knowing where the noises came from, he went to look and found a tigress lying beside a cave on the point of giving birth to cubs. Her entrails had come out and caught in the thorns, which prevented their going back again. The poor animal was whimpering in the most tragic way, and gazed dumbly at the man, as if imploring his help. The groans became more and more heartrending, till the man could no longer doubt that she was begging him to help her. At last he was unable to bear it and rushed home. 'Mother,' he said, 'I have just seen a tiger in travail whose entrails had come out. She was on the point of death. I am sure you are an experienced midwife and could go and help her.' 'This type of birth is very dangerous,' said the mother. 'If we want to help the beast the only way to make the entrails go back is to dip them in a bowl of wine.'

When they treated the tiger in this manner, four little tigers were born. The tigress was naturally very grateful, and as the old woman was going, she jokingly tapped the tigress on the back and said: 'Tigress, we are poor people and cannot afford a daughter-in-law. In return for our help you must bring us a young girl,' and the tigress nodded its head, as if it really understood.

One night, during a terrific snowstorm, a bride was crossing the mountain. Suddenly there was a roar like thunder, and five tigers rushed down the hill and closed the path. All the companions of the bride ran away, and the mother and four tiger-children carried her to the house of the woodcutter. The man heard their knocks and went to open the door, outside which he saw, escorted by five tigers, a young lady with whom he immediately celebrated his marriage. Later the family of the rightful bridegroom heard about this affair and brought a complaint before the Magistrate, accusing the woodcutter of stealing their bride. The Judge sent for the woodcutter to question him, and although he told the truth, naturally no one believed him, so that his mother had to go into the hills and beg the tigers to appear as witnesses. The Judge had them led into the hall of justice and asked them: 'Did you carry the bride to the house of the woodcutter?' All the tigers nodded their heads in admission and the accused was set free.

Some years later a rebel broke into the land with many wild beasts, which none of the generals or soldiers could disperse. The Emperor ordered the woodcutter to advance against them with his five tigers, and in three days all the wild beasts had been so bitten by the tigers that they fled away and never dared to return.

The Emperor was very pleased and accorded the woodcutter the title of 'Five Tiger General' and gave him a position on the frontier. From that time the country, which had always suffered from rebellions, had peace.

24. *The Fishing-bird*

ONE day, while a large ship lay becalmed in a broad river, a young student went down to bathe. He had forgotten to bring a towel, and as he lay drying in the sun something came flying by. He looked in the direction from which it came, and saw on the ship a young girl. She quickly withdrew her face, but her hand remained hanging out. How beautiful the fingers were! How wonderfully tender!

He then turned round to see what she had thrown, and found a sweet-smelling towel with a dollar piece inside, which was obviously put there to make it easier to throw the towel. He was quite bewitched, as if the towel had stolen his heart, and wandered up and down the river bank forgetting to dry his face or even to return home.

A breeze sprang up and the ship sailed away, but the young man followed it for many days until it arrived at a town, where the passengers and the young lady got off. He followed her to a big house, and after making enquiries, he discovered that it was the home of a retired official and that the young lady was his daughter.

We do not know what tricks the young student used, but at last he contrived to be employed as gardener in the garden of this official. Unfortunately, he was very

94

poor and his clothes were hanging in rags. Every day, while he was tending the flowers, he painted pictures, birds hopping and flying about in the most lifelike manner, on the garden wall, in the hope that the young lady would come into the garden one day to see the flowers. But neither in spring nor in summer, nor even in autumn, did she come.

One day a foreign country sent an ambassador with a rare bird to China. The envoy said: 'If anyone here can tell me the name of this bird, I will acknowledge that your country is greater than mine.' The Emperor sent for all his ministers, but none knew the bird. Just as the Emperor was beginning to utter the direst threats, someone mentioned that the official of our story would certainly know the name, but when he was brought to the capital, he did not know either. Then the Emperor told him angrily: 'If you don't discover it in fourteen days, I will cut off your head.' The poor man had no hope of learning the name in this short time, and went home to await his death.

He was no longer able to eat for worry, and at length he related the whole story to his household. They all stood gaping, except his daughter, who said: 'As I was standing once at the window that looks into the garden, I noticed some strange birds painted on the wall, which sound exactly like your description. I don't know who drew them, but we can easily enquire.'

When the official discovered that the gardener had drawn them, he sent for him and asked if it was true, and when the student admitted it, he begged him to say what the bird was called. 'It is called a "fishing-bird,"' said the young man, 'and it can swallow even the biggest fish.'

Overjoyed by his discovery, the official hurried back to the capital and said to the Emperor: 'This rare bird is the fishing-bird, which can swallow every fish. Your Majesty can ask if this is correct.' And the ambassador had to admit that it was the correct name, and to agree that China was the greater land.

On his way home, the official reflected that the gardener's knowledge was greater than his own, and, since he had saved his life, he decided to give him his daughter as wife. The student was more pleased than words can say, and after the marriage, taking his wife by the hand, he led her up to the picture on the wall and said: 'For this small hand I had to suffer so much; to endure the bites of dogs, and to wander through countless lanes; and, but for the fishing-bird, I should not be holding it now.'

25. *The Gossiping Animals*

THERE were once two brothers. The elder had a wife, but the younger was a simpleton and not yet married. The younger sowed a field of barley, but in the whole field there was only one plant, in the centre, which he thought so beautiful that he weeded it and manured it several times a day. It grew so well that soon it bore an enormous ear of corn, which the simpleton used to fondle and caress all day long. Unfortunately, just as the ear became ripe, it was carried away by a large bird. This was too much for the fool, who pursued the thief, waving his hands in the air, till fall of night. Then the bird disappeared and he was left in the wild mountains, surrounded by howling wolves and roaring tigers. Feeling nervous, he looked around till he found a flat piece of ground, where he clambered up into a tall tree and hid in its branches. At the foot of the tree, brother wolf, brother tiger and brother monkey were wont to forgather. Brother tiger said: 'It is so comfortable here this evening. Do tell us another of your stories, brother Monkey.' The monkey replied: 'I don't know any stories, but I have a piece of gossip for you.' The wolf and the tiger naturally were intrigued, and the monkey continued: 'To the South-East, about fifty miles from here, there is a small village. In it there is a young girl with an unknown disease, which no one is able to cure, and her father, therefore, has announced that the person who cures her shall have her as his wife. It is really a very simple matter, because the doctor only needs to scratch a little dirt off his spine and make three pills out of it, and the young girl will be cured the moment she eats them.' The tiger and the wolf heaved a deep sigh: 'What a pity we are not men and cannot have such luck.' But the simpleton thought to himself in delight: 'There ought to be enough filth on my back for thirty thousand pills.' The three animals related some more gossip and then went back into the wood. The next morning, the simpleton climbed down from the tree, rolled three big dark pills out of the dirt on his spine; and set off towards the South-East. He kept on asking the way, until he arrived at the village of the sick girl, where he really heard everyone saying: 'She is to marry the person who cures her.' Then the simpleton produced his pills and gave them to the girl, who was cured at once. Her father was mad with joy, and gave orders to prepare the marriage at once.

While the younger brother was celebrating his marriage, the elder brother met his death, which came about in the following manner. The elder brother's wife had always loathed the simpleton, but he was strong and could do heavy work, so that on his failure to return she said to her husband: 'The simpleton is wandering around somewhere. He ought to come home and do some work.' Her husband agreed and went out to search for him. He searched until nightfall, by which time he had arrived at the tree in which his brother had spent the previous night. He, also, was frightened by the ceaseless roars of the wild animals and climbed up into the tree. Brother tiger, brother wolf, and brother

G

monkey soon appeared, and the tiger said: 'It is so pleasant here. Do tell us the day's gossip, brother monkey.' The monkey replied: 'Yesterday someone was sitting in the tree and made his fortune by listening to us. To-day we had better make sure there is no one up there before we begin.' When the wicked brother heard that, he cowered back and trembled so violently that the branches began to shake, and the animals saw him at once when they looked up. All three of them wanted to climb up and fetch him, but the monkey said: 'Let me go. Neither of you can climb half so quickly as I,' and he jumped into the tree and flung the wicked brother on to the ground. He called out to the tiger 'Eat him up,' but the tiger refused. Then he called to the wolf 'Eat him up,' but the wolf refused. As none of them wanted to eat him, they carried him into the hills. The wolf took a piece, the tiger a piece, and the monkey a piece, and nothing remained of the brother except the head.

26. *The Fairy Grotto*

MANY years ago there lived two boys named Liu Ch'en and Yüan Chao, who were cousins. One day they went into the hills to fetch water. It was in the midst of spring, and the hills were carpeted by varieties of red and green flowers. The boys were so overcome by the beauty of the scene that they put down their pails by the stream, and set off for a walk. The country became more and more lonely, as they wandered from hill to hill, until the path finally came to an end and they found themselves at the entrance to a cave, with an enormous stone on each side, in which two fairies were seated playing chess. The two boys stood in the mouth of the cave and watched the game without saying a word. At the feet of the fairies a white hare was springing up and

down, and, much to their wonder, the two boys noticed
that each time it sprang up the flowers bloomed at the
entrance to the cave, and each time it lay down, they
faded.

When the game was finished, the fairies looked round
at the boys and asked when they had arrived. 'A
few hours ago,' they both answered, and turned to leave.
But the fairies said to them: 'Stay here in our grotto
and don't go home. No one will recognize you.' But
they did not understand what the fairies meant, and said
firmly: 'No! No! We must go home.' And seeing
that they could not persuade them to remain, the fairies
gave them each a piece of reed, saying: 'If you find
everything changed at home, come back here and point
the reed at the cave and it will open.'

They took the reeds and returned to the stream by
which they had left their poles and buckets. But all
they found was decayed earth, and tall pines were growing
on each side of the stream, where formerly there had
been open ground. In great perplexity they entered the
village, but there they could find no trace of their homes.
They asked two old white-haired men whom they saw
sitting in a meadow where the house of Liu Ch'en and
Yüan Chao was. The two old men replied: 'Liu Ch'en
and Yüan Chao were our ancestors. We are their
descendants in the seventh generation. Why do you
young fellows talk about them in this casual way?'
This was still more confusing, because how could two
young men have descendants in the seventh generation?
Perhaps the white hare jumping about in the fairy grotto
represented the seasons, and the afternoon they had
spent in the cave had lasted for four or five hundred
years. But when the two children heard the words of
the old men, they said: 'But we are Liu Ch'en and
Yüan Chao!' This made the old men so cross that
their beards waggled to and fro. They called out to
other people, who came up and beat the two boys.

99

'You young rascals,' they cried, 'how dare you come and bother old men.' The boys fled back to the cave, but the doors were fast shut. Then they remembered their reeds, but they could not recall where they had left them, and they did not dare to go back and look for them for fear the people would beat them again. They knocked and knocked, but there was no answer, and in their grief they banged their heads against the wall and died.

The Ruler of Heaven took pity on their sad fate and appointed Liu Ch'en the god of good luck, and Yüan Chao the god of ill luck.

27. *The Long Nose*

THERE were once two brothers: the elder was called Li Ta and the younger Li Hsi. They were as poor as could be, and had no good food, home or clothes. One day their mother, who lived in the same house, said to them: 'We are now so poor that if we cannot find some means of making a living only death awaits us. I am so old that life no longer has much charm for me; but you must really make an effort or you will never make names for yourselves. Just look how rich neighbour Ch'en is. When he goes out, he either rides or drives in a cart, and when he goes home, he calls for his servants and maids. That's happiness. But he made it all for himself by working hard in his youth. I can only hope that you later . . .' and tears began to course down her cheeks at the thought of her plight, and her sons mingled their tears with hers.

Shortly after Li Ta said to his mother: 'Of course we want to do something, mother, but even for stealing hens one needs rice, and we do not possess a single copper piece, so how can we begin anything? Don't weep, though, we will think of a way. Perhaps neighbour

Ch'en, who has so much money, would lend us ten dollars. It wouldn't mean anything to him. If he consents, we will leave two of the ten dollars here to keep you alive, two others will be our journey money, and the rest our capital. What do you think of that? Do you think we can manage it?' 'A brilliant idea,' the mother replied with a smile; 'go and ask for the loan.' In the end the mother herself went to the Ch'en family, and they did really give her the ten dollars. But the younger brother had a black heart, and as soon as he saw the money evil thoughts came into his mind.

The next day they carried out their plans. Two dollars were left behind for their mother's subsistence, and the rest they changed into eight thousand coppers, which they put into a bag. Then they put their things together and prepared everything for their departure.

The next morning the younger brother carried the luggage and the elder the money. After they had gone three or four miles the younger said: 'Surely the money is very heavy, brother, your shoulder must be aching. Let me take it for a while.' 'You have the luggage. Don't let us bother to change,' said Li Ta. But again Li Hsi said: 'Your load is much heavier than mine. Let's change now.' Li Ta suspected nothing and replied: 'As you are so good, we will change for a bit.' They went on for another three or four miles, until Li Hsi pretended to have a stomachache and said: 'I have a terrible pain. I must rest here for a bit. You go on in front. I will soon be well enough to overtake you.' 'Certainly not,' replied the other, 'we are brothers, and if one of us is ill the other must help him. How could I go on?' 'That is very kind of you, but put your luggage down and go and find some people to give me a little hot soup.' The brother went into the village and fetched some hot water, and on the way back he wondered what he would do if his brother died. After a while he met an old woman working in the fields, from whom he begged a cup of tea, but when he got back both his brother and the money had vanished. He wondered where Li Hsi was, but, thinking that he had recovered in the meantime and gone on to look for him, he poured away the cup of tea and went in search of him. The sun was just setting and the round moon was high in the sky, and the farther he went the more anxious he became, until finally he arrived at a pavilion, in which, being very fatigued, he decided to spend the night. The pavilion was called the 'Pleasure Haunt of the Immortals,' and on top there was a large hall. On the ground floor he could find nothing comfortable, so he went up to the hall and lay down to sleep on a stone.

Just as he fell asleep he heard the sound of voices. Now some of the Immortals were living in the 'Pleasure Haunt,' and on the fifteenth day of the eighth month they used to feast together, and it was their voices that Li Ta was hearing. One of them said: 'We have nothing to pass the time and nothing good to eat, which is so tiresome.' 'I have a stick here,' another said. 'If I knock it, it will produce all kinds of food,' and then Li Ta heard a noise and another voice said: 'That's really a magnificent meal on the table,' and it was followed by the noise of eating and conversation. Then a voice said: 'East of this there is a spring of bitter water, which the people cannot drink. Isn't it possible to turn it into ordinary water?' 'That is quite simple,' answered another that seemed older. 'If you cut down and dig up the pine by the well, and kill the green snake that lives underneath it, the water will run sweet again.' Later he heard the voice of a young man say: 'West of here there is a bridge which is still not finished after twelve years' work. I should like to know how it could be managed.' 'Do you want to know why it never gets built?' asked a deep voice. 'Underneath the bridge there are four pots of gold and four pots of silver. If they are taken away the bridge can be finished.'

102

Gradually the chink of cups, the rattle of plates and bowls, and the click of chopsticks and spoons died down, and the voices grew softer and finally ceased. Steps could be heard going away from the pavilion and dawn soon began to break. The birds were singing in the trees and the elder brother got up. He was quite famished, but suddenly he saw a stick lying in a chair, which he thought must be the magic wand. He did not bother whether it was the right stick, but gave it a blow and ordered it to produce a meal, and in a flash the table was covered with the choicest foods. He ate and drank his fill, wondering where his brother was and pitying him for not being able to share the meal.

When he had finished he took the stick and set off towards the East. In a short while he met a woman drawing water, and having walked a long way he begged her for a draught to quench his thirst. 'Please give me something to drink, mother,' he begged. 'The water here is very bitter,' answered the woman; 'no one can drink at the bitter well.' This reminded him of what he had heard during the night, and he asked the woman if the spring was really known by that name, and on her repeating it, he said to her: 'I will tell you how to make the water drinkable. Beside the well stands a pine, under which lives a green snake. If you dig up the tree and kill the snake, the water will flow as before.' The woman thanked him, and before he departed, she asked him his name and address, both of which he told her.

He went now towards the West, and after three miles, he saw a crowd of workmen building a bridge. Again he recalled his experience in the pavilion, and he asked the men: 'How long has it taken to build this bridge?' 'More than twelve years,' they answered. 'That's a long time. Why is it still not finished?' 'It certainly is a long time,' said the men, 'but whenever it is almost ready, it collapses and we have to begin again.' 'I will give you a piece of advice,' said the brother, much to the joy of the workmen. 'I can tell you the reason. Underneath the bridge are buried four pots of gold and four pots of silver. If you remove them, you can build the bridge.' The workmen thanked him again and noted down his name and abode.

The brother then took his leave and went home. On his arrival his mother asked him: 'Have you done good business?' Then he related to her in tears all that had happened to him, how he had met the Immortals and what had resulted from the meeting. Then his mother also began to weep. 'Have you still not found your brother?' she asked, and her son had to tell her that he had no idea where he was.

During the next two months Li Ta and his mother lived entirely off the stick. One day the Emperor heard that the bitter water spring had turned sweet, and that the bridge had been finished, through the advice of Li Ta. He sent his great dignitaries, who brought many treasures and gold, and at the same time Li Ta received gold and silver from the East and the four pots of silver and the four pots of gold from the West. He was now a rich man; he built a house and took a wife, with whom he lived in bliss and contentment. One day the younger brother went past as the elder was coming out. Li Ta recognized his brother in the dirty beggar and led him into the house, where he gave him new clothes and food and drink. 'You have been really lucky in the last few years,' said Li Hsi. 'I didn't make my money in business,' the elder replied, and he told his brother all that had happened since they parted.

The brother decided to follow his example, and the same evening he went to the pavilion, climbed up to the hall, and lay down to sleep. Just as he was falling asleep, he was delighted to hear the Immortals talking down below. One of them was saying: 'Last time we dined here I had a stick. Who stole it?' 'There is obviously a thief,' another answered. 'We had better go upstairs and see if he is there now.' Then the younger brother heard footsteps on the staircase, and the Immortals entered the hall and saw him lying asleep. 'Look,' said one of them, 'that's the fellow who stole my stick,' and without further ado, they gave him a thrashing, pulled his nose out twelve feet, and kicked him out of the house.

He fled home and told his elder brother what he had suffered. 'Don't worry,' Li Ta said, 'we still have the stick. I will return it to them and perhaps they will tell me how to cure your nose.'

That evening, the elder brother went to the upper hall in the pavilion of the Immortals, and soon he heard them discussing the occurrence of the night before. 'I did enjoy whipping that thief yesterday,' said one. 'His nose stretched so well.' Later on, another asked: 'How could it be cured?' 'It's quite simple,' said a third. 'One only needs to tap the stick once, call his name, and let him answer, and if one repeats this twelve times, the nose will become normal again.'

The elder brother remembered these instructions and next morning hurried home to tell Li Hsi. 'I can cure you,' he said. 'I will tap the stick and call out, and you must answer me. If I do this twelve times, you will be all right.' He took the stick and tapped it twelve times, but the younger brother said: 'It is still not enough. Knock it once more.' Then the elder tapped it once again, but now Li Hsi had a hole instead of a nose.

28. *The Bridge of Ch'üan-chou*

THE Loyang Bridge lies twenty miles outside the East Gate of Ch'üan-chou, just on the borders of the district. It was particularly difficult to build a bridge at that spot, because it is the meeting-point of the sea tides and of the river rushing down the mountains. It is said that evil spirits live in the river, and therefore not only was it extremely difficult to lay the foundations of the bridge but the boat traffic was also very dangerous. There are innumerable tales in Fukien about this bridge, but I will only relate the best known.

When the Ruler of Heaven wanted to dispose of his carnal body, he considered that the entrails were the vilest part of the human frame, and, drawing his magic sword, he split open his body and flung them into the Loyang River. But the entrails of the Heavenly Ruler were still subject to many influences, and they immediately turned into a tortoise and a snake spirit, which were always playing cruel tricks on men in the Loyang River.

Before the bridge was built, everyone had to cross over by boat. In the reign of the Emperor Shen-tsung (998-1022), of the Sung Dynasty, a pregnant woman from Fuch'ing was once crossing the river to Ch'üanchou; just as the boat was in the middle of the stream the tortoise and snake spirits sent a strong wind and high waves to upset it and sink it. Suddenly a voice cried out from the sky: 'Professor Ts'ai is in the boat. Spirits must behave decently with him.' And scarcely had the words been spoken, when the wind and the waves died down. All the passengers had heard exactly what was said, but when they asked each other's names, there was no one called Ts'ai in the boat; only the pregnant woman from Fuch'ing belonged to the Ts'ai family. All the passengers congratulated the woman, who was quite bewildered, not knowing whether to believe or disbelieve. 'If I really give birth to a son who later becomes a professor,' she said, 'I will charge him to build a bridge over the Loyang.'

Several months later, Mrs. Ts'ai really bore a son, who was named Ts'ai Hsiang. Later, about 1025, he became a professor. His mother related to him her experience on the Loyang River and begged him to think

106

of ways and means of building a bridge, in order that she might fulfil her vow. Ts'ai Hsiang was a dutiful son and immediately gave his consent, but at that time there was a law against anyone being appointed official in his own province, and as Ts'ai Hsiang was a native of Fukien, he could not become governor of Ch'üan-chou, which is in that province. Fortunately his friend, the head eunuch, conceived a wonderful plan. One day, when it was announced that the Emperor would walk in the garden, he took some sugared water and wrote on a banana leaf: Ts'ai Hsiang must be appointed official in his home town. The ants immediately smelt the honey and gathered on the characters in vast numbers, to the stupefaction of the Emperor, who happened to pass the banana tree and saw them drawn up in the form of eight characters. The head eunuch watched him reading them over and over, and quickly wrote out the decree appointing Ts'ai Hsiang to be governor of Ch'üan-chou. The Emperor wanted to punish the eunuch when he handed him the decree, but the man excused himself, saying: 'The Emperor says nothing in jest,' and Ts'ai Hsiang immediately received the appointment.

On his arrival at Ch'üan-chou, he turned plans over in his head day and night, but the waves of the Loyang River beat so high all day that no means could be found of fixing the pillars. At length, finding that, despite all his learning, he was completely at a loss, he decided that the only hope was to implore the help of the gods. He wrote a letter to the Dragon King and then asked which of his servants would be willing to go into the sea and deliver it for him. It happened that one of the servants was a drunkard named Hsia Te-hai, who, mistaking the words for his own name, knelt down and said: 'I am Hsia Te-hai, what commission have you for me?' The Magistrate nodded his head and replied: 'You want to go down into the sea. You have three days in

107

which to deliver this letter to the Dragon King. If you fail, you will receive three hundred blows,' and throwing the letter to the servant, he left the hall. The poor man was in despair at his plight, but it was too late to refuse and with a heavy heart he returned home.

At first he cursed his luck and cursed Ts'ai Hsiang, but as that did not help him much, he spent all his money on buying wine and drank and drank, until he was quite tipsy. Then he stumbled along to the river, where he planned to end his troubles by jumping into the water; but as he arrived at the river bank a breeze sprang up and, no longer having proper control of his limbs, he fell down on the beach.

The next morning, as the blood-red sun slowly rose in the East, he was wakened by the crowing of cocks, and, on opening his eyes, he found himself lying on the same spot by the seashore. But when he took the letter out of his pocket he saw that it was quite different from the one Ts'ai Hsiang had given him. Realizing that a miracle had taken place, he rushed back to the yamen in high spirits, and related all that had happened to him during the night. Ts'ai Hsiang opened the letter and saw that there was only the character 'vinegar' written in it. After a moment's thought he understood from the form of the character that the Dragon King had ordered him to lay the foundations on the twenty-first day at the hour 'yu,' and he gave orders for all the necessary materials to be ready at that hour.

Now that the time for laying the foundations had been fixed, workmen had to be engaged. On the same day, eight strange men appeared and announced that they would do all the work without payment. Ts'ai Hsiang thought that they were good socially-minded people and made no further enquiries about them, but people thought it strange that only eight workmen were engaged for this enormous work of centuries.

The twenty-first day drew near. The tides really seemed smaller in the river bed, and the workmen got everything ready; but for the last few days they did nothing but sit about on the ground and play chess. Everyone thought this too much and urged them to work, but the eight men merely replied: 'It's such a small job. Why make such a fuss about it? In any case the hour "yu" has not yet arrived.' Soon, however, the time came and the river dried up. Suddenly a whirl-wind sprang up at the place where the eight men were playing chess, sand and stones were blown in all directions, completely obscuring the sun and the moon, and none of the other workmen were able to open their eyes. When it became quiet again, everyone saw that the stone foundations were safely laid. There was also no trace of the eight workmen who had been playing chess, and it was obvious that they were the eight Immortals who had turned into men to help build the bridge.

Although the foundations had been successfully laid by the Immortals, the construction of the stonework and balustrading still remained to be done, and many more workmen were engaged to complete the great work quickly. At that time a monk named I-po, who was one of the fifteen people on Ts'ai Hsiang's Council for building the bridge, gave him the greatest assistance. Most of the plans and suggestions for laying out and strengthening the construction originated with him, and with the help of this Buddhist the design was unusually beautiful. I-po had one other faculty that caused the people the greatest astonishment. The workmen at the bridge were so numerous that sometimes there was not sufficient wood for cooking the food, and when this happened I-po stuck his foot in the stove and the flames shot up and cooked the food in a few minutes. When the work was finished he changed into an Immortal and flew up to heaven. To this day there is a temple in his honour to the north of the city where he is worshipped under the name of the monk I-po. The statue is said to be made out of his body, and for this reason the temple is called the temple of the genuine Immortal.

Although Ts'ai Hsiang expended his whole personal fortune as well as the donations of the charitable, he found that funds were still not sufficient for the completion of the bridge. Then the goddess Kuan Yin turned herself into a beautiful woman, got into a boat, and sailed up the Loyang River, where she allowed men to throw pieces of money at her. The man that hit her would become her husband; but whoever failed should have their money used for building the bridge. There were many rich young men who thought her so beautiful that money rained as thick as snowflakes about the ship, but not one single piece touched her. But at this moment Lü Tung-pin flew by on a cloud and saw Kuan Yin. He thought he would play a trick on her, and by the help of his magic, he caused a piece thrown by a small fruit-seller to touch her dress. The little man was overjoyed at winning such a beautiful wife, but suddenly the ship and the woman vanished, to the despair of the little man, who jumped into the river and was drowned. The money problem now being solved, and the leg of the monk I-po providing sufficient firewood, the workmen were able to return to work. But there were so many people that, although there was enough rice to feed them, there was a scarcity of fish, vegetables, and meat. But Kuan Yin heard about this, and through her magic arts, turned the man that had hit her, but never received her, into thousands of little fishes to serve as the daily fare of the workmen. To this day there is a kind of long thin white fish in the Loyang River which the people call Silver Fish.

When the bridge was finished everyone praised Ts'ai Hsiang, but if the tides were high the balustrades were still under the water and people had to wade over.

There is another tale about Li Wu, who later on rebuilt it.

About seven hundred years after the death of Ts'ai Hsiang, in the reign of the Emperor Ch'ien-lung (1736-1796), there was a man in the district of Ch'in-chiang of the Li Family, who was called Li Wu (fifth), because he was the fifth son. In his youth he was a ne'er-do-well, always buying things and not paying for them, which made shopkeepers more afraid of him than a tiger. There was only one butcher who not only made no objection to his debts, but even encouraged him to buy more goods. When Li wanted to buy a piece of meat, he only needed to write a receipt and the butcher gave it to him at once. Li Wu, the lazy-bones, was naturally content with this arrangement, but after it had gone on for some time, he began to wonder what the reason was.

One day he again signed a receipt for some meat, but instead of going away, he hid himself and watched. The butcher took the receipt and went slowly up to the top of a small hill. There he brushed aside the grass by the temple to the Earth God and thrust the receipt into a grave, at the same time taking out a piece of silver. Then he smoothed down the grass, and went slowly and contentedly down the hill. Li Wu ran to the place and nearly jumped for joy; for the grave was filled with pots of silver, one of which was only half-full, the other half containing the receipts that Li Wu had given the butcher in course of time.

As he was standing there, a voice called from the sky: 'This money belongs to Li Wu. To-day you have come, and I, humble spirit, can give up my post.' Li Wu understood at once and carried all the silver back home. The butcher had discovered this treasure one day when he was passing the temple of the Earth God, whom he heard saying to his wife: 'The silver under the stone belongs to Li Wu, who has still not come to fetch it. I shall have to guard it till my death.' When the butcher heard this, he looked about and at length discovered some huge pots, which, however, were only filled with pure water. He knew that the money did not belong to him, but he proposed to make use of it and used the receipts of Li Wu to fetch money from under the stone, because exactly the same amount appeared in the pot as the receipt was made out for.

Now that Li Wu had become a rich man, I don't need to tell you that he opened shops, built houses, and kept a host of male and female slaves. His chief joy was in entertaining guests, and, although he may never have had eight thousand guests, like a famous man of old, at least he had a round hundred. One day, a strange man arrived from distant parts, called K'ang Golddragon, who claimed to be able to discover buried treasures. Perhaps he was also a fabulously wealthy man, but on this occasion he came to test the habits and character of Li Wu. Li Wu, however, was a good judge of character and immediately invited K'ang Golddragon to be his guest, treating him better than anyone else. He was given basins of gold to wash his face in, and although each time that he washed he threw the golden basin into the lotus pond, Li Wu never uttered a cross or unfriendly word. After K'ang had been there several months, he disappeared one day without saying good-bye.

Li Wu, it happened, had once insulted some rogue living in the neighbourhood, and to get his revenge this man accused him of being a bandit, saying that formerly he had been a penniless vagabond, until one day he had become very wealthy. Now his house was always full of guests, and he was obviously planning a revolt. Li Wu's fortune and possessions were confiscated, and he was thrust into a wooden cage and sent to Peking for examination. When he passed over the Loyang River in the prison cart, he was soaked through by the high tide that was breaking over the balustrading. He said to the guardians with a sigh: 'If I escape with my life,

I will raise the Loyang bridge three feet.' A stone dealer and a rope dealer that were passing laughed when they heard Li Wu's oath, and they said to him: 'You will never escape! But if you return and raise the bridge three feet, we will give you the stone and the ropes for nothing,' for they had heard of the accusation and never thought that Li Wu would return alive.

After they had travelled for a long, long way, they arrived at Shantung province, where on all sides they saw fields with the stone notices: Field of Li Wu. They made enquiries, and discovered that they had been bought by K'ang Golddragon in the name of Li Wu. When he arrived in Peking his guilt could not be proved, and K'ang Golddragon made a golden snail for him, whose shell was made of gold with a living snail inside. Li Wu presented it to the Empress, who was so pleased that she worried the Emperor until Li Wu was declared innocent and sent home. There he dug up all the golden basins out of the lotus pond, looked after the fields that K'ang had bought for him everywhere, and soon became one of the richest of men. Then, in order to fulfil his oath, he engaged workmen and raised the Loyang bridge three feet higher. The fortunes of the two traders who had opened their mouths too wide were confiscated for the construction.

29. *The Tale of the Turtle Mountain*

NORTH of Chao-ch'ing lies the seven star peak, and not far west of that there is a hill that closely resembles the back of a turtle, the head of which is formed by several large stones jutting out into the water.

People say that originally there was a turtle living in this mountain, which opened its mouth every ten years. A geomancer once told a rich man that it was a very favourable district, and the man decided to take his advice

H

and bury the bones of his ancestors in this good site. He questioned the grave-seeker further, who said to him: 'Ten years ago the turtle opened its mouth. This year, on such and such a day, it is due to open it again. If you are seeking a favourable site for the grave of your parents, you must get everything ready on that night, hire a boat, and sail down the river to the Turtle Mountain. I will arrange the rest.' The man was rather doubtful of this proposal, but, being very superstitious, he eventually agreed.

The day on which the turtle was due to open its mouth the rich man hired a boat, placed the bones of his ancestors on board, and sailed towards the mountain. Despite the evening breeze the water was still as ice. Everything was indistinct in the dim rays of the new autumn moon, and the silence was only broken by the splash of oars, mingled from time to time with the rattle of wooden implements, and the coughing and low whispering of the crew. There were no other ships on the water, but two lamps were shining in the distance, and glow-worms danced around. It was a ghostly spot in daylight, but now, with the coffin filled with bones lying in the prow of the ship, it was weird enough to make one's hair stand on end. 'Are we nearly there?' asked the rich man. 'Not far,' answered the geomancer. On the shore two straw huts could be seen, with lamps, which emitted a cold but strangely brilliant light, in the window. The ship came to anchor at the Turtle Mountain, where the geomancer ordered the rich man and all the sailors to keep silence, while he carefully watched the turtle's head. The night was piercing cold. The river, checked in its course by the jutting headland, had formed a series of whirlpools, which were sucking at the ship. The waves dashed by on all sides and raced round more and more madly. Suddenly, about midnight, the rich man and the crew were terrified by a noise coming from the turtle's head, but the geomancer quickly ordered them to lift up the coffin and cast it into the boiling river, where, seized in the maelstrom, it vanished in a flash. The turtle's head opened into the water, and the moment the coffin had sunk, it closed and everything was as before. The waves became quieter, the head was as usual, the wind died down, and the new moon was still placidly shining in the western sky. The river became quiet once more, and only the coffin had vanished. The rich man gave a sigh of relief and looked round as if he had just woken up from a nightmare and was wondering where he was. 'Everything went off perfectly,' said the geomancer proudly, 'the coffin is buried and we can go home.' 'Where is it buried, though?' asked the rich man. 'Here, of course,' said the geomancer. 'Now we must drink a bowl of wine to your future luck.' 'What? You threw the coffin into the river?' 'Later you will have good luck. I congratulate you.' 'Have luck, you rascal. You have stolen my coffin. Thief!' 'Do you still not understand?' 'Thief!! Give me back the coffin.' The quarrel continued during the whole return journey, and the next day the rich man accused the geomancer before the District Judge of purloining his coffin. The Judge thought it very suspicious to throw a coffin into a river, and did not understand how a whirlpool, in which the coffin sank at once, could be considered a favourable burial site. At length he decided that the geomancer must return the rich man his coffin. The poor man had no means of escape, but he begged for the loan of the Magistrate's magic sword and for a delay of three days, which the Magistrate agreed to. Two days later he went back to the Turtle Mountain, where he mumbled some magic words and with one blow struck dead the magic power of the mountain. The water immediately boiled up and the coffin reappeared, and he lifted it on to the ship and returned it to the rich man, who was overjoyed at seeing it again. When he had it opened for examination, he found that the bones had already become covered with golden scales, which caused him bitter regrets. But the turtle in the mountain was now dead and could never open its mouth again.

The formation of the mountain, though, is still the same, and the head still juts out into the water.

30. *The True Oil*

THERE were once two cowherd boys, living in a village, who were great friends. Once when they were grazing their sheep in the same place they fell into conversation: 'It really isn't fair that we should always guard other people's cattle, and lead such a miserable existence,' said one, 'we must think of a way out.' 'Let's just sell two cows, and go off with the money,' said the other conscienceless boy, and as his companion agreed, they sold them and ran away with the proceeds. They travelled for many days, walking till they were exhausted, when they arrived at a village, on the outskirts of which lived a rich old man without any children.

The two boys sat down to rest at the door of the house, and after a time the old man came out and asked them what they were doing, and why they were sitting there. 'We are cowherds,' answered the two boys, 'but we found the work too hard. In summer we suffered from the heat, and in winter from the cold. Finally, when we could bear it no longer, we ran away.' The old man thought to himself: 'I am childless. Why shouldn't I adopt one of these boys?', and he said to them: 'Will one of you become my son?', and the wicked boy said: 'I will be your son.' But the good one thought: 'What shall I do then?' The old man took pity on him, and sent him to look after his cows, saying: 'If you guard my cows for three years, I will give you three cows.'

116

The boy agreed gladly, and the three years passed in a flash. The cowherd thought to himself: 'Formerly I ran away because my work was too hard, but here I am still herding cows,' and he went and said to the old man: 'I have looked after your cows for three years, now you must give me three.' But the old man said: 'Who said I would give you them? I said I would give you three flasks of oil,' and although the boy began to quarrel with the old man, there was nothing for him to do but tearfully to accept the oil and go away. 'I can't begin anything with three flasks of oil,' he thought, 'I had better give them to the temple.'

Thirty or forty miles from the village, in the middle of a wood, was an old temple with many monks. The abbot was possessed of supernatural powers, and therefore knew the boy would come and sacrifice oil. He announced to the monks: 'To-day a man will come and make an offering of oil. Open the main door.' The monks did his bidding, and waited at the door. For long they waited, without anyone appearing, till late in the afternoon they saw a man advancing with three small flasks of oil. They quickly announced his arrival to the abbot, who hurriedly pulled on his sacerdotal robes and went to meet him, received the flasks of oil with all signs of satisfaction, and passed them on to the monks.

When the cowherd had already gone a long way he heard someone call: 'Heh! My friend! Wait!' He did not know who it was, but he waited and his former friend came up to him and said: 'Be quick and give me back the oil.' The other replied, very worried: 'I offered the three . . . flasks . . . of oil . . . to the monastery.' But when the wicked boy heard that, he leapt on him and scratched out his eyes.

The poor boy nearly died of pain, and no longer being able to see his way, he crept and stumbled about till he arrived at a tumbledown temple. He remained lying there, and when it became dark he suddenly heard the voices of Bullface and Horsehead in the temple. 'There is a delicious smell of human flesh to-day,' said one. 'Don't talk such rubbish,' retorted the other. Bullface having been so rude, the other image did not like to insist, and after a short pause the two gods continued: 'In such and such a place there is a pair of brilliant eye pupil pearls, a blind man can see everything with them!' 'And the man who digs up the pot of gold and the pot of silver in such and such a place will become a rich man.' The cowherd listened to all they said and after a search he really found the pearls, which when placed in his eyes enabled him to see as well as before. Then he dug out the pots of gold, which he took home and became a rich man.

A year later the conscienceless boy met him again. He was very surprised to see him and asked: 'How did you regain your sight? And how did you become so rich?' The good boy told him the whole story exactly, and the other said: 'To-morrow morning I will go at once and offer some oil, and I will also become rich.' The next day he ordered forty people to carry oil to the temple, but the abbot again knew that someone was bringing oil, and he said to the monks: 'Open the side door. A little man is coming to sacrifice to-day.'

In a short time the forty men arrived with the oil, and the monks received them very politely. Afterwards, though, they asked the abbot: 'Master, so many people brought oil to-day, why did you only open the side door, while formerly, when a man brought three small flasks, you opened the main door?' 'To-day's oil and what was brought before was quite different,' he explained. 'No suffering heart brought to-day's offering, but yesterday's was the substance of a thousand heart pangs. If you don't believe me, it is easy to prove it. Open to-day's casks and water will flow out, but the others contain life blood.' And when the monks examined them it was quite true.

After the offerer had taken leave of the monks, he went to look for his men, to whom he said: 'Please scratch both my eyes out.' And although the men were very unwilling, he was so insistent that at last they did obey him. He crept into the old temple, and at midnight Bullface said: 'There is a smell of a living man again to-day.' And as the other idols made no objections, Bullface and Horsehead gobbled the wicked cowherd up.

> [Bullface and Horsehead are two underworld guards, and here they are in the position of temple guardians. The misunderstanding about Oil—Cow was caused by the similarity in sound (Yu—niu). The motive of the two people, of which the honourable one is lucky, and the wicked one imitates him, appears in countless Chinese tales. The motive ' I smell human flesh ' is just as common.]

31. *The Actor and the Ghost*

THERE was once an actor who was so brave that he feared neither wild beasts nor ghosts, and wandered far afield in the depths of the night. He was always strolling around, and one evening as he was walking along with a long trumpet in his hand, he came upon a young girl. He went up to her and said: 'Whence do you come? and whither are you going?' As the girl remained silent, he turned away; but as he was leaving she said: 'I am not a human, I am a ghost.' 'So you are a ghost,' replied the young man. 'I have always heard that ghosts could change into any form. Can you do that?' 'Easily,' said the ghost. 'Well, let me see what you can do,' said the actor, meaning her to transform herself. 'But won't you be frightened?' asked the girl, and she changed into a ghost whose long hair hung down to the ground. 'That's not very much,' laughed the actor. 'The pheasant's feathers that actors wear are much longer than your hair.' Then the girl changed into a ghost from each of whose orifices blood was streaming, but again the actor said: 'That's quite simple. If we actors use a red pencil the result is much redder.' Next, the girl changed into a ghost with enormous teeth, but the actor said: 'That doesn't impress me at all. If you can't do more than that, no one is going to be afraid of you. Try once again.' But the ghost had to confess it could do nothing more. Then the actor said: 'Now it's my turn,' and he took his trumpet and pulled it out half as long again, and he pulled a second time and made it longer, and a third time and made it longer still. Then he warned the ghost. 'Don't run away,' he said, 'I can also do tricks,' and he blew his trumpet so loud that the ghost ran away in terror. The actor went home.

From then on he no longer went out at night; but about three years later when on business he found himself far from home. He hurried on, till at eight or nine at night he found himself face to face with the ghost, behind whom were standing many other little ghosts. The moment it saw him, the ghost said: 'At last you have come. I have been searching for you for three years. I thought you must be dead. How lucky to have met you to-day, because I wanted to have a bet about our magic powers.' Then the little ghosts seized the actor and began to beat him. He thought at first of running away, but as that seemed impossible, he began to beat the ghosts, and, in beating, by mistake he also beat the ground several times. But this place happened to be a grave, out of which now suddenly a man appeared to stop him beating. The little ghosts, seeing the new ghost, ran away, screaming with terror, but the actor knelt down before the dead man and said: 'Save me. Let me sleep to-night on your gravestone.' The dead man replied: 'I am a man without sons or grandsons. If you found a society for me which every year brings me sacrifices to eat on each feast day, I will help you all your life long. I am in a very bad way.' 'I will certainly do that, if you let me sleep here to-night,' said the actor. 'I will found a club to-morrow, and at each feast we will bring you sacrifices.' The next morning the actor copied down the characters on the gravestone, and when he had looked up the man's name, origin, and family tree, he formed a large society, and every year, up to the present time, it brings sacrifices to the dead man's grave.

32. *The King of the Ashes*

A STUDENT once left home to go and take the examination in the capital. One night he arrived at a tumbled-down temple, and seeing no house far or near where he could beg for a night's lodging, he went into the ruin. Inside, three coffins were lying on the floor, and behind them was an idol, but at the back of the building he found a place where, after wiping away some of the dirt, he lay down to sleep.

He had slept till about midnight, when suddenly three spectres sprang out of the coffins and walked up to the altar in a row. The noise woke the student, who, thinking to himself they must be ghosts, wanted to lock the door, but though he searched frantically for the key, he could not find it, till finally, when the ghosts were close upon him, he hid behind the idol in a cold sweat of terror.

The three spectres were Gold-face, Black-face and Blue-face. As they came in each one called his name. Gold-face was silent for a moment and said: 'There is a delicious odour of human flesh,' and the two other spectres agreed with him. When the student behind the idol heard them say this, he was so terrified that he fell down into the incense-burners beside the ghosts and was covered with ashes. In this desperate plight he suddenly had a brilliant idea, and standing up before the ghosts he cried: 'I am the great King of the Ashes!' To which the first ghost replied: 'We have waited for you so long. How pleased we are to see you. We have a report to make. With this key you can dig up the silver treasure that now passes into your keeping.' And the student bravely took the key that the ghost handed to him.

Dawn was just breaking in the East, and the cocks were beginning to crow. The ghosts ran down, crept into their coffins, and everything became quiet again.

The student thought he had had a bad dream, but the key that the ghost had given him was still in his hand. When it was quite light, he looked down at his hand, and saw that the key had turned into a spade. Although he did not believe the story of the three ghosts, he thought he would have a try and went and dug up the ground near the coffins, and there he found a chest which contained more than ten gold and silver coins. He took them home and forgot all about the examination. One would never think that ill-fortune could be turned into good fortune in this manner.

33. *The Geomancer*

THERE was once a geomancer named Ts'ao living in T'ung-chou. He had two sons and was really an unusually good diviner; for, whenever he said of a grave that the owners would have few descendants, it was certain that if one made enquiries in the family, they really did have very few children. Or if he said that the owner would be blind, he really was blind. One day he became ill himself, and knew that he was going to die. His two sons knelt down by his bedside and said:

'Dear father, you have always chosen graves for other people and they have benefited by your choice. Why don't you choose a good grave yourself, so that we can also have a little luck?' The old man replied with a sigh: 'Naturally there are favourable sites, but you have no veins of luck,' but as his sons begged him so earnestly he said at last: 'All right. You must try your luck. When I am dead you must not raise a big mound, but wrap up my body in grass ropes and go towards the East. At the place the rope breaks and my corpse falls down, you must dig a grave and bury me. Then you must return home and prepare a terrace for the dead, on which you must place candles and cover them with the chamber-pot. On the house itself you must put a bushel, which must not be touched for seven times seven days. If you do exactly as I tell you, you will both become Emperor. But I am afraid that you will never have such luck, because you will never carry out my instructions.' The two sons thanked their father: 'Of course we will do it,' they said.

The same day their father died. The two sons secretly fastened a grass rope to his body and went off towards the East, and at the Eastern Sea the rope broke. After they had buried him, they returned home and built a terrace for the dead, on which they placed candles covered with a chamber-pot, and erected a bushel on the house. After seven days, the two sons and everyone in the house fell ill. Their whole bodies and muscles ached, as if they were being consumed by fire. There were many clever people in T'ung-chou, who noticed that all new-born children had a strange birthmark. In the Ts'ao family's bamboo garden a clump of strange bamboos suddenly sprang up.

After forty days an uncle paid a visit to the two sons. He was furious when he saw the chamber-pot on top of the candles, and said angrily: 'No wonder you are all ill, if you put such a dirty thing on the terrace of the dead.' He took away the chamber-pot himself; but, as he did so, there was a red flash and something shot up to heaven and disappeared. Everything was ruined; the illness of the brothers and of all the household was cured, many of the new-born children with strange birth-marks died without cause, and the newly grown bamboos in the garden dried up. When they were afterwards split, a small blind child was found in each knot. At the same moment a famous scholar named Ch'en Shih-hsiao, who was living in T'ung-chou, became blind. In the astrological office in Peking a real dragon was seen to arise in T'ung-chou, which if it grew up and had any success, would cause the Manchu dynasty a great deal of trouble. Therefore people were sent to T'ung-chou to kill the reptile, which was lying in the grave of Ts'ao on the seashore. They first tried by sticking iron and bronze spikes into the sand, but they could never find the dragon, until a scholar said: 'The dragon is already full grown, it only lacks eyes. Bronze and iron both have a smell and it can move away. You must use bamboo staves, and it will be killed.' The next day they did as he suggested and blood poured out of the ground. Both brothers fell ill during the month and died.

34. *The Son of the Turtle Spirit*

ONCE upon a time a turtle, who was living in a pond in a nobleman's garden, learnt after prolonged study how to change his form at will. Now you must know that the nobleman had a daughter of rare and unusual beauty, and one day, as she was combing her hair at the window, the turtle caught sight of her and fell deeply in love. He said to himself: 'As I can turn myself into a human being at will, why should I not become a young man and court the young lady?'

124

So in the night he climbed on to the bank, turned himself into a handsome youth, and went to her room, where he persuaded her to yield. From then on the turtle became a youth every night and played with the maiden till dawn, when he returned to the pond. He left no trace behind him, and even the maiden did not know that he was really a turtle, but thought instead that he was some student from the neighbourhood.

At the end of a year the maiden noticed that she was going to have a child. Her mother knew nothing about it until one day on a visit to her daughter she noticed what was the matter. She asked the maid-servant who the young man was, but the servant said: 'My mistress is very secretive; she remains in her room all day long without going out. But one day, about a year ago, I saw a young man looking like a student come out of her room. From that time he came every night and went away at dawn.' 'Is it possible?' cried the mother angrily. 'Don't you know where he comes from? How does he get up to her? You have eyes. You must once have seen how he came.' 'Really, I don't know,' said the maid. 'Mistress must try to forgive me. He comes and goes without leaving a trace. Sometimes he appears in the wink of an eye, and disappears in the same way.' 'Then he must be a spirit,' decided the mother. 'What can be done for my poor daughter?' After a moment's thought, she called her daughter to her and said: 'The man who comes to see you every night must be a spirit, but I have thought of a plan; when he falls asleep to-night, tie a thread on to his coat, and then wherever he goes, we can follow the thread to his abode and decide how to catch him. Don't fail to do this, and to-morrow we will see what happens.' Her daughter promised to do as she was told.

That night the turtle came again. The maiden had already hidden a needle and thread under the pillow, and when about midnight her lover fell asleep, she sewed the thread on to his coat without his noticing anything in his dreams.

The next morning, the turtle flew out of the window like a bird and vanished in the twinkling of an eye; but the thread flew with him through the window and into the pond in the garden. Then the father said at once: 'It can only be a turtle spirit. It must be the one my father put into the pond. But it shall not escape me; I shall kill it.' At once he called for ten workmen and ordered them to scoop the water out of the pond, and when it was empty enough to see the bottom, sure enough there was a turtle as large as a round table lying in the mud, with the red thread that led to the maiden's window fast in the folds of his skin. 'There he is,' shouted the father, and he ordered the workmen to carry him up to the edge, where he seized a knife and cut off the turtle's head so that it died. Its remains were cut up in little pieces and thrown into a corner of the garden to rot. After a few months, all the flesh was gone and only bones were left, which no one bothered about.

One day, when the maid was walking in the garden, she noticed the white bones, and told her mistress, who wept when she heard it. She said to her maid: 'It is true he was a spirit, but still he was my husband, so how can I leave his bones to lie and rot?' So she gave the maid a little yellow bag to put the bones in and hung it beside her bed. The son that was born to her in due time naturally bore no love for his grand-parents, because he was the son of a spirit. At seven years old he still had no teacher, but was allowed instead to play about the whole day long.

Now, one day a grave-seeker had found an unusually fine burial-place for one of the families in the town. According to him, there was a heap of mud in the river near the village shaped like a dragon, with a tail, a head and two horns, just like those of a real dragon, and the sons and grandsons of anyone buried there would certainly rise to high honours. Unfortunately, the current in that place was very strong, and many tales were told of ships that had sunk there, so that no ordinary mortal would be brave enough to swim over and bury the bones. The rich man consulted the grave-seeker, who finally suggested: 'If you promise to give a large reward, you will certainly find a man brave enough. We ought to announce that we are looking for someone who can dive well, and reward him handsomely if he takes the casket over.' 'That is a good plan,' said the official, nodding his head. 'We must try that.' He had a notice written out to this effect, only he wrote nothing about the bones that must be buried there, but only about a treasure, and promised a reward of one thousand pieces of gold and one thousand pieces of silver. Many people read the notice that was posted up, but all knew how dangerous the river was, and that it would be difficult to find anyone to do it.

One day, the son of the turtle spirit was strolling along, when he saw a great crowd gathered in one place, and going up he asked what was the matter. 'They are looking for someone to dive into the river and bring up a treasure. Can you do that? If you can, you will be given a large amount of gold and silver!' the boys standing by said to him jokingly. 'Bring a treasure out of the river and receive gold and silver as well? That is quite simple for me,' said the child. 'I will tear down the notice.' 'Better leave it alone,' said some older people. 'Do you know which river it is? It is the terribly dangerous Li Cha River, where so many people are drowned every year. And a young boy like you wants to dive? Go and play and don't come and talk such rubbish here.' 'But I can do it, you don't need to dispute it,' said the boy, and pushing his way through the crowd, he tore down the notice. Then the watchmen seized him and asked: 'Surely you are joking when you say you can do it?' 'Why should I joke?' the boy replied steadily. 'Would

I have torn down the notice if I could not do it?' 'Well, you must come to our Master,' said the men. 'No,' said the boy, 'first I must go home and tell my mother, then I will go with you.' 'Go there first,' said the men, 'we will wait for you here.' Swift as the wind, the boy ran to his mother, and when he had told her everything, he begged her to let him go. His mother thought: 'After all, he is the son of a turtle, he ought to be a strong swimmer.' And so she said to him: 'You can go, but before you enter the water, come back to me, because I have something to tell you.' The boy promised and went off to the rich man with the watchmen.

When the rich man and the grave-seeker saw a seven- or eight-year-old child coming, they were very surprised, but they thought that, having torn down the notice, he must be sure of himself. They sent for wine, and while he drank, the rich man said to him: 'What we wrote in the notice was not quite the truth. We want to ask you to take the remains of my grandfather and bury them in a favourable spot. Now in the river there is a dragon formed out of sand, with his mouth always open. I will give you the casket which contains the remains of my grandfather, and you must dive to the bottom of the river and place it in the dragon's mouth. If you can do that, you will receive the promised reward of one thousand pieces of gold and one thousand pieces of silver.'

'That is quite simple,' said the boy. 'I can certainly place the bones in the dragon's mouth.' After the meal, he took the casket and went home to tell his mother. His mother suddenly remembered the bones of her own husband, and with a smile she took the little bag with the bones of the turtle and gave them to her son, saying: 'These are the bones of your father. Take them to the bottom of the river and put them in the dragon's mouth, and hang the other bones on his horns. Don't forget to do this, and don't mix the bones.'

The boy promised to follow her instructions and went to the river with the two packets, where the rich man and the grave-seeker were waiting. The boy called out to them and plunged into the river, at the bottom of which he soon arrived. There, sure enough, was a mud dragon, more than six feet long, with a head and a tail, and his mouth wide open, as if he wanted to swallow something. The boy took the two packets out of his breast-pocket, and threw his father's bones into the dragon's mouth, and hung the bones of the rich man's grandfather on the dragon's horns. Then he shot up again and swam to the bank.

When the rich man and the grave-seeker saw that he had returned safely, they knew that their plan had succeeded, and they were very glad. They brought him back to their house, and gave him dry clothes and delicious food and wine, and when he had finished, they sent him home with one thousand pieces of gold and one thousand pieces of silver.

When the boy was ten years old, his appearance suddenly began to change, and he became quite out of the ordinary, and much cleverer than anyone else. Finally, he became Emperor and the son of the rich man was his minister.

35. *Chu the Rogue*

CHU, the good-for-nothing, was a regular rascal, prepared to play pranks on all and sundry. One day the sun was blazing in the sky, and he called out: 'Sunshine P'usa, I never sent for you. How dare you come uninvited into my room! I will complain to Yü-huang ti.' The Sunshine P'usa was very frightened by this threat, and said: 'Please don't complain. There is a pot of silver in front of your house, you can take that,' and when Chu really found a pot of silver, he no longer wanted to accuse the sun.

The next night the moon was shining, and he said to it: 'Moonlight P'usa, I never sent for you. How dare you enter my house without permission! I will complain to Yü-huang ti.' 'Please don't do that,' said the Moonlight P'usa in a terrible fright. 'Take the pot of gold behind your house and say no more about it,' and as he did dig up the pot of gold, Chu the Rogue kept silent.

One day he went into the temple of the Plague Gods. 'You are jumbled together in threes and fours,' he said to them. 'You are certainly bad men. I will complain to Yü-huang ti.' But the Plague Gods were not so meek as the Sun and Moon Gods. When they heard Chu's disrespectful words, they complained to Yen-lo-wang, the King of Hell. Yen-lo-wang happened to be in the Judgment Hall at this moment and he sent the bee spirit up to earth to fetch this wicked man. But Chu was very clever and pasted paper over all the holes in the doors, walls, and windows. He only left one small hole, which he covered with a pig's bladder. When, therefore, the bee ghost arrived, it searched in vain for some opening until it came upon the small hole. 'Trapped!' it cried out, as it found itself inside the bladder, but Chu chortled with glee.

When Yen-lo-wang noticed that the bee spirit had been gone for several days, he ordered the one-legged spirit to go up to Earth and catch Chu. Unfortunately Chu also knew about this and filled his house with prickly things and sat down in the middle of the thorns. The one-legged ghost found Chu sitting in his house doing nothing and dashed in; but the thorns ran into his foot, and being unable to run away he was taken prisoner by Chu. Yen-lo-wang soon noticed that the one-legged spirit also failed to return, and mounting his thousand-league horse, he went together with Oxhead and Horseface to the house of Chu. Chu knew beforehand of his coming and gave his wife exact orders what to do. She went to greet Yen-lo-wang herself with a smile on her face and invited him to dinner.

After the meal, Chu took an old water-buffalo out of the stable. As he got on to the animal to ride down to the Underworld, as he had arranged with Yen-lo-wang, his wife hung two glowing arrows on its back, with the result that the buffalo, maddened by the sudden pain, rushed away so fast that Yen-lo-wang's thousand-league horse could not keep up with it. Yen-lo-wang called out to Chu to stop, and then asked him: 'What kind of buffalo is that? I never knew that they could run so fast.' 'It is a thousand-league buffalo,' answered Chu without turning a hair. Yen-lo-wang was very surprised and begged Chu to allow him to try it. Chu agreed, but warned him casually: 'My buffalo only knows its master. It only runs fast with me.' 'Is there nothing to be done to make it think I am you?' asked Yen-lo-wang. 'Perhaps it would be deceived if you put on my clothes,' answered Chu, and he gave his clothes to Yen-lo-wang, who put them on and got on to the water-buffalo, which refused to move a step. Chu, however, was seated on the thousand-league horse, dressed in Yen-lo-wang's clothes, and he gave it a blow and soon arrived in Hell, where he placed himself on to the throne and said to the Rakshasas and other small servant ghosts: 'Chu the Rogue is following me on a water-buffalo. Beat him the moment he arrives.'

The spirits did not know that the man on the water-buffalo was the King of Hell. They did not ask his name, but pulled him off his mount and thrashed him, until Oxhead and Horseface arrived and explained what had happened. Don't you think it was a good joke, to give the King of Hell a good beating? But mad with rage, he climbed on to his throne and ordered the little spirits to heat up the cauldron of oil for Chu to be boiled in.

When the spirits brought the oil, Chu asked them: 'Do you want to become rich?' And when they all asked him how it could be managed, he continued: 'You see, Yen-lo-wang is a stupid man. One only needs a few pints of oil to boil one man. I suggest that you leave enough oil to roast me and then sell the rest. Won't you become rich then?' The little spirits were very pleased at this idea, and sold the spare oil at once. Just at this moment the order came to boil Chu, and burning to show their zeal, they cast him into the cauldron. But he did not cry out, because he held himself up on one side with his head and on the other with his feet, and although Yen-lo-wang went on stoking the fire, he could not boil him to death. In despair he ordered the little ghosts to drag him along to the Yin-Yang River and leave him there to freeze to death.

On the bank Chu called out as loud as he could for someone to ferry him across. There was a carp in the river, who was so sorry for Chu that he offered to carry him himself to the Upper World. Chu looked at the carp and thought: 'What a fine carp. I must catch it and sell it for wine,' and he called out: 'Brother Carp! Please tell me how I can cross over.' 'It's very simple,' answered the carp. 'You get on to my back and are carried across.' 'But your back is so slippery,' said the rascal. 'I am afraid of sliding off. I don't think I dare go, unless you agree to a suggestion of mine. I shall tie a rope round your body, and hold one end myself. Then I won't drown if I fall in.'

The carp allowed itself to be bound, and Chu rode safely over the river with the rope in one hand. But when he arrived in the Upper World he dragged off the poor carp and sold it to buy wine.

36. *The Infection*

IT is a custom in Kuang-tung that all grown-up girls should lie with a man before their marriage. In this way the man that was with her first receives the poison in her body, and in a short time he is covered with red spots and great poisonous ulcers, which soon spread all over and kill him. This custom in Kuang-tung is called 'passing on the infection.'

In the village of Kao-fu, not far from Wu-shih, lived a Mr. Ma, who travelled about the province on business. He had no luck, though, and lost all the money he had taken with him. Finally he was reduced to such straits that he no longer had the wherewithal to return home, and there was nothing for him but death. While begging for money, he reached the house of a rich man, whose daughter had just arrived at a marriageable age. Since this girl had not yet passed on the infection, no one wanted her as a wife, which worried the rich man so much that he felt as if a stone was lying on his heart. While he was pondering on his troubles, the beggar appeared, and they at once offered him one hundred cash as a reward if he would pass the night with his daughter. Ma was delighted, because Shao-hsing people consider the first night with a girl the most enjoyable, only he wondered why a beggar should be offered such a pleasure and be paid for it as well.

The young lady's room was beautifully clean, and its occupant was so far from being ugly that the young man fell in love with her at sight and confessed his passion. She saw at once that he was a stranger fallen on evil days, and not wishing to belong to him, she said in a friendly tone: 'You don't come from these parts and you don't know our customs. All virgins have to give themselves to another man before anyone will demand their hand in marriage. But the man who first possesses the girl soon breaks out in boils all over his body and dies. If the girl does not do it, she herself falls ill, but I am warning you because I do not want to be responsible for your death.'

Ma at first was worried by the danger, but then he said: 'Sister, by forbidding me to do what is necessary you sacrifice your own life. How could I ever repay you? But, sister, look how miserable and ruined I am; I have no money for returning home. Let me remain with you, and then you can marry another man without a qualm.' Deeply touched by the moral and noble words of the beggar, the young lady replied: 'I cannot accept your offer to die for me, merely because you have no money. I want to make a proposal; if you agree, I will give you the money to return home. These are my requests: you must swear brotherhood with me; you must tell me your abode; you must not sleep with me to-night. Then I will soon fall ill and my father will turn me out of the house and I can beg my way to you. You must swear to receive me.' And while she spoke sorrow overcame her, and tears rolled down her cheeks like a broken string of pearls.

Ma agreed to her conditions, and after receiving a large sum of money he returned to Shao-hsing without taking leave of the rich man. The rich man now thought his daughter was safe from the infection, and he looked around for a suitable match; but a few years later, she broke out into red spots which soon became poisonous. Her father was furious, because now he knew she had not given herself to the beggar, and moreover, girls who catch the disease though remaining chaste enjoy an evil reputation. He was not willing to endure the shame and turned her out of the house, but she had expected this to happen.

The poor girl was very weak and ill, and as she crept along the streets all day she used to hope that the God of Death would give her his hand. But then she thought of her adopted brother, Mr. Ma, who was living in Shao-hsing, and she went on; but, being quite penniless, she had no choice but to beg her way to the village of Kao-fu. There she asked for the Ma house, not having heard that Ma meanwhile had become one of the richest people in the village.

After his return from Kuang-tung, by dint of careful living and hard work, he gradually saved money, till finally he was quite well off. He often wondered whether the maiden in Kuang-tung, who had saved his life and sworn brotherhood with him, had married in the meantime or not. Had she really fallen ill? Deep in these thoughts, he walked out of his door just as a woman was going by with filthy clothes and sores all over her body. She asked him: 'Please, sir, is there a Mr. Ma here?' 'There are many,' answered Ma; 'which one do you want to talk with?' 'I want to see the one who was formerly a merchant and lost all his money,' answered the beggar woman. 'Why do you want to see him?' asked Ma, 'and how do you know he had troubles in Kuang-tung?' Then the poor girl told Ma of her misery, and he sighed deeply and tears coursed down his face. He looked at her and saw how her beauty had been killed as the first cold in winter nips the plants, and he groaned: 'My dear sister! poor sister! It is all my fault,' and he led her into his garden. Mrs. Ma was very kind and treated her very well, for her husband had told her the whole story. He in the meantime had become quite unrecognizable, for while he had been dried up and thin as a rail before, he had spread out and was now quite fat.

Soon after, the girl's disease became much worse. The wounds smelt disgusting, and hot breath rose from her mouth. She called for Ma and said to him: 'Brother, I fear I am not much longer for this life. My illness is growing worse. After my death, don't have a great funeral, but bury me simply without much expense.'

135

Ma was overcome by the gloom of the room, and, after promising to comply with her wishes, he went out.

During the night, her mouth became so dry that she was unable to speak. In her agony she drank anything she found, but she was still thirsty. Then she saw an old cracked wine-jug into which a fiery red snake had fallen. But this by no means deterred her, and swallowing down the whole jugful, she ended by collapsing on the floor.

Ma had been very worried about her during the night, and hurried across to see how she was. As he entered her room there was no sound to be heard, and thinking she was dead, he hurried over to the bed; but she was lying on the ground, quite well, and lifting her up, he laid her on the bed. After she drank the wine, the ulcers disappeared, and eventually she was quite cured. Ma took her as his second wife, and they all lived together peacefully for many years.

37. *The Amazing Adventure of a Scholar*

EVERYONE was celebrating the New Year except the scholar, who was so poor that he could not even buy firewood, and he had been sent into the woods by his wife to fetch some. He chopped for a long time, but finding nothing but dried sticks, he eventually climbed up to a high peak to cut down something better. On his way down to the valley he passed a large cave in which a tribe of monkeys were playing. One monkey was just entering the cave with a golden plate piled high with pearls and precious stones, and the scholar thought he would try to deceive the monkeys and steal their treasure. He cast down a large rock, which terrified most of the animals, but a clever one glanced up, and seeing a man standing on the crag, he rushed up and dragged him into the cave. Inside it was very spacious, and in every respect resembled an ordinary palace. The monkeys carried the scholar before a large monkey and then departed, but the ruler treated him very well and entertained him for several days. One day the monkey turned into a handsome man and said to the scholar: 'This evening we are going to the theatre. Do you want to join us?' 'To what theatre?' asked the scholar. 'In the Emperor's palace,' said the monkey. 'That is too far away; how can we get there?' asked the scholar. 'Don't bother about that. Just shut your eyes, and when I tell you to open them we will be there,' and before the monkey had finished speaking, the scholar found himself in a magnificent theatre. There was a large audience composed of the highest officials in the land, but the scholar soon became tired of watching and said to his companion: 'What shall I do? I can hardly keep my eyes open, from sleep.' 'All right,' said the monkey, 'I will show you where you can take a nap,' and he led him through to the women's apartments, into the bedroom of the Chancellor's daughter.

A little later the young lady came home from the theatre with her maids and went into her bedroom, where she found a man lying on the bed behind the curtains. She was so astounded that for a long time she could not utter a word, but on looking closer, she saw the stranger's beautiful eyes and eyebrows and realized that he was no ordinary man. She dismissed her maids at once to prevent them noticing anything and reporting the matter, and then said to the stranger: 'Who are you? How dare you get into a young lady's bed!' The scholar nearly fell out of bed at the shock, and asked breathlessly where he was and how he had got there. 'This is the palace of the Chancellor, and I am his daughter,' the young lady told him. The poor man was horrified to hear this, but eventually he decided that his only hope was to tell the young lady everything. She forgave him at once, because they had fallen in love at first sight, and she decided to hide him in the clothes closet for the moment, to which she brought him food every day. The maids, though, soon became suspicious, and observed everything through a crack in the door. The news gradually spread through the house, until it reached the ears of her mother, who immediately rushed off and accused her daughter of improper conduct. But when she saw that the man was both respectable and handsome, she became calmer and ordered her daughter to tell her the whole story from beginning to end. She also did not know what to do, but she ordered her daughter to keep the matter secret till she had thought of some plan; for it was obvious that sooner or later it would come to the ears of the Chancellor.

One evening the mother plied the Chancellor with wine until he was quite drunk, and then said casually: 'In such and such a case, what would you?' And she told him the whole story. 'There is no difficulty about that,' said the minister, 'the couple should get married and then everything would be all right.' 'Do you mean that?' asked the mother. 'Am I accustomed to lie?' asked the Chancellor crossly, and with this assurance the mother quickly wrote out a statement and gave it to the Chancellor, who, being quite drunk, signed it without a word. A few days later he heard of the scandal about his daughter, and was so furious that he wanted to kill both her and the scholar. Fortunately, since the mother was able to produce the paper signed by him, he could do nothing about it, and three days later the marriage was gaily celebrated and a large entertainment given in the house of the Chancellor.

38. *The Wicked Rich Man is turned into a Monkey*

MANY, many years ago there was a rich man living alone with his wife without any children. He bought a maid-servant. Although he was very rich he had a heart of stone and never gave away a farthing in charity. He considered poor people more despicable than dogs, and he not only refused them money and food, but also cursed them, shouting: 'You ought to have perished rather than come here.' And if the beggars did not take themselves off, he drove them away with a stick.

You can imagine how brutally he treated the young slave girl. If anything displeased him he cursed her and beat her, sometimes so badly as to draw blood. The whole day long the house rang with the crack of whips and foul language, and soon all his neighbours nick-named him 'the cruel.' The maid-servant, however, served her master well and faithfully, but when alone she sighed to herself: 'Oh, Lord! Why have I come here? What an awful life I have. Will I never have any better luck?'

The Immortals and the gods heard about the cruelty of the man and his wife, and wanted to discover the truth. One of them turned into a barefooted, scurvy-headed beggar, and went to the rich man's house, clad only in a few tattered rags, and called out at the door: 'Mother, father in the house. Help me. Give me something to eat, I am so terribly hungry.' It happened that the old people had gone out and only the maid was at home, heating the stove. She used rice straw as fuel, and occasionally there were some grains left in the ears. She had been collecting them for some time and now she had a bag full of over two thousand grains. So sorry was she for the miserable beggar that she gave him the bag, but she warned him saying: 'Take the rice away quickly. My master is a villain. If he sees you there will be trouble, although the rice I am giving you I collected myself.' When the Immortal saw that she had such a kind heart he did not go away, but gave her a handkerchief. 'You must wash your face with this,' he said, 'but be careful not to let other people use it.'

Just at this moment the two old people returned. Seeing a beggar, they shouted at the maid: 'What have you given to the beggar, slave?' They tried to beat the beggar, who ran away when he saw what they intended; but the poor girl received another dreadful whipping from her master.

From then on she used to wash her face with the handkerchief every day, and her heavy dark face gradually became whiter and more beautiful. Her master was very surprised and questioned her very closely. She knew she could not keep the matter secret and therefore told him the whole story: 'The only reason why my face becomes white is that I wash it with the cloth that the beggar presented me with in return for the rice.' When the couple heard her, they asked her angrily: 'So you did give the beggar some rice. Can't you give the cloth to us?' The servant was very frightened, because the beggar had told her that she alone and no one else might use the handkerchief, but she knew that if she refused she would receive another beating from her master, and so she respectfully handed it to him with both hands.

Next morning the old couple both washed their faces with it, hoping to become as beautiful as their slave girl. But as soon as they had used it, their faces and whole appearance changed, and eventually hair grew all over their bodies and they turned into monkeys. They ran off into the mountains and were never seen again.

39. *The Dissatisfied Benefactor*

IN a certain village there was a very rich family, the head of which was always doing good deeds. In summer he bought fans and medicine to distribute; and during the winter he made large quantities of padded clothes, which he gave to any poor person suffering from want or cold. He repaired bridges and built roads, and without a doubt innumerable people benefited by his kindness. His fame spread from his own village to the next, and gradually there was no one in the whole district who did not respect him for his charities.

Eventually his renown spread so wide that it reached the ears of the Immortals in Heaven. Wanting to test him, one cold winter's day, two of them transformed themselves into two shoeless, half-naked beggars and stood outside his house, chattering with cold. Suddenly, and heaven only knows for what reason, they began quarrelling, and from quarrelling they came to blows.

The rich man, who was seated in his house, hearing the sounds of combat, quickly went to the door, where he saw two miserable beggars. He went up and separated them, and then ordered the servants to bring them clothes, shoes, and socks, and to prepare some food for them. At the good news the beggars ceased fighting.

They both ate extremely slowly on purpose, so that the sun went down and night fell before they had finished. Then they said to the rich man: 'It is dark now, master, and we have no home. Cannot we stay the night here?' Their benefactor granted their request without any hesitation. 'That's quite all right,' he said. 'Just remain here. Everything is ready,' and he sent them off to sleep.

But the beggars intentionally behaved in the most disgusting manner; they spat all over the bed, and the next morning, after eating breakfast at the rich man's house, they went off without saying good-bye and without expressing their thanks in any way. They thought that their benefactor would certainly get angry with them now and curse them. But he was a really good man; for after breakfast, when he did not see the beggars, he merely told the servants to clean up the room and wash the bedclothes, and never said a word against the two strangers.

Just behind his house there was a well. One day a maid-servant was fetching water, when the rich man came by and said jokingly: 'How pleasant it would be if the water in the well was wine, but as inexhaustible as the water.' The next time the girl fetched water she noticed to her surprise that it was yellow in colour, and at the first sip she knew that it had really turned into wine. She reported the matter to her master, who was even more surprised than she. From then on they began to sell wine, and to sell it much cheaper than the shops.

One day a man came to buy spirits. 'Why,' he asked the rich man, 'do you have no spirits, if you have yellow wine?' After the customer's departure, the rich man thought to himself: 'How pleasant it would be if the water in the bucket would turn into spirits; we could sell it,' and while he was speaking the water in the bucket was suddenly changed. Now they sold brandy and were even richer than before.

One day a man asked them for some grape husks, but the rich man did not know where to get them from. The buyer said to him: 'You have wine, how do you mean that you have no husks? It's merely that you don't want to sell them.'

The man went off in a temper, leaving the rich man pondering over the matter. 'It really is stupid to have wine, but no husks. It would be nice if I could have some.' Suddenly he saw the two men who had formerly fought outside his house and afterwards had eaten and behaved in such a foul manner, and he had a great shock when they said to him: 'It is true that you are kindly and charitable, but you are too grasping. First you had wine, then you wanted spirits, and now you are demanding husks. There are no contented men in the world. From to-day the wine and the spirits will vanish; and husks are not in stock,' and just as the man was going to answer, they disappeared. He hurried round to the back of the house, but the spirits in the bucket had become water again and the well water had ceased to be wine.

40. *A Bottle full of Ants*

ONE evening, a man said to his wife: 'On such and such a mountain there is a large tree, and underneath the tree is buried a jar full of silver coins. On top of the bottle lies a stone. I thought of digging it up this evening, but I prefer to go to bed a little earlier and dig it out at the first streak of dawn to-morrow.' A near neighbour, who lived in the next house, heard him say this, and rushed off to dig up the jar at once. At the place mentioned, he found a large tree, and soon he came upon a big stone, underneath which he found a heavy jar. He put in his hand to feel what was there, but to his horror felt nothing but ants. This made him extremely angry, and shutting up the jar again, he ran back to the house of the man and the woman. He climbed on to their roof, and loosened several tiles at a place that was over a hole in their mosquito net; then he shouted out: 'You lied to me. Here are the ants for you to eat,' and he tipped up the jar. But he heard nothing but the clink of falling money. This roused the husband and wife, who said: 'How extraordinary! Gold is raining down from Heaven.' The neighbour caught the word 'gold,' and having some doubts he looked into the jar, inside which there was still one piece of money, the wages for his work.

41. *Gold-hair becomes Minister*

'GOLD-HAIR' was the nickname of Liu Ta, because his hair was so blond. His parents died soon after his birth, and having no brothers or sisters, he was brought up by his uncle. When he grew up, he had no desire to study or learn anything, but merely wanted to play about. This annoyed his uncle, who refused to give him a copper. No longer being able to get any money, Liu Ta went to his uncle and said: 'Uncle, I want to go away and study. Please give me two hundred ounces of silver.' He appeared to be quite serious, so his uncle said: 'I am so pleased to hear that you intend to study. I would even give you three hundred ounces if it was necessary.'

Liu Ta took the money, and wandered through the land for two years until it was all finished. When his uncle saw him returning with empty hands, he asked him: 'Here you are back again. What have you learnt in the meantime?' Knowing that his uncle would ask him this question, Liu Ta had considered the matter, and decided that the best way of preventing his deception being made public was to say he was an accoucheur, for who has ever heard of a male midwife? He therefore told this to his uncle, who was horrified at the trade he had learnt, but could only say 'good.'

Shortly after, the wife of the Emperor, the Empress, had a very difficult confinement; after three days the child had still not been delivered and the Emperor summoned all the midwives in the Empire, but none of them was able to help. Then the Emperor issued an order: 'Anyone that enables the Empress to bring a living child into the world will be made an official.' This announcement spread abroad, until it reached the village of Liu Ta, where his uncle advised him to go to the palace and try his luck. Liu Ta had no wish to go, but his uncle urged him, saying: 'Why did you learn midwifery, if you won't go now?' And Liu Ta thought to himself it could not do any harm to have a try and he might become an official.

On his arrival at the capital, he announced why he had come, and the Emperor sent him to see the Empress. 'That is not difficult,' Liu Ta said. 'Please buy me a couple of dolls.' Then he sat down facing the Empress, seized a doll, and said continuously: 'Little Emperor, come out. Come out quickly, little Emperor.' He was so ridiculous that, in spite of the terrible pain, the Empress was compelled to laugh and the child was born at once.

The Emperor wanted to reward Liu Ta, but all the grandees at court dissuaded him: 'He has not rendered any great service,' they said. Just at that moment an official informed the Emperor that the ruler of the barbarians had revolted. The officials now all asked the Sovereign to entrust Liu Ta with the campaign against them. The Emperor said to him: 'The leader of the barbarians has revolted; you must go and drive him off. If you succeed, I will give you a post.' Liu Ta was far from pleased when he heard that. 'How can I fight?' he thought. 'If I go out to battle, I shall be killed; but if I stay here, I shall die just the same, so I might as well see what turns up,' and he said to the Emperor: 'Agreed, I will go there alone. I don't need one single soldier,' and the Emperor granted his request.

Liu Ta rode off to the battlefield on his horse, but from afar off he could distinguish the ranks of the enemy, which terrified him to such an extent that he began to shake all over. His terror communicated itself to his horse, which soon became very restive and knocked him off against a tree. To save himself, he caught hold of a bush, which came up by the roots, and the effort made him fall down again into a manure bucket. Fortunately, though, it had a handle and he lifted it up in his hand. When the barbarians saw a horseman advancing towards

K   145

them with such an enormous, many-pointed lance in one hand, and a huge smoking cauldron in the other, they were overcome with terror and reported the matter to their king, who immediately ordered a retreat.

Liu Ta returned to the capital and announced to the Emperor that the barbarians had retired, but the ministers again prevented his receiving a reward. 'He has not done anything remarkable, the enemy retreated of their own accord,' they said. The Emperor therefore said to Liu Ta: 'I am going to ask you to guess something. If you are successful, I will give you an appointment at once,' and pulling out a sack, he continued: 'Guess what I have got in here!' There being no means of knowing, Liu Ta was in a terrible state and kept on repeating with a sigh: 'Oh, Gold-hair! Gold-hair!' but the Emperor understood 'Gold cat,' and opening the sack he said: 'Correct. Now I will reward you.'

42. *The Tale of the Silver Men*

IN olden times there lived a man of the name of Li. He was so rich that he had eight silver men cast, which he kept in his treasury.

But his sons and grandsons wasted his wealth, and when it was all finished, they cut a bit off the bottom of the silver men. Naturally the latter were enraged at this treatment, and one day they could stand it no longer, but turned into eight young men and went off. They came to a ferry, where they asked the ferryman: 'Do you want to be rich, old fellow?' 'We poor people are happy, if we have enough to eat,' answered the old man; 'how can we dream of riches?' Seeing that the ferryman had no vein of luck, the silver men crossed the river and continued their journey. A little later they met a merchant. 'Do you want to be rich, brother?' they asked. 'If I can earn enough to buy my daily bread,

146

I am content,' answered the man. 'What's the use of dreaming about riches?' He also had no vein of luck, and although the silver men asked all and sundry the same question, there was no one that wanted to become rich, and failing to find a resting-place anywhere, they eventually returned to the Li house.

On their return to the ferry the boatman recognized the youths as the transformed silver men, because the news of their leaving Li's house had spread abroad. As they were stepping on to the bank and not paying much attention, he seized his opportunity and hacked off a finger with his knife. He found that it really was pure silver, but when he wanted to cut off another bit, he saw that they had gone too far to be overtaken. 'I have not gained great riches,' he said with a sigh, 'but at least I have got my passage money.' When the Li family saw the silver men coming home, they greeted them with tea and wine, burnt incense and paper money, and prayed to them: 'Don't run away again. If we have not got the luck to keep you, who has?' And from that time the silver men remained with the Lis.

43. *The Dark Maiden from the Ninth Heaven*

THERE was once a very poor man living in a deserted kiln, who worked when he found anyone to employ him, and otherwise collected firewood in the fields or dung on the roads. He lived all alone; sometimes he earned no money and had to go hungry; at other times he was able to save a few hundred coppers.

At New Year everyone buys the things they need for the festival: fish, meat, wine, vegetables, incense, fire-works, inscriptions, and many more things than I can describe. On New Year's Eve the poor man took the

147

200 coppers he had saved and went into the market. He looked about, but could not find anything that pleased him, until he saw a picture of a beautiful girl hanging on the wall, which so entranced him that he could not take his eyes off it. 'Do you want to buy it?' asked the shopkeeper, and when he nodded, he told him that the price was 600 cash. The poor man did not hesitate, but rushed home, and took all his savings, amounting to 500 coppers, out of a niche. 'If I also use the 200 in my pocket,' he thought, 'that together makes 700, and I can buy two bushels of rice as well.' He ran back to the market, bought the picture, and then spent the rest on a bushel of rice and three white cabbage heads, which he took back to the kiln. Next morning, when everyone was wishing each other a happy New Year, a beautiful picture was hanging up in the old kiln with a large plate of cabbage in front of it. The poor man humbly knelt down and bowed to the lovely woman.

From that day, before every meal and whenever he went out or came in, he used to bow to the picture. Nothing unusual happened for about six months, only the picture made him feel very contented and soothed him whenever he felt tired.

One day he arrived home exhausted and very hungry, to be greeted, as he opened the door, by a delicious odour of food. He made his bow and went to open the pot, which he found full of steaming hot rice. At first he was too frightened to eat, but eventually he placed an offering before the picture as usual, and ate until he was satisfied. In the afternoon he went out to collect firewood, but the food was again ready on his return. He wondered who could have done it, and next morning he merely pretended to go and collect dung, and hid instead behind the kiln and watched to see if anyone went in. After a while no one had entered, but he heard someone moving about inside, and creeping up to the door he peeped into the room, where he saw a beautiful girl standing by the stove making a fire. On the wall there was nothing but a piece of smooth white paper. He was trembling with excitement, but he did not know what to do. In the end he stepped back, coughed, and then walked noisily up to the door, and when he entered, the picture of the beautiful girl was once more hanging on the wall, and the pot was full of half-cooked food, with a fire still burning underneath.

That afternoon he went out again and waited until he heard light footsteps moving across the room, followed by a soft rattling of the cover of the pot, the noise of water being poured into a basin, the chink of flint and firetongs, and the wheezing of the bellows. With bated breath he crept up to the door and burst in, and, quickly rolling up the picture, he hid it out of sight. When he looked round he saw a beautiful girl standing by the fire, at whose feet he went and flung himself down. He remained kneeling till she raised him up, saying: 'Since this has occurred, we might as well live together, and then you won't need to be alone so much.'

The girl looked after the house so well that their money increased almost as if it grew. After six months they had so much gold and silver that they decided to build a house with halls, and pavilions, and terraces, and to fill it with many beautiful clothes and treasures. Here they lived happily together, and everyone that went past wondered: 'How strange. Six months ago there was only a deserted kiln here. Who has built this marvellous palace?'

The husband kept on asking his wife who she was, but she only laughed and gave him no explanation. Once when he bothered her too much, she said, half joking, half serious: 'I am the dark maiden from the Ninth Heaven. As a penalty for some fault I had committed I was condemned to descend to earth for a few years.'

But when he asked her for how many years, she did not reply.

Three years passed and a daughter was born to them, which made them happier than before. One day, however, the wife suddenly became troubled, as if something very important had happened, and later she ceased to eat. Fearing she was ill, her husband wanted to send for a doctor, but she refused to see anyone, and merely asked him casually: 'Did you keep the roll of white paper? I should so like to look at it again.' The husband thought that after living with him for three years and bearing him a child she would no longer want to leave him, so he said no more and fetched the roll; but no sooner had he unrolled it than his wife disappeared and the beautiful girl had returned to the paper.

He flung himself down and wept, and his little daughter wept too, but the maiden on the picture did not move. He hung it on the wall and worshipped it as before, and later his daughter did the same, but she never returned to life.

When the old people heard this, they said: 'The appointed time that the dark maiden from the Ninth Heaven was destined to spend on earth having passed, she was able to return to Heaven.'

44. *The White Sheep Spirit*

EVERY evening people crossing over the Mountain of Yellow Mud would see an old man, clad all in white, walking about in the moonlight and politely entering into conversation with travellers, whom he would beg to tarry a while. Woe betide those that did; for he was an evil spirit, who used to bewitch and devour people. Gradually the number of people eaten by him assumed alarming proportions, but no one knew how to rid the district of this pest.

150

Eventually the matter was brought to the notice of Lü Tung-pin, who turned over in his mind methods of destroying the ogre. When the moon had risen, he buckled on his magic sword and went down to the Yellow Mud Mountain. In the silvery beams of the moon, he saw the white shadow of a man moving about on the mountain. A cold wind was blowing and not a soul was to be seen in any direction. He clambered up the hill, but the ghost saw at once that he was no mortal man, but Lü Tung-pin with his bottle gourd on his back, and without loss of time it turned into a white bird and flew off towards the East. Lü quickly turned into a bird of prey and pursued him to the edge of the sea. Seeing Lü in pursuit, the spirit turned into a large white fish and plunged into the water, but Lü turned into a cormorant and chased him across the sea, and was just on the point of seizing him when the fish swam to the shore and turned into a cinnamon tree. Finding the tree, however, too noticeable, he turned into a stone and hid himself among a great pile of rocks. By this time Lü Tung-pin had arrived, and slowly loosing the string on his bottle gourd, he picked out a white stone from among all the others. The ghost was now caught and could neither flee nor change into something else. It assumed its proper form, that of a white sheep, and was led away by the Immortal.

45. *The Narcissus*

THERE was once a rich man with broad acres and two sons, who spent his days in pursuit of pleasure; but one day he passed away and his sons divided his possessions.

The elder brother presumed on his rights as the eldest (for the younger was a simpleton and easily deceived), and claimed all the fields and all the money, only allowing his brother a piece of rocky dry land, quite unfit for cultivation. The younger brother was too dutiful to protest, and accepted his miserable portion. But he could not do anything with his piece of land, which was barren and covered by boulders, and did not have a drop of water. He could neither plough nor sow, and naturally he did not have enough to eat. Eventually he was forced to mortgage his land and live from coarse rice and roots.

When his mortgage money was finished, he had nothing more. For several days he went hungry, but at last he could bear it no longer and ran off to his brother to borrow a little money. But the elder, in spite of his riches, had no love to waste on his brother and ended by excusing himself from giving a cent. The poor man went out into the street, and began to weep. He did not weep in vain, for the sound reached the ears of Yü-huang ti, who said quickly to his Minister: 'There seems to be a man weeping bitterly down on Earth; hurry down, and ask him what it is about.' 'It would be better to invite the local god to make enquiries,' answered the Minister. The Jade Emperor sent for the local god, who mounted a cloud and came up to Heaven to explain the matter.

When the Jade Emperor had heard the explanation, he smiled gently and said: 'He really is a faithful brother. But how can we help him? I think it would be a good idea to send him the Narcissus.' 'But if other people copy him he will become as poor as before,' protested the god. 'Oh, no!' said the Emperor. 'The Narcissus only grows on a sandy bank.' 'But everyone has sandy banks,' said the god. For a moment the Jade Emperor was at a loss, but at last he said: 'I know of a way of preventing other men imitating him. I will speak a magic formula over the flower before I give it to him. It will then only bloom if it is planted in his field. If it is transplanted, it will flower the same year, but never again, however carefully it is tended. People will have to buy new ones every year. Don't you think that is a good plan?' 'Brilliant,' agreed the local god, and taking the Narcissus in his hand, he sailed down to Earth, where he changed into an old man carrying a staff and went up to the younger brother. He asked him what he was crying about, and the young man told him the whole story. The god listened to the end and then said to him: 'Heaven does not desert upright men. Here is the Narcissus from Heaven; plant it on your stony bank and soon people will be marvelling at your riches.' 'How can one earn money with flowers?' asked the young man. 'Other people can also sow them, and in a year's time no one will buy mine any more.' 'Not at all,' said the god. 'The Jade Emperor has already arranged that; other people will be unable to grow them. Every year they will come and buy yours.' 'Has Yü-huang ti really given me such a treasure?' he turned round to ask, but the god had already disappeared. Then he realized that the old man must have been a visitor from Heaven, and he said a prayer of thanks.

He planted the flowers as he had been bidden on the stony bank, and soon their luxuriant growth covered the whole slope. At New Year they produced lovely scented white flowers, which pleased everyone so much that they wanted to buy them, and thus the younger brother earned a large sum of money. The buyers thought that, after buying them, they would never need to get any more, but the old plants never flowered twice, and every year they had to buy more from the younger brother, who gradually became rich. He was able to buy good clothes and have costly food; but during this time his elder brother, no one knows how, became poorer day by day, until finally he had nothing left. The younger brother pitied him and presented him with a few plants, but the most they produced was a few miserable leaves and never a single flower, and though he continually gave him seed, the result was always the same. From now on the elder brother could just keep body and soul together if he worked the whole day, but the younger led a leisurely life and became daily richer.

46. *The Two Bells*

FORMERLY the big bell of the temple on the Southern Mountain and the big bell from the K'ai-yüan temple used to fly out to meet each other every day at midnight, one being a male and the other a female. One morning the bell from the K'ai-yüan temple was flying home when it saw a woman washing bed-sheets in the stream. It fell down into the water and cried: 'If you want to lift me out again, you must find ten women with ten sons to do it.' The women were found, but just as they were lifting the bell on to the bank, a bystander shouted out: 'One of the ten sons is a bastard,' at which the bell slipped back into the water and remains to this day buried in the sand, no more to be seen.

47. *How the Faithful Wife became Eternal through the Cruel Emperor*

THE Meng family garden adjoined the garden of the Chiang family, and was separated from it only by a wall. One year the Mengs planted a pumpkin on their side of the wall, and the Chiangs did the same on theirs. Both plants climbed up the wall, and at the top they joined together and became one plant.

After the pumpkin had bloomed luxuriantly, it developed a huge fruit, and when it became ripe, both

154

families wanted to pluck it. After a long discussion it was decided that each should take a half; but when they cut it open, they found inside an unusually pretty little girl. The two families looked after her together, and gave her the name Meng Chiang.

This happened during the reign of the wicked, unjust Emperor, Ch'in Shih Huang-ti. He was afraid at this time that the Huns would break into the land from the north and not leave him any peace, and in order to keep them in check, he decided to build a wall along the whole northern frontier of China. But his architects were no good, for no sooner had he built one piece than another fell down, and the wall made no progress. Then a wise man said to him: 'A wall like this, which is over ten thousand miles long, can only be built if you immure a human being in every mile of the wall. Each mile will then have its guardian.' It was easy for the Emperor to follow this advice, for he regarded his subjects as so much grass and weeds, and the whole land began to tremble under this threat.

An ingenious scholar went to the Emperor and said: 'Your method of building the wall is making the whole country tremble. It is quite possible that revolts will break out before it is finished. I have heard of a man called Wan. Now since Wan means ten thousand, he will be enough, and you need only fetch him.' The Emperor was delighted with this suggestion, and sent to fetch Wan at once, but Wan had heard of the danger and run away. Meng Chiang was now a grown-up girl. One clear moonlight night she went into the garden to bathe in the pond. In the joy of the bath she said to herself: 'If a man were to see me now, I would willingly belong to him for ever, whoever he was.' Wan happened to have hidden in a banana tree in the garden, and hearing Meng Chiang's words, he called out 'I have seen you,' and Meng Chiang became his wife. But while they were happily seated at the wedding feast, the soldiers arrived, and the heartless brutes seized him and carried him off, leaving Meng Chiang behind in tears.

In this way she was separated from Wan even before she had been married, but in spite of this she loved him and thought of nothing else but him. She was just as attached as other wives to their husbands. Eventually, careless of the fatigues of the journey, she travelled over mountains and through rivers, to find the bones of her husband. But when she saw the stupendous wall, she did not know how to find the bones. There was nothing to be done, and she sat down and wept. But her weeping so affected the wall that it collapsed and laid bare her husband's bones.

When the Emperor heard of Meng Chiang, who was seeking for her husband, he wanted to see her himself, and her unearthly beauty so struck him that he decided to make her Empress. She knew she could not avoid her fate, and therefore she agreed on three conditions: First, a festival lasting forty-nine days should be held in honour of her husband; secondly, the Emperor, with all his officials, should be present at the burial; and thirdly, he should build a terrace forty-nine feet high on the bank of the river. There she wanted to make a sacrifice to her husband. On these three conditions she would marry the Emperor. Ch'in Shih Huang-ti granted all her requests at once.

When all was ready she climbed on to the terrace and began to curse the Emperor in a loud voice for all his cruelty and wickedness. Although this made the Emperor very angry, he held his peace, but when she jumped from the terrace into the river, he flew into a rage, and ordered his soldiers to cut up her body into little pieces and to grind her bones to powder. But the little pieces changed into little silver fish, in which the soul of faithful Meng Chiang lives for ever.

48. *The Mason wins the Prize*

THERE once was a woman whose son was a mason. One day a Magistrate sent for him to mend the roof of his house. The Magistrate had a very beautiful daughter, who, when she heard that the roof was being mended, went out with her maid to watch.

The mason fell in love with her at sight and purposely cut his finger on a tile so that drops of blood fell upon her. When the young lady saw that the mason had wounded himself, she told her maid to fetch a piece of cloth and a needle to bind it up. Naturally the mason imagined that she had fallen in love with him, and when he arrived home he threw himself on his bed and fell ill, and every day became worse.

His mother, very worried at his condition, asked him what was the matter. The mason replied: 'If you promise to do what I ask you, I will tell you, otherwise I must die.' The mother having promised, the mason told her how he had seen the daughter of the Magistrate and fallen so deeply in love that he wanted to marry her.

His mother said hesitatingly: 'How can we arrange that? She is the daughter of an official and will never be willing to marry you.' But the son had thought of a plan, which he explained to his mother: 'You must take a wooden clapper and beat it in front of the Magistrate's gate until someone comes. Tell them that you must see the Magistrate himself, then explain what I desire. You must go there every day until they can no longer bear the noise and open the door.'

His mother took a wooden clapper and went and banged at the door of the Magistrate's house, which made the servants so nervous that they begged her to go away. But she continued knocking until at last they asked her what she wanted. 'I want to speak with your master,' she said, and although they assured her they could arrange

157

the matter themselves, she insisted on seeing the Magistrate in person till finally the servants, at their wits' end, had to let her in.

When the Magistrate came and asked what she wanted, she related the story of her son's passion and illness, and begged him to allow her son to marry his daughter. The Magistrate thought the matter over for a moment and then replied: 'That can be arranged, but first your son must bring me three precious things. The first is a pearl from the mouth of a dragon, the second the shell of a turtle spirit, and the third a golden-haired lion. If he succeeds, I will give him my daughter.'

The old woman went home, and no sooner had she entered the house than her son was cured. He ran out to meet her and asked: 'Mother, have you seen the Magistrate?' 'Yes,' she answered, 'but there is no hope. He wants three precious things: a dragon pearl, the shell of a turtle spirit, and a golden-haired lion. Only on these conditions will he give you his daughter.' 'That is quite easy,' said the son. 'I will go and get them now.'

He started out towards the West, for he thought that such rarities were only to be found in the land of the Buddha in the Western Heaven. He had been journeying for several days when a dragon suddenly barred his path. He asked the dragon why he would not let him through, and the dragon replied: 'You are on the way to the land of the Buddha in the Western Heaven. If you promise to ask the Buddha a question on my behalf, I will now let you through.' 'Just tell me what it is,' said the young man, 'and I will ask him.' 'You must ask the Buddha why the dragon at such and such a place, who has been morally perfecting himself for over one thousand years, may not ascend to Heaven?' The mason noted his words, said good-bye, and continued on his way.

A few days later he was stopped by a turtle spirit, who

refused to let him proceed. He begged the tortoise to let him go, as he was on his way to the Western Heaven, and when the tortoise heard where he was going, he promised to release him if the mason asked a question for him. 'Of course I will do that,' said the mason, 'if you will tell me what you want.' 'You must ask the Buddha why the tortoise at such and such a place, who has been morally perfecting himself for over one thousand years, cannot yet ascend to Heaven?' The mason promised to do this, and the turtle set him free.

He went on for nearly a fortnight until he reached a temple, where he went in to rest. On the altar in front of the gods was sitting a golden-haired lion, and as that was exactly what he was looking for, he went up and begged the animal to help him. The golden-haired lion nodded his head in answer, so the young man made an agreement with him to come on the day of his marriage and sit at his father-in-law's table. Then he continued on his way.

At last he arrived at the land of the Buddha in the Western Heaven, and was granted an audience with the Buddha himself. He asked about the dragon and the tortoise, and the Buddha said: 'The dragon cannot ascend to Heaven, because he has two pearls in his mouth, and all the other dragons only one. If he spits out the superfluous one he can ascend to Heaven. The tortoise cannot ascend because his shell is too rough. If he can change it for another he can come.'

The mason was very pleased with these replies, because now he had found the three precious things he needed to marry the maiden. He thanked the Buddha and set off home, only stopping to tell the tortoise and the dragon what the Buddha had said, and to receive from the former his shell and from the latter a pearl.

On his return, he at once sent the two objects over to the Magistrate, and promised to produce the other on the wedding day. The Magistrate could no longer withhold his consent and gave him his daughter. On the wedding day the golden-haired lion appeared and all three presents stood on a table in the guest-hall and were the wonder of the guests.

After the wedding the two loved each other dearly. The husband remained the whole day at home with his wife and could not be separated from her for even a quarter of an hour. One day the wife asked: 'Why do you never work?' The husband answered: 'Because I cannot bear to leave you.' 'Then,' said the wife, 'I will paint a picture of myself for you always to carry with you, and you can always look at me, just as if you really saw me.'

From that time, when the husband went out, he always took his wife's portrait with him. One day, when he had taken out the picture to look at it, there came a sudden gust of wind which tore it out of his hand. Farther and farther flew the picture, until finally it fell into the Emperor's palace, where it was found by the Emperor himself.

'Is there really such a beautiful woman?' asked the Emperor. 'You must seek her out and I will make her my wife.' The head eunuch searched, high and low, until at last he discovered her name and where she lived, and brought her to the Emperor. As she was leaving her husband she consoled him, saying: 'It is not so bad. We will meet again later. In three years come and see me with a large onion, six feet long, and a dress made of chickens' feathers, and everything will be all right.'

When the wife arrived at the palace her face became hard as stone and she ceased to smile. When the Emperor wanted to visit her she told him she was ill, and finally his passion faded and she was left alone in her house.

Time passes quickly. Three years went by in a flash. During this time her husband had sought everywhere for an onion six feet long, and day and night he sewed

160

the dress of feathers. When both were ready he put on the dress and went to the palace to see his wife, who burst out laughing when she saw him coming. The Emperor noticed her beautiful smiling face and heard her happy laughter, and half pleased and half surprised, he asked: 'I have not seen you laugh for three years; why do you laugh so much at this stupid man?' Then she answered: 'If you were to put on a dress of chickens' feathers and carry an onion more than six feet long, I would laugh at you too.'

The Emperor thought that was quite simple and removed his fine robe and ordered the man to take off his feather dress. But as soon as they had exchanged their clothes the wife called in the head eunuch and ordered him to kill the man with the feather dress. The Emperor, in the feather dress, was too terrified to say a word and was beheaded by the eunuch. Then the mason became Emperor, and husband and wife lived happily ever after.

49. *Husband and Wife in this Life and in the Life to come*

THERE were once a husband and a wife who loved each other dearly. One day the wife died. Not being able to forget her, the man at last decided to go in search of her. He had heard people say the dead become ghosts and live in Spirit-land. So he left his home and set off towards this land. After a short while, he went into an inn and asked the waiter which was the best way to Spirit-land and how he could find his wife there.

'It is only one day's journey from here to the Land of Ghosts,' said the waiter. 'If you go quickly, you can get there and back in a day. When you arrive go straight to the well. She will certainly come to fetch water and then you can see her.'

The husband followed his advice and started the next day. Everything happened as he had been told. He went to the well, seated himself on the edge and waited. Then he saw a beautiful woman coming with a pail of water. It was his wife, who was looking just the same. He called out and took hold of her, but she did not look at him, and never even raised her head. She behaved just like a stranger, drew her water, and returned home. Sadly and with drooping spirits the man returned to the inn, where he told the servant how his wife had not recognized him and paid no attention to him at all.

'Of course, yesterday I forgot to tell you,' said the servant; 'return to-morrow and take a small piece of money. When she draws water throw the coin into her pail. Then she will speak to you.' After a few hours' sleep the man went off full of joy, and waited at the well. Everything went off as he had been told. He threw the money into the pail, and she began to speak to him. She seemed to remember that she was his wife, but she said to him: 'Return home. I have become a spirit, we cannot be husband and wife again,' and she slowly walked away. The man did not want to let her go and hurried after her, and as the sun was sinking below the hills they arrived at a small village. She turned round and said to him: 'My dear husband, don't come any farther. In front of you lies my house. I am now married to an official in the Underworld. He is very cruel, and if he sees you, he will certainly eat you. Please go home now.' But the husband would not and could not tear himself away. 'Very well,' said the woman, 'I will conceal you in my house. I will say you are my brother. . . . If he offers you some food, watch to see whether I eat it, and then act accordingly. There are many things, poisonous worms and frogs, which you can't eat.'

Shortly afterwards the ghost arrived. As soon as he reached the doorway he shouted: 'I smell human flesh. I smell human flesh. Who has come to the house?' and he showed his teeth and stretched out his claws to search for the stranger. 'It's only my brother,' explained the wife. 'Oh, all right, my brother-in-law. Be quick and get tea and dinner ready!'

They greeted each other, and the ghost did not eat the man. Fortunately, during the ten days he spent there, the ghost had to go to the office of the King of the Underworld every day, and they were able to be alone. But the wife said to her husband: 'My dear husband, we can't become married again, and as we can't do anything here, we had better flee.' So one day they ran away, and after travelling for over ten days, they arrived in the Upper World. They stopped outside a house, where the woman said: 'I am so thirsty. Wait a moment, I will go in and get some tea. Each of us must take half of this coin.' After she had gone in the man waited and waited, but although he waited till nightfall there was still no sign of her. Feeling very angry, he went into the house and asked the owner whether he had seen his wife, but the man denied it. 'But I saw her go in myself,' said the husband, very mystified.

Just at that time the owner's wife had given birth to a daughter, and the crying of the little child was audible indoors. The husband refused to go away and became a workman in the house. It was very strange, no matter who carried the baby it began to cry; but if the workman took it, it ceased at once. Also, no one could open the right hand of the girl from her birth, so great was the strength in her fist. She grew very quickly, and eventually, when she was seventeen years old, the workman opened her hand, and inside lay half a coin, which fitted exactly into his own piece and made a whole coin. They became engaged and were soon husband and wife again.

163

50. *First discuss the Price when the Pig is Dead*

THIS proverb is known all over South Fukien, and it is applied to people who don't first think a matter over, but only bargain when everything is finished. There is an old story about it, which I will now tell you.

Once upon a time there lived in Ch'üan-chou a Mr. Chin and a Mr. Yi, who were such close friends that they became blood brothers. Unfortunately, Chin fell ill and died, which so upset Yi that he stood weeping beside the coffin of his friend and wanted to end his own life. From then on he thought only of his friend, but there was nothing for him to do.

Hard though it is to believe, the tale of his sorrows had reached the Underworld, and one night Chin appeared and talked to him in a dream. He related how he had become an official in Hell, which made it easy for them to meet; Yi only needed to take a siesta and utter a few magic formulas, and his soul would find its way to the Underworld, where he could talk with his friend. Then Chin told him the magic words and vanished.

Soon after, Yi woke with the words still in his mind. He was delighted at the devotion of his friend, and the next afternoon he carried out his instructions exactly. He lay down on the bed, spoke the magic formula, and in a short while found himself in the halls of the Underworld, where his friend was waiting to greet him.

Now that Yi had discovered a means of reaching the Underworld, his affection for Chin daily increased, and every day he took a rest and went to meet his friend.

One day Yi's beloved grandson was taking a nap with him. This seven- or eight-years-old child was a good mimic, and when he heard his grandfather's words,

164

he copied them exactly and also arrived in the Underworld. Yi was so occupied with his friend that he paid no attention to his grandchild, who wandered around in the halls. The child loved playing, and ran outside to join a crowd of children who were taking pigs' caps off the wall, putting them on and jumping about. He also took one and began to run about, till he had vanished who knows where!

During his conversation with his friend Yi quite forgot that his grandson had been with him, and on his return to the Upper World he called out to him, but could not wake him. The child was as one dead. Suddenly he remembered that he had taken him with him, but midday being past, it was too late to fetch him. I don't need to tell you what a state the whole house was in.

Yi had to wait till the next afternoon before he could lie down in his bed and visit Chin again. He enquired at once about his grandson, but Chin had to fetch the lists of the living and the dead before he had any idea where the boy had gone to. In these books he discovered that he had been reborn as a pig. The boy had not understood what the other children were doing with the pigs' caps, but thinking they were playing with them, he had put one on his head. He had, as a result, been reborn as a pig in Mr. So-and-So's house. Yi was horrified by this news, and begged Chin to help him. Chin thought for a long time and then said to Yi: 'You must return to the Upper World and go quickly to Hsing-hua fu. There you must find the house where a sow has just produced thirteen pigs, and you must take one with a white star and kill it. Your grandson will then be able to return to Earth as a man.'

On his return home, Yi gave orders not to bury his grandson. During the night he went to Hsing-hua fu, where he found the house with the thirteen piglets. When he found the one with the white star, he said at once he wanted to buy it, and then slaughtered it without further ado. His behaviour surprised the peasant, but Yi soon arranged the price with him, and when he reached home his grandson had returned to life.

51. *The Unnatural Mother*

ONCE a very beautiful girl disappeared. Her mother was unable to eat or sleep for worry, and went about the whole day asking where her daughter was. One day she was sitting in the yard bemoaning her loss when a sparrow flew down on to the roof and began to twitter. 'Dear sparrow,' the mother said, 'if you know where my daughter is and can lead me to her, I will give you a bushel of roasted beans.' So the mother tied a red string on to the bird's tail as a sign, and they set off on their search. But the bird flew much quicker than the woman and was always waiting for her. Finally, it flew up to a cave in the mountains, where it sat down on a stone and chirruped. A girl came out of the entrance and was much surprised to see the red string on the sparrow's tail: 'Where did you get the red string from our house?' she asked. 'Your mother gave it to me,' said the bird. 'She will soon be here herself.' And while they were speaking, the mother arrived.

'What are you doing here, my child?' she asked. And the daughter answered: 'I was going for a walk in the village, when an ape came up and carried me off. He will be here in a moment, so you must hide, because if he sees you he will eat you up!' The mother just had time to hide under a jar before the ape appeared. He sniffed and said: 'Why is there such a smell of human flesh?' His wife tried to conceal it from him, but eventually, seeing there was nothing to be done, she told him the truth: 'My mother is here, but fearing lest you

166

would eat her, she hid under a jar.' The ape, however, was very pleased: 'Your mother has come?' he said. 'Tell her to come out quickly. I want to meet her,' and he went and turned up the jar. The daughter said to him 'That is your mother-in-law,' whereupon they embraced, and were very happy. The ape then said 'To-day, we have nothing good to eat. I will buy some meat and wine,' and he went out.

The mother and daughter took this opportunity to run away. The daughter told her mother to cook a pot of lime, and when the little monkeys saw it, they asked: 'Grandmother, what is that?' 'It is a good eye medicine,' she said, 'but it isn't for children.' 'But we want some,' said all the little monkeys. So she covered their eyes with lime, and then said to them: 'Go into the sun and let it dry,' and when it was dry, they could not open their eyes. The mother and daughter fled, taking with them all the gold and silver of the ape.

When the old ape came back and saw the little ones could not open their eyes, he asked them what had happened, and they told him the whole story. Their father boiled a great pot of water, and told the children to wash their eyes, but afterwards there was a red rim all round.

From now on, every morning, the old ape took the children down to the house of their mother. He sat down on the millstone in front of the house, and in a sad voice began to sing his song: 'Ape-Wife! Ape-Wife! It is unnatural to leave your children. Your children weep, your husband is sad.'

The girl began to be frightened, as well as being affected by the tragic song. She evolved a plan with her mother, and one night they made the millstone red-hot. In the morning the ape came as usual with his children, but when the little ones sat down on the stone, they jumped up with a scream. 'What's the matter?' cried the ape. 'I will sit down,' but he also leapt up with a scream of pain, and all together they fled home. When they looked at each other, all the hair was burnt off their behinds.

They never returned to look for their mother again. And from that time all monkeys have bare behinds.

52. *The Greedy Minister*

ONCE upon a time a schoolboy found a snake's egg lying in the road. He thought it very pretty, and not being sure whether it was a bird's egg or a snake's egg, he carried it along with him and wrapped it up in cotton wool. A few days later the egg cracked, and a thin, small snake crept out. The boy played with it the whole day long, and he loved it so dearly that he never let it out of his sight. He even took it to school, where he played with it secretly during lessons.

Swiftly as an arrow flies the time; day after day goes by. The snake grew a fine skin, and became bigger and bigger till it would no longer fit into the shoe that the boy had hidden it in. But he was not afraid and continued to play with it.

One day, the teacher noticed him and said to himself: 'What is that boy always doing? Why doesn't he pay attention?' And going down to the boy's place, he found the shoe with the snake in it, which reared up angrily at the sight of the stranger. The teacher was terrified by the snake, and keeping his distance, he said in a trembling voice to the boy: 'Where did you get the snake?' 'I raised it from an egg,' answered the boy. 'I am not frightened of it, we have been friends for a long time.' Then he told his pet to raise its head, and at the sound of its master's voice the snake was no longer frightened and lifted its head at once. 'Drop your head,' said the boy, and it sank down again. The teacher said no more, but allowed the boy to play with the snake.

Later, the boy went to the capital to take his examination, but he could not take the snake with him. As he was leaving, he said to it: 'I have looked after you all these years. You might give me a present in return.' Then the snake spat up a huge pearl, which gleamed in the dark. So bright was it, that it dazzled the eyes. It shone in the dark like the sun and everything was visible in its light. It was an incomparable treasure. The boy was delighted, and after thanking the snake again and again, he set off on his journey.

He went to the capital, where he took one of the first places in the examinations. Now he was no longer a young student, but a famous, grown-up man, a professor. He thought to himself: 'It will be best to offer my pearl to the Emperor, for then he will make me a high official,' and he gave it to the Emperor.

The result was even better than he expected; the Emperor was so delighted with the pearl that he was appointed Chancellor. But now he was never contented although, after the Emperor, he was the greatest man in the land, because he no longer had his treasure. How nice it would be if he could get another, and with this idea he asked leave to return home to ask the snake for another pearl.

Full of anticipation he went into the hills where the snake lived. The snake smelt the smell of human flesh and came up, hissing and spitting, to swallow him, but when it recognized its master it became quiet again. When the Chancellor explained his reason for coming it opened its mouth wide, whereupon the Chancellor, thinking it was going to spit out another pearl, quickly stepped forward, but the snake shot out its head and swallowed the greedy man.

53. *The Bear's Husband*

ABOUT two miles south-east of my house is the village of Huimin, which the peasants call 'Wang P'ing's Home-coming.' In the village nearly all the inhabitants are called Wang, and they tell the following tale about themselves.

Wang P'ing, their ancestor, in his youth went off on a trading journey. One day when he was on the sea a terrific storm sprang up, which drove the ship hither and thither right off its course. At last it was driven against a mountain, and Wang P'ing was seized by a bear-woman and carried off into the hills. They became man and wife, and every day the bear-woman shut Wang up in the cave and went to look for food. When she came back she told him to pick out what he wanted to eat. Several years passed in this manner and two children were born to them. The bear-woman thought that Wang P'ing was no longer homesick for China, and in any case it was almost impossible to escape, so gradually she let him go out and no longer shut him up in the cave.

One day when the bear-woman had gone hunting, Wang P'ing wandered down to the seashore with his children. Suddenly he saw a ship lying on the beach, and finding that the sailors were all Chinese, he related his experiences to them, and begged them to weigh anchor as soon as possible. The sailors did as he asked them, but they were not far from land when they saw a large animal waving and screaming on the beach. Wang P'ing paid no attention at first, but the bear-woman jumped into the sea and swam towards the ship, which so terrified Wang that he prayed to the God of the Sea: 'God of the Sea! Send us a favourable wind. If I escape safely I will build you a large temple as a thanksgiving for saving me, and I and my children and grandchildren will worship you for ever.' As he finished speaking a wind sprang up, the sailors hoisted the sails, and the ship shot away like an arrow from a bow.

On arriving home Wang P'ing built a temple, which still exists in the village; but one cannot decide whether it is the temple that Wang built or another which was built later. In no other place is there, or has there ever been, a temple in honour of the Sea God.

54. *The Three Copper Pieces*

THERE was once a tobacco pedlar who travelled around with his pole on his shoulder and sold his tobacco for a small profit.

One day he met an old man in tattered clothes with a long beard and white hair. The old fellow called out: 'Young man, give me a wad of tobacco!' and with these words he stretched out his arm and seized the pedlar's box. This enraged the pedlar, who would have beaten him if they had not been in the public street, but when he saw that it was a poor old man his anger left him. The old man took a handful of tobacco, but no sooner had he stuck it in his pipe than it vanished, and the pipe did not become full until he had rammed the whole supply into it. Then he lit it, contentedly puffed a cloud of blue smoke into the air, and throwing the pedlar three copper pieces, disappeared.

The man threw the coins crossly into his basket and went home. But the farther he went the heavier his basket became, and on turning round he found it filled with copper pieces. He divided them up between the two baskets and continued on his way, but by the time he reached home both were full. He placed the money in his money-box, but that overflowed, and the surplus had to be put in the corn-bin, which in a few hours was also full. He now decided to give up his trade and open a pawnshop with his money, and he sat about the whole day and rejoiced in his good fortune.

Some time after an old man entered the shop with a few things to sell. He wanted three copper pieces for them, no more and no less, and he refused silver or dollar pieces. The pawnbroker thought that a man who only wanted three coppers and refused to accept the value for his goods could not be quite right in the head; but he opened his chest and gave him the three coppers, and the old man went off with them.

But strange to say, from now on the money in the chest remained as it was and no longer increased. The old man had taken his three magic coppers away with him.

55. *The Helpful Animals*

THERE was once a poor youth who went to fish in the river every day, but was never able to make a good catch. One day he took a broken piece of an iron pot, and realizing that it was a treasure, he took it home and hid it in an iron box, which he hung upon a beam. From that time he became daily richer. One day he engaged as servant a man who had come from beyond a river and beyond a sea. This servant wondered how his master had become so rich, and was sure he must possess some treasure. After a long search he at last found the box hanging on the beam, and secretly opening it during the night, he stole the piece of the iron pot and fled away over the river and over the sea to his own home. From now on the young man became daily poorer and the thief daily richer.

One day the cat in the young man's house said to the dog: 'Master always used to give us meat and rice, and we always got our share of what he ate. Why do we now only get soaked rice?' 'Master's treasure,' answered the dog, 'was stolen by a thief who lives beyond a river and beyond a sea. As he cannot get it back, we must fetch it for him.' The cat agreed to this plan, and they set off. When they arrived at the sea the dog did not know how to get across, but the cat said: 'We cats always can think of a plan. How do you propose to cross?' The dog replied: 'We dogs also have plans.' Then they both swam across, and on their arrival at the river they crossed it in the same manner.

Then the cat suggested: 'Wait here. I will bring you a bone, and drink a little fish soup myself, and then we can steal the treasure.' They ate and drank, and about midnight the cat crept into the thief's house, went to a mouse-hole, and asked the mice: 'Will you help us to steal the treasure?' 'Certainly,' answered the mice, 'but where is it?' 'It is inside the iron box that is hanging from one of the beams,' explained the cat. 'We must first consult our adviser, who will certainly know of a good plan,' said the mice. The adviser was an old one-eyed mouse. She ordered the mice to clamber up the beam and gnaw through the rope that fastened the box. The noise they made woke the wife of the thief, who asked her husband: 'What is gnawing there?' Half-asleep the man answered: 'How should I know?' But after a while the box fell down with a bang, and she said to him again: 'Do get up and see what's the matter.' 'Oh, go to sleep, it's nothing,' said her husband, and turning over, they were soon deep in slumber. But the mice nibbled a hole in the box, through which one of them crept, took the fragment, and gave it to the cat and the dog. Each of them wanted to carry it, but eventually the cat took it, because he did not trust the dog.

When they arrived at the river the cat took the fragment in his mouth, but half-way across it slipped out

173

of his mouth and sank to the bottom. The dog scolded him, saying: 'You said I couldn't be trusted with it, and now you let it fall into the water.' The cat naturally had no reply, but he dived into the river and caught a water-rat, who, full of terror, asked the cat if he was going to eat him. 'No,' said the cat, 'I won't eat you if you dive to the bottom and bring me back the broken fragment.' The water-rat agreed to this proposal at once, and diving down he soon retrieved it. The cat took it again, and they ran on and on until they arrived at the sea.

Then the dog said: 'You carried the fragment over the river, I must carry it now.' Not wanting to quarrel, the cat allowed the dog to take the fragment and carry it over the sea, but just in the middle the fragment slipped out of his mouth and fell into the water. They swam to a mudbank where they angrily blamed each other, till a fight ensued, during which they were both coated with mud like water-buffaloes. The Dragon King, who was sitting in his palace, heard the shouts and sent a messenger to ask what the matter was. He soon learnt that they were quarrelling about a broken bit of iron, and as the piece in question had just fallen into the court of his palace, the Dragon King ordered a servant to return it to them. The cat took it again, and the dog swam behind, and when they arrived at their master's home, the cat placed the piece on the table.

But when the wife saw the cat, who was as filthy as a water-buffalo, she flew into a temper and shouted: 'Monster, when one becomes poor, domestic animals become as foul as corpses,' and she gave the cat such a blow that it fell down dead, and the dog met the same fate. But when they were both dead, the treasure returned to the place it had come from, that is to say, the sea.

56. *The Little People*

THERE are many people in Ching Ting that own brownies. They are beings that one can hear but not see, and they have no shadow. They work for other people; and if, for example, you are planting flowers you only need to plant one to show them, and they finish the rest of the field. They have a passion for sweeping, so that the houses of people that have brownies are always specially clean. If, on arrival at such a house, you take off your shoes at the door, there is no dust to be seen when you look round, by which you know there are brownies in the house. Brownies are caught in the following manner: You bury at the cross-roads two different species of creatures, like millipedes, snakes and other beasts, and then dig them up several days later and put them in an incense-burner, and you will find brownies. Every year they like to eat a human being, and if, when their master makes accounts with them on New Year's Eve, there is still something owing, he must give them a man. For this reason, on New Year's Eve, if they have broken a cup, their master must pretend they have broken twenty and reckon it against them, and tell them to wait till next year for their feast. If he no longer wants them, he can marry them off, though if they refuse to marry there is nothing to be done. If they consent, he prepares a packet of silver, a packet of powder, and a packet of incense-ash—these are really the brownies—and drops them in the road. Whoever wants it just picks up the silver. Sometimes people who don't know about it pick the silver up by mistake, and then the brownie goes with them. It prefers living in the cooking-pot, and for this reason people who are afraid of brownies put a little water into the pot after cooking.

There is still another story about them.

A poor man once found a packet of silver, and a packet

of powder lying in the road. He knew it was the dowry of a brownie, but he wanted the silver and not the imp. He was afraid, though, that it would follow him, and therefore he seized the silver and dashed down to a river, because brownies can't cross the water. When he arrived at the river, the imp had already climbed on to his sun-hat, but both the hat and its occupant were carried away by the stream. Later the hat was hung up by someone on a tree, which withered at once. The poor man gradually became rich with the silver, but one day he was walking along the river bank with his son when the boy pointed at the withered tree and asked his father: 'Why is the tree withered?' The father told his son the story of the brownie, but the imp was still in the tree, and when he heard that this rich man was his old enemy, he sprang on to the ground, seized his soul, and ate it up. From then on, the rich man grew thinner and yellower, and eventually he died.

57. *The Faithful Official*

HSÜAN CH'ENG lies on the southern bank of the Yang-tzu-Chiang, and every year at the golden-plum time there was a terrible flood; the people were powerless against this recurrent disaster and gradually came to look upon it as belonging to the nature of things. On one occasion during the last dynasty the Earth God appeared to Governor Ch'en in a dream three days before the flood was due, and said to him: 'For the last thousand years there have been two iron oxen buried on the summit of Mount Hua Yang. This year, in the sixth month, they are planning to go down to the sea with the flood. Now I am afraid that if the iron oxen join the river, men and fields and villages will sink beneath the flood and the land will become a great lake. You are Governor here and cannot look calmly on while the people are destroyed;

you must do your duty and prevent this calamity occurring. If you knew nothing about it, it would not be your fault; but since I have told you, you must do something. I know in what manner you can save the country, but I doubt whether you are willing to sacrifice yourself.' The Governor replied at once: 'I am father and mother of my people and am ready to help them. If I can save them, my own life is of no account.' 'If you really love the people, you deserve the highest praise,' said the God. 'The only thing for you to do is to inscribe the names of the people in your district in a book, and when the flood arrives at the town walls, you must jump into the water with the book. There is no other means of averting the danger. I beseech you to think over my suggestion.' But without further thought, Governor Ch'en agreed to the sacrifice. At that moment, he heard the watchman's gong and woke up to find that it was just midnight, but his dream was clear before his eyes in the smallest detail.

Soon the cocks began to crow and it became light, and the Governor called in his assistants that were on duty. 'During the night, two iron oxen have come out of Mount Hua Yang,' they announced, 'but as they are not running about, we don't think that they will do much harm.' The Governor was much affected by the news, because it agreed exactly with his dream. He related his experience to the officials and ordered them to prepare a list of all the inhabitants in the district within two days. The under officials worked day and night on receipt of the bad news, and sent the lists to the Administration. On the third day, there was a terrible explosion on Mount Hua Yang: two enormous water-dragons broke loose, the iron oxen began to fight, and at the same time the water burst through the dykes and covered the land with a sea several feet deep. The villages and fields to the north soon sank beneath the waves, and within half a day the water had risen to the top of the city wall. Then

Governor Ch'en climbed on to the wall to look around, and at the sight of the still rising water he clasped the book in his hand and with one cry sprang into the waves. To the great surprise of everyone, a moment later the flood began to sink, and the victorious iron ox and the water-dragons vanished.

After the great flood was over, the people of Hsüan Ch'eng built a temple in honour of Governor Ch'en, who had given his life for them; and to spread his fame abroad, they offered sacrifices. The iron ox that had fallen in combat was carried into the town and erected as a memorial, and both the temple and the ox are there to this day.

58. *The Big Bell of K'un Ming*

THERE is a very old bell-tower built on the South wall of the town of K'un Ming. The tower is more than ten feet square and inside there is a big bell, so big, in fact, that only one man can go round between the bell and the tower. The bell is still very useful, because it is rung whenever there is a fire. It has a loud and powerful tone, which makes the ear-drums tremble, and which can be heard all over the district.

It is not known for certain where the bell came from; but the tale goes that when the bell-tower was built no beam could be found strong enough to support it. Many, many workmen tried their skill, but no one could find a means of hanging it. One day a Taoist appeared and made a beam out of sawdust and water, and hung the bell safely upon it. On his departure, he said to the people: 'Please do not sound the bell until the third day after my departure.' But the people rang it on the morning of the second day instead of doing the monk's bidding. The priest had just arrived at the Big Beam bridge, forty miles from the town, and at the sound of

178

the bell he said angrily: 'The ring of the bell could have spread for three hundred miles if the people had listened to me. Now it will only reach forty.' For this reason the bell can be heard at the Big Beam bridge forty miles away, but no farther. The Taoist is said to have been Lu Pan, the God of Carpenters.

59. *The Magic of the Mason*

THERE was once a rich family whose head, Chang Pao, was called by everyone the 'Rich.' He had two sons and three daughters, but the eldest was just fourteen years old and the younger only two. One day, Chang Pao decided to build a new house, and engaged masons and carpenters, who worked for many days till the house was almost finished. Chang's wife was a good woman. She prepared good food for the workmen's daily meal, and as well as meat, she gave them spices and sauce, and other tasty morsels, all cooked together in a delicious stew. The workmen were really unusually well-treated, but, in spite of that, the ungrateful brutes considered themselves ill-used and said: 'This miserly family won't even give us fresh meat to eat, nothing but old pork and chicken, which no one could stomach.' And for this reason, the masons and carpenters were in a bad humour.

Finally, they began to hate their employer, and to regard him as their enemy. One day one of the masons decided to call a meeting, and he sent his companions round to make everyone come without fail, since there was something very important to discuss. And while they were eating dinner, he summoned them all again. After dinner they all arrived and the caller of the meeting was elected chairman. He stepped forward confidently and said: 'I have called this meeting to-day because our employer treats us so badly. The food is a disgrace: we have worked for many days now without getting any fresh meat. We must really revenge ourselves. Think over what we can do.' All agreed with him, but after a long time no one had any suggestion to make. 'Think a little quicker,' said the chairman, 'it is already late.' But the men still sat silent, and no plan was suggested, till finally the chairman said: 'If you can think of nothing, I will tell you my plan. My plan is to build a ship of clay, and to place on it a rower, with a bamboo pole in his hand, and to fill it with notes and coins. Then we must place the ship over the door, in the eaves of the newly-built house, so that it faces outwards. In this way, the house will have no more luck, and gradually the owners will become poorer and poorer, till finally they will no longer have enough to eat.' When the workmen had heard the plan, they all shouted: 'That's what we will do, and you shall carry it out alone.' This was what the chairman had intended, and as it was already late, they went home.

Three weeks later, the house was finished and the master mason had carried out all his plans. The masons and carpenters went away to other people to build other houses.

After Chang Pao moved into the new house, not two years passed before he was in a bad way. He was always quarrelling or injuring someone, and each time he lost a great deal of money. He and his wife were very worried, but they could not understand why everything went so badly. At the end of ten years, Chang and his family were as poor as church mice, and could scarcely afford three meals a day. Then his eldest son fell ill and died, and one after another of his daughters passed away, till finally he had only the one boy, who had been two years old when the house was built.

This year it was terribly hot, so hot, in fact, that you could never do without a fan, and many people died. Then Chang Pao died, and his wife and son felt themselves more poor and lonely than ever.

One afternoon, the woman was sitting in the house doing nothing, when suddenly a man appeared outside and cried: 'Hallo!' Not having any idea who the man was, she was very frightened, till he said: 'I am old Chen Ts'ai, the master mason, who helped to build your house ten years ago.' Now she knew who he was, and as it was dinner-time, she cooked him some food, and gave it to him, saying: 'I used to give you finely sliced meat, but now we are so badly off I can only give you tasteless stuff. Please excuse me.' When the mason heard that, he realized that far from having treated him badly and given him bad meat, she had been extremely generous, and after the meal he asked for a ladder, and, climbing on to the roof, he turned the prow of the ship round. 'From now on you will be more successful, and become rich again,' he said. Then he went away.

Two or three years later, luck returned to the house and the family became prosperous again.

60. *Wang San, the Ever-Poor*

THERE was once a man called Wang San, who was terribly poor. Except for one unmarried sister he had no relatives. One day this sister, who had gone to collect fuel or wash clothes, did not return at dark. Wang searched everywhere, but there was no sign. For ten days he hunted for her, and then he thought she must either have been eaten by a tiger or drowned in the river, and he mourned her.

One day, more than a year after her disappearance, Wang went into the hills to collect wood. He was following the river when his attention was caught by a lotus leaf that was drifting along, floating quickly if he walked quickly, slowly if he walked slowly, and stopping if he stopped. Thinking this was very peculiar, he went up to look at the leaf, and noticed some white cabbage leaves in the same place. This surprised him still more. 'Who on earth can be washing cabbage in these wild trackless hills?' he wondered, and he followed the lotus leaf up stream, until it was caught on a sharp rock. There he saw a girl washing cabbage in the river, and when he looked carefully, he recognized his own sister.

In great excitement he ran up and asked her how she had got to this place. She took off the apron she was wearing and told him to step on to it. 'I was taken prisoner by the God of Riches, and am now his wife,' she said. 'I had gone into the hills, when suddenly a dark cloud enveloped me and carried me off to a cave. Come with me, and we will ask the God of Riches to give you a little of the enormous store of gold and silver in the cave.' Wang went to the cave with this sister, but the god had not yet returned. She gave her brother some food, and then there was a knock at the door. 'That is the god,' she said. 'You smell of human flesh, so you had better hide,' and she shoved him into a dark spot. As the god came in, he sniffed loudly and said: 'Why is there such a smell of man here?' His wife answered lightly: 'How could a man come here?' But the God of Riches was not deceived and said: 'You are not telling the truth. If I find anyone now, I will kill him.' Then the woman flung herself down at his feet and said: 'My brother is here. Please forgive us.' 'Why do you hide your relations when they come here?' asked the god. 'Fetch him at once.' Wang San came out of his hiding-place, and the god gave him delicious fish and meat to eat. That evening before the god went to bed, Wang's sister said to him: 'My brother is so terribly poor. Every day you are showering riches on different people, can't you spare him a little?' But her husband answered: 'It is not that I do not want to give him anything, but he is destined never to have money during his life, and I can do nothing about it.'

The next day the god set forth as usual to distribute

182

riches. Wang got up, ate breakfast, and then, as he had nothing to do, wandered round the cave. On his way he passed heaps of gold and silver, some of which he stretched out his hand to take, but a snake, which had been sleeping on the heap, woke up and struck at him, which so frightened Wang that he fell down in a swoon.

His sister searched everywhere for him till at last she discovered him lying unconscious near the golden mountain. Knowing that the snake had frightened him to death, she waited for her husband to come home, and then begged him to bring her brother back to life with the magic weed. The god said: 'You see, I was quite right. Your brother is not fated to have any money.' But he fetched the magic weed, and the sister brewed a soup to give to Wang, who was restored to life at once.

The next morning the God of Riches went out again. Wang San told his sister he wanted to return home, because it was too dangerous with her. In spite of the god's warning that Wang would never have any money, she gave him two strings of cash and two ounces of silver, so that at least he would be able to open a small business.

Wang placed them both in his pocket and set off home, but on the way he felt something squirming about in his pocket, and found two hideous frogs. In a rage he flung them into the pond, but then he felt two snakes in his pocket, which wriggled out and disappeared in the grass. When he searched for the money, there was nothing there, and realizing that he was fated to remain poor, he allowed the two frogs, which were the two silver ounces, and the two snakes, which were the two strings of cash, to run away.

PART II
LEGENDS, MYTHS, JOKES, ANECDOTES

61. *Faithful even in Death*

THE village of the Liang family and the village of the Chu family were close together. The inhabitants were well-to-do and contented. Old Excellency Liang and old Excellency Chu were good friends. A son was born to the Liang family, who was given the name Hsienpo. Being an unusually quick and clever child, he was sent to the school in the town. At the same time a daughter was born to the Chu family, who besides being very clever was particularly beautiful. As a child she had a love of reading and studying, and only needed to glance at the book to know a sentence by heart. Old Chu simply doted on her. When she grew up she wanted to go away and study. Her father tried in vain to dissuade her, but eventually he arranged for her to dress as a boy and study with Hsienpo. The two lived together, worked together, argued together, and were the best of friends. The eager and zealous Hsienpo did not notice that Yingt'ai was really a girl, and therefore he did not fall in love with her. The reason was that Yingt'ai studied so hard and was so wrapped up in her work that her fellow-students paid no attention to her. Being very modest, and never taking part in the children's jokes, she exercised a calming influence over even the most impudent. When she slept with Hsienpo, each lay on one side of the bed, and between them stood a bowl of water. They had arranged that whoever knocked over the bowl must pay a fine; but the diligent little Hsienpo never touched it.

If Yingt'ai changed her clothes she never stood about naked, but pulled on her clean dress under the old one, which she then took off, and finished dressing. Her fellow-students could not understand why she did this, and asked her the reason: 'Only peasants expose the body they have received from their parents,' she said.

'It should not be done.' Then the boys began to copy her, not knowing her real reason was to prevent them noticing that she was a girl.

Then her father died, and her sister-in-law, who did not approve of Yingt'ai studying, ordered her to come home and learn home-work. But Yingt'ai refused and continued to work.

But the sister-in-law, fearing lest she might fall in love with Hsienpo, used to send her from time to time babies' things, swaddling clothes, children's clothes and covers, and many other things. The students became very curious when they saw the things, and Yingt'ai could only tell them that they were the things she herself had used as a child, which her sister-in-law was now sending her to keep.

The time passed quickly. Soon Yingt'ai and Hsienpo were grown up. Yingt'ai still dressed as a man, and being a well-brought-up girl, she did not dare to ask Hsienpo to marry her; but when she looked at him her heart was filled with love. His delicate manner attracted her irresistibly, and she swore to marry him and none other. She proposed the marriage to her sister-in-law, who did not consider it suitable, because after her father's death they had lost all their money. Against Yingt'ai's will she arranged a match with a Dr. Ma, who belonged to a newly-rich family in the village. Yingt'ai objected strongly, but she could do nothing about it. Day after day she had to listen to complaints; she was without filial piety, she was a shameless decadent girl, a disgrace to the family. Finally she could bear it no longer, but her sister-in-law still feared she might secretly marry Hsienpo, and she urged the Ma family to appoint a day for the wedding. Then she cut off Yingt'ai's school money, which forced her to return home.

Everybody attacked Yingt'ai, who was obliged to hide her misery. Weeping bitterly, she said good-bye to Hsienpo, who accompanied her part of the way home.

As they separated, Yingt'ai sang a song which revealed that she was a girl and that she wanted to marry him. But the good, dense Hsienpo did not understand her hints. He did not see into Yingt'ai's heart, and tried to comfort her by telling her that one must return home some time, and that they would soon meet again. Yingt'ai saw that everything was hopeless, and went home in tears.

Hsienpo felt very lonely without his companion, with whom he had lived day and night for many years. He kept on writing letters to Yingt'ai, begging her to come back to school, but he never received a reply. Finally he could bear it no longer and went to visit her. 'Is Mr. Yingt'ai at home?' he asked. 'Please tell him his school friend, Hsienpo, has come and wants to see him.'

The servant looked at him curiously, and then said curtly: 'There is no Mr. Yingt'ai here, only a Miss Yingt'ai. She is to be married soon, and naturally she can't leave her room. How could she speak to a man? Please go away, sir, for if the master discovers it, he will make a complaint against you for improper behaviour.'

Suddenly everything was clear to Hsienpo. In a state of collapse he crept home. There he found, under Yingt'ai's books, a bundle of letters and essays which showed him quite clearly when he read them how deeply Yingt'ai loved him, and also that she did not want to marry any other man. And through his stupidity, his lack of understanding, the dream had come to naught. Overcome by remorse, he wept the whole day; Yingt'ai was always before his eyes, and in his dreams he called her name, or cursed her sister-in-law and Dr. Ma, himself, and all the ways of society. Through not eating or drinking he fell ill, and gradually sank into the grave.

Yingt'ai heard the sad news. Now she had nothing more to live for. If she had not been so carefully watched she would have done herself some injury. In this state

189

of despair the wedding day arrived. Listlessly she allowed herself to be pushed into the red bridal chair, and set off for the house of her bridegroom, Dr. Ma. But when they passed the grave of Hsienpo, she begged her attendants to let her get out and visit it, to thank him for all his kindness. On the grave, overcome by grief, she flung herself down and sobbed. Her attendants were afraid of her doing herself some injury, and urged her to return to her chair, but she refused. Finally, after great persuasion, she got up, dried her tears, and bowing several times in front of the grave, she prayed as follows: 'You are Hsienpo and I am Yingt'ai. If we were really intended to be man and wife, open your grave three feet wide.'

Scarcely had she spoken when there came a clap like thunder, and the grave opened. Yingt'ai leapt into the opening, which closed up again before the maids could catch hold of her, only leaving two bits of her dress in their hands. When they let these go they changed into two butterflies, which flew up into the air.

Young Dr. Ma was furious when he heard that his wife had jumped into the grave of Hsienpo. He got people together and had the grave opened. But the coffin was empty, save for two white stones. No one knew where Hsienpo had gone to with Yingt'ai. In a rage the grave-violators flung the two stones on to the road, where immediately a bamboo with two stems shot up. They were shimmering green, and swayed in the wind. The robbers thought this was magic and cut down the bamboos with a knife, but as soon as they had cut down one another shot up, till finally several people cut down the two stems at the same time. Then they flew up to heaven and became rainbows.

Now the two lovers have become Immortals. If they ever want to be together, undisturbed and unseen, so that no one on earth can see them or even talk about them, they wait until it is raining and the clouds are hiding the sky. The red in the rainbow is Hsienpo and the blue is Yingt'ai.

62. *Wen Shu and P'u Hsien, the Two Immortals*

ON either side of the gilded image of the Buddha in the central hall of a Buddhist temple stand two gods, one young and one old. They represent the Boddhisatva Wen Shu and the god P'u Hsien, and I will now tell you the story of how they gained their position.

When Wen Shu was only fifteen or sixteen years old, his best and dearest friend, P'u Hsien, was over thirty. They were both aware of the sin and misery on earth, which made them despise this orb of red dust and no longer desire to be reborn to suffer in it. So they set off together in search of the truth.

They passed through wild mountains and savage valleys, seeking some quiet place where they could attain perfection. But to their great sorrow they could find nothing suitable. Just as they were discussing what to do they heard in the distance the sound of a weeping woman, whose sobs drifted along to them at intervals on the wind. Deeply moved, Wen Shu proposed to P'u Hsien that they should go and see what was the matter. They learnt that a peasant family lived in the valley in which they were, and the woman was weeping because her husband had just died, leaving her a pretty young widow with three children. Having no relations to help her, the poor young woman wept the whole day and prayed to Heaven for help all night. The account of her troubles touched Wen Shu, who said to his companion: 'How pitiful is this poor child. We must settle here to perfect ourselves in the Law and at the same time to help the poor woman a little.' 'No, that is

191

impossible!' answered P'u Hsien. 'If we want to follow the Law we must give up all idea of women. No one could safely live near such a beautiful companion. Look, there is a nice temple on the mountain-top. I will go there, cut off my hair, and perfect myself as a monk. If you want to remain here, do as you like, but please excuse my leaving you.' P'u Hsien took leave of his friend, and set off to the steep peak he had indicated, but Wen Shu decided, in spite of P'u Hsien's disapproval, to remain where he was and help the peasant woman.

It was the farm that troubled the widow most, for she thought: 'Who will do the hard work now my husband is dead? And if we no longer reap the rice and the corn, we shall have nothing to eat.' And the longer she thought the sadder she became, and tears coursed down her cheeks. But now, naturally, she was consoled, because Wen Shu had offered himself as a labourer without demanding a farthing for his work.

Wen Shu was now very busy; he got up every morning with the fiery red sun and worked in the fields till evening, and even on his return he helped to wash the rice and to clean the vegetables and to do all kinds of domestic work. At night his bed was a heap of straw in the corner of the kitchen, because there was no room elsewhere. But even then he did not sleep, but sat with crossed knees reading the Holy Scriptures, and reciting the name of the Buddha to perfect himself. When the other peasants saw him working for a pretty widow, they used to call out to him: 'Look, the young fellow has begun an affair with his mistress. Obviously he sleeps with her at night, and has to work himself to the bone during the day. If a young man and a young woman live together little ones soon appear.' Although Wen Shu heard this dirty gossip, he paid no attention to it, and relied on the proverb, which says: 'If you do nothing wrong by day, you need not fear someone who knocks on the door by night.' He never thought of quarrelling with them, but called out laughing that they were too clever.

Swift as a stream passes the time. The widow's children grew up. On the wedding day of her eldest son the whole house was filled with lamps, and everyone was very gay. In the evening Wen Shu went to the widow and said cheerfully, but in a serious tone: 'Mistress, I wish you all good luck. I have helped you for many years, but now that your children are grown up you can live without my help. What will you give me as a farewell gift?' 'Please tell me truthfully what you would like,' said the widow. 'I will give you anything you want.' 'Then I would like to spend the night with your newly-married daughter-in-law,' answered Wen Shu. The widow had never expected him to make such a familiar request, and it put her in a difficult position, since she could hardly allow it. But she thought to herself that Wen Shu was the great benefactor of the family, and that he had always behaved in the most exemplary fashion, living as a vegetarian with the object of becoming an Immortal, and if he slept in the same room as the young wife, he certainly would not do anything shameless or improper. Finally, after carefully explaining the matter to her daughter-in-law, she granted Wen Shu's request.

That evening Wen Shu and the young bride went into the bridal chamber, where the red candles were burning brightly, and the happy wedding night began. But happiness makes the time fly by, and when the girl was woken by the crowing of a cock with the light shining into the room, there was no sign of Wen Shu to be seen, and to her terror a three-foot golden image of the Buddha was lying in his place on the bed. At the news, everyone, old and young, came into the room to see the figure, and the tale of the miracle spread abroad. Wen Shu's span of life had been completed, and during the night he had ascended to heaven as a Boddhisatva.

N

Meanwhile, after P'u Hsien had separated from Wen Shu, he climbed up to the temple on the peak, where he shaved his head and became a monk. With peace in his heart he read the Scriptures and perfected himself, and several years later when his teacher, who valued P'u Hsien highly, left this world, he appointed him in his will to be the new abbot of the community.

One day, on a journey through the air, Wen Shu passed this temple, which he recognized as the abode of his friend, P'u Hsien. Stepping off his cloud, he changed in an instant from a Boddhisatva to a beautiful young maiden; for, as the saying goes, the law of the Buddha knows no boundaries. Then he changed some angels into bearers, and climbing into a litter, he was carried into the temple with incense and candles in his hand.

P'u Hsien was seated in the Hall of Meditation, when an acolyte announced the arrival of a lady, come to burn incense. He hurried off to greet her, but she sacrificed so slowly that the sun had set before she was finished. This made the abbot slightly suspicious, but since she was attacked by pains in the stomach, he had to take her into the guest-room and let her lie down on the bed. In the middle of the night, the pains became so acute that she said groaning to P'u Hsien: 'I have such pains. The only cure is for a man to clasp me in his warm body or I shall die. Please have pity on me and save my life.' 'Noble lady,' answered P'u Hsien, 'you are mistaken. We are monks here, who worship the Buddha and strive after Immortality. How can we grant your request? You will soon feel better if you sleep a while.' In this way the woman was consoled, and, as the pains had only been caused to tempt P'u Hsien, they were gone long before dawn.

But Wen Shu wanted to try P'u Hsien once more, to see if he was not greedy. Before getting into his litter, he dropped a pair of golden bracelets into the basin.

194

After conducting the maiden to the door, P'u Hsien returned to the room, where he saw lying in the basin two wonderful, gleaming bracelets, made, as he ascertained, of pure gold. His first thought was to run after the girl and return the jewels, but eventually he decided she had probably not noticed their loss and he might as well keep them as an offering for the temple. Then he heard the voice of a god say out of the clouds: 'Women you no longer love, but to gold you are still attached. Wen Shu wanted to help you, but now you must labour for another twenty years.' And P'u Hsien had to perfect himself inwardly for another twenty years before he could ascend to heaven and become a god.

63. *The Marriage of the City God*

IN the town of Chieh-yang there is a custom whereby once a year all the gods are carried into the open. On this day altars are erected everywhere, on which offerings are made to the gods, and at the same time plays are performed for several days on end, to provide them with the amusement they most enjoy. Sometimes as many as twenty pieces are performed on one day, and the excursion of the gods is always a very gay occasion.

One day it was the holiday of the City God. His image was carried outside the East Gate of the town, where everyone hurried to greet it. Two young girls were standing outside a house door gossiping about this and that, and one of them said: 'Look! The old boy is quite handsome. If I knew a young man who looked like that, I . . .' but her sister-in-law interrupted with a laugh and ended the sentence for her: 'wouldn't mind marrying him.' They were only joking, though, and it never occurred to either of them that it would ever come true.

At the end of the day, the god's statue was carried

195

quietly back to his temple, but during the night, when everything was peaceful, he turned into a young man and visited the girl.

The next morning, on awaking from a dream, the girl found a man's black shoe beside her bed. In a great fright she ran off to tell her mother all that had happened, and the mother was also very worried and said to her daughter: 'If he comes again to-night, cut a piece off his coat.' During the day, a rumour spread through the town that the City God had lost a shoe.

That night the girl put a pair of scissors close to the bed. It was already late in the night when she had another dream, so delicious that at the moment of parting she almost forgot her mother's orders to cut off a corner of the stranger's coat. The next morning she heard people saying in the street that the City God had lost a piece of his coat.

Thus it went on from day to day, with the girl becoming daily thinner, for the City God visited her night after night, and shortened her rest. Finally, she died and became the companion of the god for ever.

For this reason, the City God is always carried to Feng-wei Hsiang, the home of the girl, and there offerings are made to him, because he is the stepson of the family there.

64. *The Tiny Temple of the City God*

MANY, many years ago, perhaps even during the Ch'ing Dynasty, there was a terrible summer drought at Hang-chou. The sun blazed down the whole day out of a leaden, cloudless sky, the plants hung their heads and dried up, and men were unable to sleep at night for the heat.

The people prepared to offer prayers for rain. They cleaned a place for the sacrifice, where day and night were heard the beating of drums and the clang of gongs and the murmur of the Holy Scriptures. The people fasted all in vain; the sun shone hotter than before, and the sky was still clearer. The rice harvest was already ruined, but now the wells dried up, which was even worse. They burned incense and prayed again, but again their efforts were useless. Amid scenes of wild excitement the peasants collected in bands of hundreds and thousands and decided to go to the District Governor and demand rain from him. They set off for the Yamen, where they did not wait for permission to enter, but burst past the watchmen in great numbers. The Governor soon appeared and asked them what they wanted. 'We beg the noble Governor to order heaven to send us rain,' they shouted, and, wanting to avoid further trouble, the Governor agreed to help them.

But it was a difficult matter; he was no god to conjure up rain at will. But having given his promise, he must find some means. In this sad mood he prepared for bed, but his thoughts were too troubled by the problem for sleep. He got up, washed, and without breaking his fast, he told his servants to fetch the City God. Then the living man and the plaster image were placed together on chairs and loaded with chains like criminals. A huge crowd gathered to see the spectacle, for the people believed the Governor was sacrificing himself for his people. The Governor explained: 'In the Upper World I am ruler of this province, and in the Underworld he is ruler. But since he does not care that men are dying of thirst, I have had both of us placed out in the sun to see whether his plaster body or my flesh and blood collapses first.' These words were greeted with wild applause. All day long the Governor sat in the sun, but towards evening he retired to bed completely exhausted, and in his dreams the god appeared to him and began to talk: 'I am a being of the Underworld,' said the god, 'and its concerns are my affair. The

Upper World is your affair. I consider it outrageous that you want my plaster body to fall to bits.' 'It is not my wish alone, but the wish of the whole people,' answered the Governor. 'They are on the point of death and have begged me to intercede for them. If you would only take the trouble to save Hang-chou, we should be ever so grateful.' 'My powers do not reach to making rain,' replied the god. 'If you really wanted to help Hang-chou, you could,' insisted the Governor, but the god continued to deny his ability in face of all these protests. Finally, however, he said hesitatingly: 'I really can't send for rain, but if you want, you must . . .' 'What must I do?' asked the Governor excitedly. The god was unwilling to explain, but having already said more than he ought, he continued: 'If you succeed in getting rain, you must on no account betray me, or I won't tell you anything,' and until the Governor had given his word of honour not to mention the god, he would not say another word. Then he whispered cautiously: 'Just before dawn at the fifth watch, you must go alone to the Yü-huang Mountain, six or seven miles from the town, where you will see three monks approaching. Let the first monk go by, and seize the second, before he can run away. Then make your request, but you must not say it was I who told you.'

The Governor was so excited after this interview that he leapt out of bed, to the surprise of his servants, who rushed up to find out what the matter was. He could scarcely wait for the end of the next day, and the more he prayed for the sun to set, the slower it seemed to move. He went to bed at five o'clock, but rose again quietly at midnight, and crept out of the Ch'ing Po Gate, on the way to the Yü-huang Mountain. When he arrived at the top he took a short rest after the tiring climb, but at the fourth watch, being midsummer, it became quite light, and looking round, he saw three monks coming towards him. When they were quite close he dashed out, and, allowing the first monk to go by, he seized the second by the arm.

'What's up?' asked the monk. 'Why have you seized hold of me without any reason?' For a moment the Governor was too worried to utter a word, fearing lest he might have seized the wrong man, but finally he said: 'Noble Yü-huang ti, help my people of Hang-chou. Help us, we are dying of thirst. Save us!' 'You have really made a mistake,' answered the monk; 'how could you imagine a simple monk like me to be Yü-huang ti? Stop talking rubbish and let me go.' But the Governor continued: 'Great god, pity the people of Hang-chou. Give us a little rain, or I will kneel down and never get up again,' and tears poured down his cheeks like two strings of pearls. Yü-huang ti's heart was touched by his devotion, and he said: 'Get up! Get up! I will look after the rain for you, but on one condition.' 'Yes, anything,' answered the Governor, hurriedly drying his tears. 'How did you know I was Yü-huang ti?' asked the god. 'I knew that myself,' answered the Governor. 'That is not possible,' answered the god. The Governor was very troubled now, for he thought to himself: 'If I don't tell the god, he won't give us any rain; if I do tell him, I shall break my word'—breaking one's word is very bad, of course, but—and after a long inward battle, he decided his word was less important than the well-being of the people, and he confessed to Yü-huang ti: 'The City God told me.' 'Good,' said the monk, 'the rain will appear at once.' The Governor dropped the god's hand so as to be able to thank him, but the three monks had already changed into wind, and he had to content himself with making three obeisances to Heaven. Then he hurried back to the town, and on his arrival at the Ch'ing Po Gate, rain began to fall. It poured and poured and the people were overjoyed.

In the evening the City God arrived and bitterly reproached the Governor for his betrayal, becoming even angrier when the Governor tried to explain there had been nothing else for him to do. 'You deserve death,' he shouted, but seeing the offender seated unmoved, he went on more calmly, 'but it is too late for regrets. I came to-day to ask you a favour.' 'What is it?' asked the Governor; 'I will do anything you ask. I will never break my word again.' 'I have been ordered to such and such a place on military service,' explained the god ; 'I want you to take care of my household. I must depart to-morrow, but when the newly-appointed City God arrives, I want my family to have some abode, and then they will be quite content. Good-bye! See you in the next life!' And he disappeared.

The Governor could no longer sleep, and calling his servants he sent them to look for a house. Finally they found one with three rooms in the sheep-market, and in it they placed the god's wife, his children and all his household. To-day it is called the 'Tiny Temple of the City God.'

65. *The Man who cuts down the Cinnamon Tree*

THERE was once a young man who loved all animals and living things. One day as he was walking along he found a swallow that had fallen down at the edge of the road. It hopped about, twittering sadly, and pitying the poor bird, the boy carefully picked it up and carried it home. He nursed it with tender care, and a few days later the leg was sound again. To show its gratitude the swallow made a bow to the boy and then flew off, but shortly after it came back with a yellow pumpkin seed in its beak, which it presented to its benefactor. The boy planted it in the garden, and day by day the plant grew stronger and stronger, and hidden among the leaves was an enormous yellow pumpkin. When at last it was ripe, the boy gathered the fruit and split it, and to his great astonishment a stream of shining gold and glittering silver came flowing out.

The tale of this miraculous occurrence quickly spread through the countryside, and everyone praised the kindness of the young man. Only one ugly child in the neighbourhood became ill with envy, and his mouth watered at the tale of such riches. He thought he would also rear a little swallow and get the same reward. It was easy money. So he knocked down a swallow that was sitting on the roof, and cared for it as carefully as the other boy had done. When the bird was cured it really did bring him a pumpkin seed, which he planted in an open space in front of the guest hall.

How excited he was when a yellow pumpkin grew underneath the leaves. But on opening it he received a terrible shock, because out stepped a smiling well-dressed old man, with a bill in his left hand, and a pen and a box of red ink in his right. He had a genial expression and said quietly to the boy: 'You wicked child! How could you be so covetous? But as you worship gold so much, you can come along with me.' Then he wrote something in the green register, took the boy by the hand, and climbed on to the runners of the pumpkin, which suddenly shot up like a ladder into the sky for the two people to step on. Beneath them the runners dried up as they passed, so that one could go up but not down. Before long they arrived at the 'Palace of Boundless Cold' in the moon. The roads were made of shimmering jade set in silver, the palaces of gleaming gold and agates, and everything was so bright that one could not keep one's eyes open, and so vast that one could see no end. Still more wonderful were the enchantingly attractive fairies, who danced to the accompaniment of heavenly music. Their ineffable beauty bewitched the eyes and ears of the boy, who quite forgot where he was. After he had looked round for a while, he asked the old man to take him back again. 'You want to return, do you?' asked the old man. 'Very well. If you cut down the cinnamon tree here, you can return home, otherwise not,' and fetching a white silver axe, he handed it to the boy.

In great excitement the boy rushed off with the axe to look at the cinnamon tree, which was made of gold with branches festooned with precious stones and agates. He thought to himself: 'If I have to cut down this tree I can take it home, and then I won't need to work for the rest of my life.' He raised his axe and cut a large notch in the trunk, but as he did so he felt a sharp pain in his shoulders, and looking round he saw that he had been bitten by a silver-white cock. In a rage he drove it away, but when he looked at the tree there was no sign of the blow he had given it. He gave it another slash, but again the cock bit him, and again when he had driven it away, the cut was no more to be seen.

So it went on; and he remains there to this day, because the tree never receives more than one cut.

If one looks up at the moon on a clear night one can dimly see many trees and people; and that is connected with our story of the naughty boy in the Palace of Boundless Cold.

66. *The Girl on the Green Tree*

NORTH of the Yi-lu Mountain, in the house of the Shao family, there was a most remarkable tree. It was green at all seasons of the year and every morning a number of round pieces of copper fell down, which could be used as money when pierced with a hole. The future daughter-in-law, who was living in the house, was made to pierce the holes, and she had to rise very early and beat the holes with a hammer until sunrise. Then her mother-in-law appeared and sent her into the hills to collect wood, without allowing her anything to eat. The poor girl's hands were covered with blisters from piercing the holes, and they used to pour with blood; it was worst during winter, when she used to lose ever so much blood. She only had two ragged garments to put on for collecting wood. One day an icy wind was cutting her to the bone, and, overcome by the thought of her miserable existence, she sat down on a bank and began to weep. At the sound of her tears, an old man came out of the pine-wood and asked her why she was weeping. 'At my home there is a remarkable tree,' she told him. 'Every morning many pieces of copper fall off it, and my mother-in-law forces me to pierce holes in them so that they can use the money. It is terribly hard work and my hands always begin to bleed.' The old man pointed at the mountain peak and said: 'Have you never seen the stone man? He stretches out his finger in the direction of your house, which causes the copper to fall off the tree. If you knock off his finger, the tree will die.' When the old man departed, the girl thanked him again and again and then picked up her basket of wood and went home. But later she secretly slipped a hammer into her basket and knocked off the stone man's finger with one blow.

The next morning, the mother-in-law saw that the strange tree had withered and died. She at once suspected her daughter-in-law of the deed and began to rate her soundly: 'You wretch! If you won't let my tree live, I won't let you live.' The poor girl ran out of the back door in a terrible fright and did not dare to return. During the winter, there was nothing to eat in the mountains and she was reduced by her terrible hunger to chewing pine-needles. After she had followed this diet for several months, she found to her astonishment that long white hairs appeared all over her body and she was able to fly around in the air.

The Girl on the Green Tree

Just outside the gate of the Chung-en temple stood a marvellous pine, whose branches grew again as soon as they were cut off. The monk in the temple noticed that several days running the needles on the magic pine were missing, and he wondered who could be eating them. The next evening, instead of going to sleep, he watched through a crack in the door. Half the night had already passed and the moon had just risen, when he heard a whistling sound, and an extraordinary being dropped down on to the tree, stretched out its lips and began to eat the pine-needles. In the moonlight the white hairs on its body glistened like a white fleece, and the monk was uncertain whether it was an Immortal or a ghost. The next evening, therefore, he placed a table laid for dinner under the tree, and the hot smell of the food rose into the branches. He was sure that if the being was an Immortal it would certainly eat nothing ; but if it was a ghost, it would gobble it up. About midnight the monk, who was keeping watch with his magic sword, saw the being swoop down to the tree. It glanced down at the ground and on all sides, and then flew down to the table, seized a fish in one hand and a piece of meat in the other, and stuffed them into its mouth. Then the monk opened the door, raised his sword, and called out: 'What kind of ghost are you?' The white-haired being ruffled its hairs and tried to fly away, but it could no longer leave the ground. It knelt down and said: 'I am the daughter-in-law-to-be of the Shao family.' The monk waved the magic sword again and said: 'If you want to be the daughter-in-law of the Shao family, how can you do such things?' In a trembling voice the white-haired girl replied: 'I killed their magic tree, for which my mother-in-law wanted to kill me. I ran away in terror, and there being no other food, I always ate pine-needles. After two months, white hairs grew all over my body and I was able to fly, but there are too few trees in the mountains, and in any case the needles have a bitter taste. This pine tree, however, has a delicious flavour, besides which the supply never fails. Fearing lest someone see me in the daytime, I have flown here at midnight for the last ten days. To-night I saw the table spread with food under the tree, and not having tasted any human food for three months, I could not resist taking some, your honour. But after I had eaten the fish and the meat, I could no longer fly. Please forgive me, your honour.' The old monk lowered his sword and said: 'If you are really the Shao family daughter-in-law, you can stay in the temple to-night, and to-morrow I will send you home.' 'I can't go home,' said the girl. 'I am terrified of my mother-in-law's stick.' 'Don't be afraid,' said the monk. 'I will arrange that,' and the girl remained in the temple.

The next day, the monk saw that the girl was only covered by a few rags, and before taking her home, he gave her a few old clothes. Her mother-in-law received her back out of respect for the monk and did not beat her. After she had eaten oil and salt for more than two months, the white hairs disappeared and she was the same as before.

(*Note.*—The Yi-lu Mountain in Hupeh Province.)

67. *An-chih kills the Snakes*

BY the side of the road stood a large hollow tree in which lived two evil snakes. Nearly everyone that passed this way was eaten by them. It was said that if they wanted to eat a man they only needed to make a sound from far off, and the man died. No one was able to harm them.

After a long time the Earth God of this district heard of the matter and complained to Yü-huang ti, the Pearly Emperor, how evil and dangerous these snakes were. Yü-huang ti was naturally very angry and ordered the

An-chih kills the Snakes

Thunder Earl and the Lightning Mother to kill the snakes. But the snakes were too poisonous, because when they saw the Thunder Earl and the Lightning Mother coming against them, they spat out poison, which rose into the air and destroyed the cloud on which the two gods were riding. They could not approach, and even when they came in the night, the snakes were so careful that one was always keeping watch, and there was nothing to be done.

When Yü-huang ti received the report of the two gods he was so angry that his hair stood up on end. He called all the Immortals together and consulted with them how to kill the snakes. The merciful goddess Kuan-yin suggested: 'I have heard that there is a very skilful bird-catcher on earth called An-chih, who can shoot down the wild ducks from the sky. If you send the Thunder Earl and the Lightning Mother the snakes will watch them in the sky, and An-chih will be able to shoot them unawares. Perhaps this will be successful.' Yü-huang ti agreed to this subterfuge and gave orders to carry it out, and Kuan-yin appeared to An-chih in a dream and fixed the day that he was to kill the snakes on.

On the appointed day the male snake was really killed by An-chih, but when the female heard the shot, she quickly lowered her head and breathed at him. Fortunately Kuan-yin was near by and sent a strong wind which blew An-chih twelve miles away, so that he avoided the poison. The female, however, was furious with him for killing her husband and swore to have her revenge. She turned herself into a beautiful girl, and the Emperor made her his Empress.

One day the snake Empress pretended to be in great pain and declared that only the liver of An-chih, who had killed the snake, could cure her. The Emperor sent An-chih an order: 'In consideration of the great service performed by An-chih in killing the snake, he is to come to court and be appointed an official.' But

206

Kuan-yin knew of this and told An-chih again in a dream that he must kill the Empress.

The Empress wanted to see her enemy before he was killed, because she was afraid that the Emperor might have deceived her. The Emperor hid behind a curtain while An-chih had an audience with the Empress. As he came in she said in triumph: 'An-chih! An-chih! You killed my husband, but now I am going to eat your liver,' but before she had finished speaking, there was a shot and she fell back dead on the bed. The Emperor lifted the curtain and rushed into the room, where he saw a huge snake lying on the bed. After An-chih had related the whole story to him, the Emperor in his fear wanted to keep him, but An-chih said: 'When you go to bed, you need only call my name three times and your fear will leave you,' and with that he took his leave.

It is said that it was just New Year when An-chih killed the snakes. For this reason the people of P'u-chiang at New Year do not say 'go to bed,' but 'go to rest' (An-chih) in remembrance of this story.

68. *Tales of the San Kuan*

MANY years ago Mount Yün-t'ai in Chêkiang Province was completely surrounded by the sea. On the summit of Mount Ling-chou lived a rich man named Ch'en Kuang-jui. One day his wife was feeling ill and wanted to drink some fish soup. Ch'en bought a large carp, but as he was preparing to cut it up the fish suddenly began to weep. This was more than Ch'en could bear, and he ordered the cook to carefully cut off three scales and then put the fish back in the water. The cook prepared a soup with the three scales and Mrs. Ch'en was cured.

Ch'en Kuang-jui wanted to go to the South to assume

his official post. He engaged a passage on a large merchant ship, whose captain, however, was the pirate Niu Hung. As soon as the ship had passed the bridge of the nine dragons at the outer headland he threw Ch'en into the sea and tried to compel his wife to live with him. Naturally the wife was disgusted with his proposal, and she contrived to be left in peace by telling him that she was expecting a child. Niu Hung, however, pretended to be Ch'en Kuang-jui and took up his post with his wife.

Mrs. Ch'en was really expecting a child, and after three months a son was born to her. Fearing lest the cruel Niu Hung would harm her child she wrapped it up in red and white silk, and placed it in a wooden pail. She then bit her finger and wrote a letter in her own blood, which she hid in the pail, and dropped the child into the river. From that time she pretended to be ill, and refused to live with Niu Hung.

The monk in the temple of the Golden Mountain had risen early and was watching the waves dancing on the river, when suddenly he heard the soft crying of a child. The sound gradually came nearer, until he saw something dark being driven towards the mountain by the waves, from which the crying seemed to come. He went down to the foot of the mountain, where he saw a child, wrapped in red and white silk, lying in a wooden pail. He carried it up to the temple, and when he saw the letter written in blood, he knew where the child had come from. He put the letter away and kept the little castaway as his disciple, giving him the name of T'ang-seng (floating monk), because he had floated ashore.

When T'ang-seng was fourteen or fifteen years old all the little temple novices used to mock him: 'Floating Bonze! Floating monk! Man without name or family!' they cried. T'ang-seng wondered whether he had really had no parents, and one day, being no longer able to bear the uncertainty, he ran to ask the monk. The

monk gave him the letter written in blood, from which
he learnt that he belonged to the Ch'en family, that his
father had been thrown into the sea by Niu Hung, and
that his mother was still living in shame. Tears came
into his eyes and he wept over the misfortunes of his
parents, but the monk comforted him: 'Your father is
not really dead,' he said, 'he is now in his old home in
Mount Ling-chou,' for the monk was a supernatural
being and could foretell the future. T'ang-seng dried
his tears at the welcome news and took leave of his
teacher on the same day. He thrust the letter into his
pocket, and went in search of his parents with a wooden
fish-clapper in his hands.

During the last ten years Mrs. Ch'en had continued
to feign illness, but her longing for her husband and her
child had ended by making her a real invalid. For
several days she heard someone beating a wooden fish
outside the garden wall, every beat of which went straight
to her heart. She said to her maid: 'Go to the garden
gate and see who is beating a clapper.' The maid came
back to tell her that it was a fifteen-year-old monk, and
for some reason the woman pitied him and told her maid
to let him in. The monk knelt down before her and
said: 'Are you not Mrs. Ch'en?' She admitted it,
and asked if he wanted alms. The monk shook his
head and produced the letter, at sight of which the
woman began to weep, for she now knew that the young
monk was her son. T'ang-seng related to his mother
how he had become a monk on the Golden Mountain,
and how he had discovered where she lived, and at last
he told her that his father was not dead, which made
Mrs. Ch'en so happy that she ceased to cry. She was
afraid, though, that Niu Hung would discover her son
and injure him, and therefore she told him to go and
find his father, and ask him to send a report to the
Emperor to have Niu Hung arrested. T'ang-seng took
leave of his mother and went across the sea and over

o

hills, beating his wooden fish, until he arrived at Mount Yün-t'ai.

We must now return to Ch'en Kuang-jui. After he was thrown into the sea by Niu Hung, a young man carried him off to the Crystal Palace, at the same time continually thanking him for saving his life. Ch'en asked him why he called him his saviour, and the young man answered: 'I am no other than the third son of the Dragon King. I had turned myself into a carp and gone for a swim in the sea, but I was caught by a fisherman and sold to you. Did you not save me then?' The young man brought him to the Dragon King, who knew already that Ch'en had saved his son's life. He was very friendly to him, and kept him in the Crystal Palace for ten days.

Ch'en gradually began to feel homesick, and wanted to return home. The prince said to him in secret: 'Don't accept gold and silver from my father, but ask for the little box on the table.' Ch'en went to the Dragon King and asked leave to depart, and though the king pressed him to stay, he remained firm. Then the king sent for gold and silver, but Ch'en merely shook his head, until the Dragon King asked him what he wanted. 'I want the little box on the table,' he said. The king did not seem very pleased at this request, but Ch'en being the saviour of his son he could not very well refuse it. The third prince escorted him up to the Yün-t'ai, and then took leave of him and returned to the Dragon King. Ch'en went back to the Ling-chou Mountain, and on arriving home he opened the little box. Inside he found three flower-pots, which turned into beautiful laughing maidens. One said: 'I am the eldest daughter of the Dragon King.' The second said: 'I am his second daughter,' and the third said: 'I am his third daughter.' They all three became Ch'en's wives, and two or three years later they each bore him a son.

Encircled by the sea on the Yün-t'ai Mountain, Ch'en knew nothing of the outer world. He often thought of his former wife, but did not know whether she was alive or dead. One day, when he was sadly thinking of her, T'ang-seng appeared beating on his wooden fish, and from him Ch'en learnt that his wife was still alive, and that the pirate Niu Hung was administering his post in his name. Needless to say, Ch'en was infuriated by this news, and he engaged a ship on the same day to go to the capital and make a report to the Emperor. With the soldiers he was given he went to the South and killed Niu Hung.

He took his wife back with him, and the nine people lived together in the greatest happiness. There is still a Palace of Harmony standing on this point, which was built in memory of Ch'en. Formerly the palace was in Ling-chou, but after it had been burnt down three times, it was rebuilt at this place. T'ang-seng, though, was a monk and could not always live with his family. Hiring a boat, he left the Yün-t'ai Mountain and travelled about the world.

Being grandsons of the Dragon King, the three sons of the princesses all wanted to be appointed princes by Chiang Tzu-ya at the investiture of the gods. The eldest son said to the youngest: 'Brother, go and see if the old man has also given us an appointment.' The youngest son went to Chiang Tzu-ya, who had appointed them to be the three officials (San Kuan), and without delay the youngest son took the place of honour as Inspector of Heaven. After a while, when his brother did not return, the eldest said to the second brother: 'Brother, go and see what has happened to our brother.' The second, however, also learnt that he had received a post and became Inspector of the Waters. Seeing that his brothers did not return, the eldest son finally went himself. He saw his youngest brother in the place of Inspector of Heaven, and his second brother as Inspector of the Watery Realms, and only the post of Inspector of Earth was still vacant. He ought to have received the post in Heaven, but his brother was already seated in it, so in an ill-humour he took the only one remaining. Later the people built a temple on the outer-cape in honour of the three brothers, and one can see that the eyes of the Inspector of Earth are still red with anger.

After his death, Niu Hung thought of nothing but injuring the descendants of Ch'en Kuang-jui. Before many years had passed, he was reborn as Excellency Chin, and he deceived the Emperor, saying: 'The people of Yün-t'ai are becoming so overbearing, they will certainly soon rebel. I beg you to transport them to the Interior and set a watch on them.' The Emperor believed his minister and sent orders that all the inhabitants of Yün-t'ai were to be moved into the Interior. The three officials received no more incense, and to avoid starvation moved to Shansi. Eighteen years later, the Emperor permitted the people to return to their homes and the officials were given their sacrifices again.

(*Note.*—This tale is found in various forms in Chinese literature, particularly in the novel, *A Journey to the Western Paradise*.)

69. *The Mother of Heaven*

ONE day the Ruler of Heaven had some important business in a distant part of his realm, which would keep him busy for three days. He therefore transferred all his duties to the old Mother of Heaven, and asked her to look after everything in his absence. 'But for these three days you must grant man's every wish,' he warned her, and the Mother of Heaven smilingly nodded in agreement. She left her palace, mounted a cloud, and travelled round everywhere to attend to the wishes of man. As she was passing a river, she heard a man say:

'Heavenly Father! Send wind. If a wind blows, I can sail away.' She ordered the wind to blow and went on her way. Soon she arrived at a large wood, where she heard someone calling: 'Heavenly Father! Please tell the wind to stop. If it goes on any longer, all my pears will fall.' This was too much for the Mother of Heaven, and she returned to her palace.

The next morning she set off again, and heard an old voice saying: 'Heavenly Father! Send rain. If it rains, I can sow my beans.' She sent a heavy rain, which lasted all day. But in the evening on her way home she heard a young girl say with a sigh: 'Heavenly Father! Please send fine weather. All my ginger will rot otherwise.' The Mother of Heaven could bear it no longer, and with a groan she returned to her palace and during the third day kept her room.

In the evening the Ruler of Heaven returned from his journey, and she related all that had happened and begged him to forgive her. But he said generously: 'It isn't very difficult. You must send a strong wind to blow in the rivers, and a gentle breeze on the pears. Rain must fall during the night in order to sow beans, and the sun shine during the day to dry the ginger.' The Mother of Heaven agreed at once, but asked with a smile: 'Why didn't you tell me before?'

70. *The Two Earth Gods*

IN a certain district there was an Earth God on the South Mountain and another on the North Mountain, but being stationed in such out-of-the-way places, it was long since they had received incense or any other form of sacrifice, and both were on the verge of starvation.

One day the Earth God of the Southern Mountain saw a young cowherd go past his temple, and, without a moment's hesitation, the god stretched out his hand and stroked the boy's body several times. On arriving home, the boy began to burn all over and became very ill. His family were distracted with worry, but suddenly they heard a voice saying from the boy's mouth: 'I am the God of the Southern Mountain. I have come to drive away the illness, which has been caused by the mountain spirits. If you go to the temple of the Earth God and cut a piece off the camphor tree in front of it and give it to the boy to drink, he will be cured.'

The people all cast themselves on to the ground when they heard that the Earth God was present, and the father of the boy followed his directions to cut off a piece from the camphor tree, boiled it, and gave it to his son to drink. A quarter of an hour later the invalid had recovered. The next day the family sent a pig's head, five beasts of sacrifice, and various other gifts, to thank the god for his favour. The god was overjoyed at the success of his plans and sent a servant to invite the God of the Northern Mountain to dinner.

On receipt of the invitation the god hurried across at once. At the sight of the choice meal his mouth began to water and he begged his host to tell him by what means he had acquired such a repast. 'A man cannot always stay poor,' said the Southern God proudly. 'One only needs to think out a plan.' 'Do come to the point and tell me how you did it,' said his guest. 'Don't be in such a hurry, I will tell you later. We are terribly hungry now.' But during dinner, the Southern Earth God related the whole story to his guest, who noted every word so as to imitate him and have some luck himself.

By a fortunate chance a cowherd went by his temple on the following day. The god stroked him several times as he had been told, and he noticed that the boy received a terrible shock. He ran home and became very ill, whereupon the god spoke out of his mouth as follows: 'You must go to the temple of the Earth God of the Northern Mountain and cut a piece off the camphor tree near by, cook it, and give it to the sick boy to drink.'

The father naturally rushed off to the temple, but, although he searched everywhere, he could find no camphor tree behind the temple. He stood dumbly wondering what to do, when he remembered that the image itself was made of camphor wood, and he decided, therefore, to cut a piece off the god; but, thinking that it would be too painful in front, he lifted up the god's dress and cut a bit off his behind. This he boiled and gave to his son with the greatest success, for the boy became well at once. Unfortunately this man was desperately poor, he could scarcely earn his daily bread, so that it never occurred to him to offer a sacrifice to the Earth God. The god, however, thought that they were bad people, from whom he had not only received no benefits but even injury, and the more he thought about the matter the angrier he became, until he decided to vent his ill-humour on his neighbour. He hobbled over to his temple, where the god looked at him in surprise and then asked: 'I have not seen you for so long, brother. How altered you are.' The Northern God did not even take the time to sit down, but launched into an account of his misfortunes to soothe his mind. But the Southern God was not at all sympathetic, and laughed till his sides ached. 'Ha! Ha! You must be careful what kind of family you choose. If you never even thought about that, you also can have had no idea that there is no camphor tree near your temple. If one is so stupid and gets injured, it is no good blaming it on someone else.'

71. *The Empress of Heaven*

ALTHOUGH she was only a seven-year-old girl, she already possessed supernatural powers. Her father and her two brothers were merchants, and each time that they were overtaken by a storm during the sea-crossing, she rescued them from the waves without anyone noticing it.

One day her father and brothers were once more on the sea, when a terrific storm sprang up. She felt very troubled at their great danger, and her soul immediately left her body and hurried to their assistance. Being half an Immortal, she arrived in an instant at the sea, where the waves were beating as high as the sky. The ship was pitching and tossing in all directions, and the passengers, pale with terror, were thinking that their last hour had come. The daughter grasped her brothers in her arms and her father in her mouth, and fled over the sea. It made no difference to her whether the sea was deep or shallow. The three castaways only saw a little girl appear through the winds and the waves to save them, and they thought that she was an Immortal; they had no idea that she was their own little girl.

Before leaving she had been talking with her mother, who was frightened out of her wits when her daughter broke off in the middle of a word and her body became stiff and cold. The mother thought she had fallen ill and began to sob and weep, but there was still no sound. After she had been calling and fondling her for a long time, the girl suddenly said: 'Yes.' 'Wake up, child,' said the mother, 'I nearly wept myself to death.'— 'Father is dead.'—'What are you saying?' cried the mother.—'Father and my two brothers were overtaken by a terrible storm on the sea and the ship sank, but my soul hastened over the water to save them. I grasped my brothers in my two hands, and caught my father's

216

clothes in my mouth. But you wept and called for me, until my heart was touched, and I had to answer 'Yes,' whereupon my father dropped out of my mouth. I would otherwise have saved him, but immediately after his fall he was hidden by the waves and I could find no trace of him. I managed to save my brothers, but, alas! father is dead.'—'Is that really true?' asked the mother. —'Yes.'—'Oh woe is me, woe is me!'

Soon after, the brothers came home. Weeping, they clasped their mother in their arms and told her how first their father had been saved and later drowned. The daughter reproached her mother, saying: 'You are to blame for the death of my father. Look, my feet and hair are still moist.' The mother embraced her children again.

The daughter was sorry for her mother's widowed state and swore an oath never to marry. She tied her hair together and waited on her mother till her death. After her death she became an Immortal. She became protectress of merchants and ships on the rivers, and is particularly worshipped by them.

72. *The Ruler of Earth*

I HAVE heard that the Ruler of Earth was once a man who was famed for his ability in driving away white ants. Not only were there none in his own house, but he drove them away from all the neighbouring villages. The white ants were afraid that he would exterminate their whole race and made a report to the ant king. The king accepted their petition and said to the man: 'I have never stolen your corn; I have never stolen your rice; why are you destroying my whole race so brutally?' But the man paid no attention to the king, and continued to destroy the white ants as before. The ruler of the ants soon saw that no attention had been paid to his warning, and he decided to use other methods. He led his whole forces to the man's house and devoured him alive, and their hate being still unsatisfied, they carried his remains to a dark place near the soul tablets in the Hall of Ancestors and covered it with sand to prevent its being found. It was not till much later that his relatives found the body and erected a tablet on the spot, where he was worshipped. In remembrance, they called him the Ruler of Earth, but later people imitated them without knowing the reason, and nowadays there is an altar for sacrifices to the Ruler of Earth in every home.

73. *The Monk with the Bag*

DURING his youth the 'Laughing Buddha' lived in a monastery at Fenghua in the province of Chêkiang. Even when eating or sleeping he carried a bag with him, and for this reason the people called him 'The monk with the bag.'

Once upon a time—I have forgotten exactly when—the God of Fire descended on to the temple, which in a short time he reduced to a heap of ashes. There being no money with which to rebuild it, the abbot ordered the monk with the bag to collect some. He set off with his wooden fish-clapper and his bag, and one day he arrived at the house of a widow. She was the owner of a large mountain covered with trees, which had not been felled for over one hundred years. They were very big now and the monk begged the widow to give him a bag full of them. Thinking that the monk was making a joke, because after all a small bag won't contain many trees, she gave him permission at once.

The monk engaged a few workmen, cut down all the trees on the mountain, and slipped them into his bag. It was extraordinary to see large and small trees vanish into it without a shadow of them appearing inside. It was just like the bottomless cave in the novel, *A Journey to the Western Paradise*. The widow was horrified when she heard the news and rushed off to the mountain, but every tree had been cut down and there was nothing left but the branches, which had been cut off. She thought to herself: 'Up till now I have lived from the sale of these trees, but with them all cut down, I shall soon die of starvation,' and she knelt down before the monk. 'Don't kneel down. I know what you are thinking about, but you will have your trees again in three years' time,' he said to her with a smile. She only half believed his words, but three years later the mountain was really covered with trees as big as before.

Whither did the trees go? He conjured them away to a small well in the temple. Now that the building materials were ready he did not need to collect any more money, but returned to the temple to supervise the workmen. The temple was to be made bigger than last time, and since the time allotted for building was very short, no carpenter was willing to undertake it. The monk had to appoint the magician Lu Pan.

Lu Pan ordered his pupils to take the wood out of the well, but they were careless and overlooked one beam, which was to serve as the centre pillar. The monk wanted to test Lu Pan and, kneeling down before him, he asked if the building material was sufficient. 'Just right,' answered Lu Pan, 'not too much and not too little.' The work now began, but when it was almost finished, Lu Pan found to his horror that one beam was missing, and although he calculated again and again he could not get it right. Having already said there was sufficient wood, he did not dare ask the monk for any more, but the only thing he could think of was to make a centre pillar out of the chips of wood that had fallen down, and, wonderful to relate, it could not be distinguished from a real one. The monk secretly admired the skill

219

of Lu Pan, and Lu Pan the magic of the monk, and in this manner the great task was finally achieved.

74. *Lü Tung-pin sells Coffins*

IT was once again New Year. Lü Tung-pin took a coffin, changed into a dirty old beggar, and went round, calling out: 'Coffins for sale, good cheap coffins. Won't you buy my coffin, old man? Won't you take it, mother? Do you want one, cousin? Or you, brother?'

It is an old belief that New Year's Day is decisive for the whole year, and men and women, young and old, must be careful of their words and deeds, for there are easily quarrels and fights. This is very important for beggars, and everyone received Lü with the words: 'How dare you sell coffins on New Year's Day, you wretch.' 'Do you want to be thrashed?' 'You obviously want to die, selling coffins on New Year's Day.' 'You ought to have your feet cut off.' 'What, you haven't gone yet?' 'Wait a moment, and I will burn you.' 'Be off with you now. We old things can't keep up with you, but the youngsters will overtake you.'

The poor beggar received nothing but curses and blows, but he did not worry. He wondered if all people, without any exception, were so hateful. After passing several more houses he came to the home of an old peasant with numerous sons and grandsons. This man bought the beggar's coffin and gave him something to eat as well, and afterwards Lü went on his way. The peasant polished up the coffin and said contentedly: 'Isn't it pleasant to receive an official post and money on New Year's Day?' (a pun on the word 'coffin').

Shortly afterwards all the children in the neighbourhood fell ill, and many died, since no one could find a cure. The eldest grandson of the peasant also caught the illness and died, and the peasant loved him so much that he laid him out for burial in the coffin he had bought at New Year. But, strange to relate, the moment the child touched the side of the coffin he came to life at once. The peasant was overjoyed, but he thought it was a chance occurrence. Soon after, his other grandsons fell ill and died of the same disease, but all came to life again when they touched the coffin, and the peasant realized what power it possessed.

The news of the miracle spread abroad and everyone marvelled at it. Now, if a man's child died, he did not weep but went and tried the old peasant's coffin, which never failed to reanimate the corpse. The parents gave the old peasant many valuable presents out of gratitude, and eventually everyone whose child had died willingly gave him money for the privilege of using the coffin. People from far and near came; the peasant was always travelling round, and for a long time he had no peace. But when the plague was over the old man had become quite rich.

75. *Lü Tung-pin as Patron of Barbers*

THE 14th of April in the old calendar is the birthday of Lü Tung-pin, and all barbers in the town sacrifice to him on that day. The custom originated in the Ming Dynasty.

The first Emperor, Chu Hung-wu, had a scalp disease; every day he sent for a new barber to come to the palace and shave him, but none of them could do it without hurting him, and he had innumerable barbers executed.

All the barbers in the land were in a desperate state, not knowing what to do. They sent a plea up to Heaven, and when the Jade Emperor received it, he sent Lü Tung-pin down to Earth. Lü Tung-pin changed into a barber, turned his magic sword into a razor, went to the palace, and after he had shaved Hung-wu, not only did the Emperor feel no pain, but his disease caused him no more trouble.

At first the barbers marvelled at the cure, but gradually they all learnt that the man who had shaved the Emperor was the envoy of Heaven, Lü Tung-pin. They thanked him again and again and gave him the post of Hairdressing God. Ever since, Lü Tung-pin has been worshipped by every barber and is considered ancestor of the trade.

76. *Lü Tung-pin as Beggar*

ONE day Lü Tung-pin changed into a beggar once more and came down to beg in Ch'ao-chou. He went to every house, but no one gave him a copper. This made him very angry, and, taking up his place in the door of a shop in the middle of the main street, he shouted out: 'You with your few stinking coppers play the rich man and despise me. You will never get any money.' The shopkeeper merely laughed at him: 'If you have money, why do you come here to beg, you swindler?' he said. 'Why should I have no money? I merely don't need any.' 'Where is your money, then?' 'I have a pot of silver buried in your shop. We can dig it up together.' 'And if there is nothing there?' 'Then you can beat me.' Not knowing whether to believe him, the shopkeeper began to dig at the spot indicated, and about three feet below the ground he really found a pot of silver. He at once planned to keep it and said craftily: 'That's my silver, I buried it here twenty years ago. You can't pretend it's yours.' 'All right, you can keep it,' said Lü Tung-pin, and went out into the street. 'Underneath this busy crossroads there is also a buried treasure,' he said. 'Please dig it up.' 'You are mad,' said the shopkeeper; 'how can there be a treasure buried at the crossroads?' 'Don't talk so much. Dig it up and see. If there is nothing, you can punish me,' said Lü. The shopkeeper sent for some workmen and told them to dig up the crossroads, and sure enough, they found another jar of silver. Lü Tung-pin stroked his beard and asked with a smile: 'Did you bury some more money twenty years ago?' 'Who can tell, if someone in this busy old town didn't bury silver at the crossroads?' said the shopkeeper. 'It is no proof that you can change earth into silver.' 'All right, we will go down to the river and try there,' and Lü proceeded to the river bank with the shopkeeper, followed by a crowd of inquisitive people. He vaguely pointed at the ground and said: 'A jar of silver is buried there. Dig it up quickly.' Everyone was longing to know the result, and they dug so quickly that in a minute they found a large jar of silver. Dumbfounded, they stood with open mouths and shook their heads; even their eyes were riveted with surprise. Then Lü Tung-pin asked with a laugh: 'What do you say now? Did you bury this treasure twenty years ago? Answer me, you clever tradesman,' but the man was too ashamed to reply, and, stroking his chin, Lü continued: 'You see that I can have money; but I do not need it. You have made a little money, which you use to put on airs and despise the poor. Don't you think I have the right to despise you also?' The shopkeeper blushed to the roots of his hair and tried to stutter a few words of excuse, but Lü Tung-pin suddenly vanished. Several people asserted that he was carrying two glass jars on his coat, which proved that he was the Immortal. Later a temple to Lü Tung-pin was built on the spot where the silver was found, and an inscription was erected over it: 'He can find treasure.'

77. Lü Tung-pin tests the Ascetic

ONE day Lü Tung-pin changed into a beggar with a festering leg, and went to test a man who had been endeavouring to become an Immortal for ten years.

He came hobbling past the hut of the ascetic and called out: 'My foot itches so. Help me! Help me, old man!' The ascetic came out when he heard him, but he nearly fainted at the dreadful appearance of the beggar. 'You want my help?' he asked. 'That is quite simple. Do you want some food, or clothes, or money? Just tell me what you want and I will give it to you. I'm not a miser.' 'No! No!' said the beggar. 'Well, what do you want then? Tell me what it is,' said the saint. 'If, old man, you put your lips to my leg and suck the pus out of the wound, it will become healed at once. I prayed to the gods, and they told me in a dream that you alone could cure me.'

The ascetic knit his brows and wondered whether he would be able to do something so revolting. 'Can no one save you but I?' he asked. 'The gods told me in a dream that you were the only man,' answered the beggar. For a long while the ascetic hesitated, but at last he said: 'A human life is worth one thousand pieces of gold. I will try.' 'I will for ever be indebted to you,' said the beggar. Having made his decision, the ascetic knelt down and licked the wound, and when he had finished the leg was quite healed, and a moment later the beggar disappeared. Now the ascetic knew that he had met an Immortal, and he knelt down on the ground and sent up a prayer of thanks to Heaven.

The next day the ascetic himself ascended to Heaven as an Immortal so as to thank his benefactor.

78. *The Tale of a Pig*

A MAN once died, and appeared before the Prince of the Underworld, Yen Wang, whom he asked in what form he would be reborn. As he had no particular preference, Yen Wang led him into a large hall and told him to choose for himself. Inside he saw the skins of every kind of animal hanging up in rows. The white looked a little too much like mourning garments, which made him fear that people would mock him in the Upper World. He did not like the mottled ones either, they looked too parched, not elegant. Then he saw some pinky-white skins—they were human—the colour of which was certainly very pretty; but again he thought that people might laugh at him, and really they would be rather difficult and impractical to put on. At last he found a black skin, rather like a foreign jacket; the colour was just right, the cut perfect, so he mentioned his choice to Yen Wang, pulled on the coat, and was reborn. But on opening his eyes for the first time, he was appalled to find himself lying in a filthy dirty pigsty, and then he looked at himself and saw that he had become a little black porker.

79. *Why does Li T'ie-kuai have a Poisoned Leg?*

MANY people say that the Immortal Li T'ie-kuai was once an ordinary man. One day he bought some garlic in the street and put it in his bag, which he carried over his shoulder. He was passing a temple of the Earth God, when he saw several Immortals eating red pills of immortality. He wanted to eat some too, but could think of no way of arranging it. Suddenly he had an idea; he tapped his bag and said to them: 'The pills that you are eating are too small; just look how big my pills of immortality are. I will help you to eat up your little ones, and then you can have some of my big ones.' Seeing the pills in his bag, the Immortals invited him to come and eat with them, and Li shoved the pills into his mouth with both hands and laughed inwardly, because he could not laugh openly with his mouth full. Soon all the little pills were gone and the Immortals said to Li: 'Now let us have your big pills.' Li opened his bag, tipped his garlic out, and said with a laugh: 'Make a good meal now.' The Immortals were not annoyed at being deceived, but climbed on to a cloud and flew off to the Mountain of the Volcano, and having eaten the red pills, Li T'ie-kuai was able to go with them. When they arrived at the Volcano, the Immortals flew very high; but Li being only a beginner could not reach great heights, and he lost one of his legs, which was burnt off in the fire. That is why he has a poisoned leg.

Other people say that, when he was young, he was very poor, and his mother ordered him to go into the hills every day to collect wood. The wood that he collected, though, was only sufficient for one day, which caused his aunt to say: 'What are we going to burn when it rains?' One day it really did rain and there was no wood in the house. His aunt cursed him: 'Lazy devil,' she said, 'to-day we will use your foot as fuel.' Now Li T'ie-kuai had already learnt some tricks from the Immortals in the hills, so he went to the fireplace, sat down, and stuck his foot into the fire, which blazed up much brighter than with wood. When his aunt saw him she shouted out: 'Are you mad? I was only joking when I said you ought to stoke the fire with your foot; I didn't mean it seriously,' and at the same time she pulled his foot out of the fire. But that was a grave mistake, because the bottom part of the leg fell off and naturally became poisoned. If his aunt had not pulled it out, he could have taken it out when the food was cooked and there would have been nothing to see. The aunt used the burnt-off leg to brush up the cinders.

80. *How Chang Kuo-lao became an Immortal*

CHANG KUO-LAO was a dullard and very poor. He had one brother and a sister-in-law. The brother did business away from home, and Chang Kuo-lao went out every day to collect firewood.

One day, being tired of collecting wood, he curled up to go to sleep under the arch of a bridge; but just as he was dropping off, he heard a voice say beside him: 'Hurry up and brush the planks of the bridge, the Immortals are coming by.' He pulled himself together and looked around, but seeing no one in sight, he lay down again. But just as he was falling asleep, he heard again: 'Be quick and tidy up the bridge; the Immortals are coming by.' He got up again, and as he did so, there came a wind, which blew all the dust away from the bridge. Soon some men went by dressed in filthy clothes and with faces begrimed with dirt. Chang laughed to himself, because he had pictured the Immortals as something quite different, but soon after he saw another approaching the bridge. The man had a festering leg and an iron crutch in his hand and a huge bottle gourd tied round his waist, just like the Immortal Li T'ie-kuai. Chang seized hold of him and said: 'You are an Immortal! Give me some marvellous thing, or I won't let you go.' Li shook his head and replied: 'I am not an Immortal. They were the people that have just gone by.' But Chang did not believe him, and said: 'They didn't look like Immortals, but you are the image of Li.' Seeing no way of escape, Li scratched some dirt

227

off his spine, rolled it into a pill, and gave it to Chang, saying: 'Go to a fishmonger and buy rotten fish and stinking crabs. Take them to your home, put them into a bowl, and drop in the pill. In one minute all the fish and the crabs will come to life again.' Chang was very pleased and thanked him for the wonderful gift. 'But,' he said, 'if you have deceived me, the least I shall do will be to smash your gourd when I meet you again.'

On his return home, Chang said to his sister-in-law: 'To-morrow morning prepare some food for me and lend me some money. I want to open a fish shop.' The woman answered: 'You are far too stupid to open a shop.' But Chang insisted, saying: 'Everyone has a nose and two eyes, why should I alone be incapable of doing business?' And she could find no further excuse. The next morning she rose early and prepared a meal for Chang. When he had eaten, she gave him the money, and he took a pole and a basket, and went down to the sea, after arranging with the fish shops for the sale of his fish.

About midday Chang came home with two baskets of rotten stinking fish and crabs. His sister-in-law began to scold him when she smelt the fish. 'You filthy idiot,' she said. 'How could you buy such muck?' Chang, however, paid no attention to her, but put the fish into a pail of water and dropped in the pill, and when he dipped in his hand he felt them jumping about like live dragons. He began to clap his hands with excitement at his success, and his sister-in-law could hardly believe her eyes.

Sea fish and crabs die if they are taken out of water, and the tradesmen all sold dead fish, except Chang, who sold living ones, and naturally everyone wanted to buy his. His gains were much larger than other people's, because dead fish only cost a few coppers. After this had gone on for four or five days, the other fish shops became very worried: 'We all see quite clearly,' they said, 'that Chang buys dead and rotting fish: how can he sell live ones? If he brings back fish to-morrow morning, we must investigate the matter.' The next day they all gathered at Chang's house, where they saw him put the dead fish in a bucket; then he stuck in his hand and the fish came to life again. Dumbfounded, they all rushed up to Chang and asked: 'How do you do it? What do you do?' But Chang said: 'There is a treasure in the bucket'; whereupon they all rushed at the bucket and tried to secure the pill, but seeing that they wanted to steal it, Chang stuck it into his mouth; and, when they even tried to force open his mouth, he swallowed it, and they had to return home no better off than before.

Having swallowed the pill, Chang himself became half immortal. One day he said to his sister-in-law, who was cooking dinner: 'I am longing to see my brother, so I think I will pay him a visit now, and have dinner on my return.' 'Don't talk such nonsense!' his sister-in-law answered. 'How can you visit your brother? He lives over one hundred miles away.' But Chang said: 'If you won't believe me, I will bring something back as proof.' He went out of the door, and arrived at his brother's house as quickly as if he had flown. 'Why have you come?' asked the brother. 'I wanted to visit you,' answered Kuo-lao. 'If you have any torn clothes or holes in your socks, I will take them back to your wife to be mended.' The brother had no torn clothes, but Chang went into the house, tore a large hole in a pair of trousers, and ran off. His brother thought sadly: 'Age has not made him any wiser.' On the way home, Chang fell in with the Immortals he had met on the bridge. 'Did you like the thing I gave you?' Li of the iron crutch asked him. Chang thanked him profusely, and Li continued: 'We are thinking of paying you a visit to-morrow. You live on the east side of the bridge, don't you?' 'Perfect,' said Chang. 'I will expect you to-morrow, then.' When he reached home, dinner was just ready. He took his brother's trousers out of his pocket and gave them to his sister-in-law, saying: 'My brother wants you to mend these for him. By the way, some good friends of mine are coming to dinner to-morrow, so please sweep the steps and prepare some tea for them.' At first his sister-in-law thought he must have stolen the trousers somewhere, but when she looked carefully she saw that they really were her husband's trousers, and she thought to herself Chang Kuo-lao must really have learnt some tricks.

The next morning she had cleaned the door and the guest-room and was sitting in the kitchen making tea, when she heard Kuo-lao say: 'Ah! Here you are,' and she saw some dirty fellows, in ragged clothes, entering the house. Once again she was angry with him and grumbled: 'He goes about with such dreadful people.' When they had sat down, Chang ordered food, but Li of the iron crutch said: 'Don't bother, we have brought our own,' and one of the Immortals lifted something that looked like a dead baby out of a torn basket, and one of them tore off an arm and ate it, and another a leg, and Chang, being asked to help himself, tore off two ears and gobbled them up. The sister-in-law nearly fainted when she came in with the tea and saw them eating a dead baby; for she did not know it was the magic ginseng root. Chang offered them tea, but Li refused: 'We don't want any tea,' he said. 'We will have some noodles,' and each of them went to the stove in turn and blew his nose into the pot. Then they added water, made a fire, and produced snow-white noodles, which they consumed sitting round the fire, each dipping his hand into the pot and picking some out, though the sister-in-law almost fainted at the sight of the filthy muck they were eating.

The meal over, they climbed on to a cloud and flew up to Heaven, and Chang Kuo-lao followed them on a little black donkey. When he got out of the house, though, he also mounted a cloud and flew up to Heaven. From that time Chang Kuo-lao became an Immortal; but if he travels about the heavens, he still rides on his little black donkey.

81. *Lu Pan builds a Temple*

ONE day, many years ago, Lu Pan, the God of Carpenters, was chatting with his sister, the Goddess of masons, and Lu Pan was boasting of his great prowess. 'I don't even take one night to build a house,' he said. But his sister replied that she could build a pagoda in even less time. They went on wrangling for a time, until at last Lu Pan said: 'You really must not tell such lies. How could anyone build a pagoda in one night?' 'You needn't exaggerate so much,' retorted the goddess, 'no one can build a house in twelve hours.' 'I will build you one this evening, if you won't believe me,' said Lu Pan, and from words they came to deeds and to a test of their powers, Lu Pan agreeing to build a house and the goddess a pagoda. They left each other delighted over the bet, and Lu Pan chose a site on the west of the town, and the goddess one on the east.

The goddess's task was easy and her pagoda was finished before cockcrow, because the ground was littered with tiles, which she carried over to the building without loss of time. Then she ran off to the west to see how her brother was getting on, but he was by no means finished. She had been fearing that he would do better than she, but when she saw that he had not yet finished, she became very jealous and imitated the crowing of a cock. All the cocks near by began to crow at once, and soon the whole town was ringing with their cries. Lu Pan was very cross when he heard them, because when he counted his wood he found that two ridge beams were missing.

He quickly rolled two substitutes together out of sawdust, and then rushed off to the east to see how his sister's pagoda was getting on. Half-way there she met him and said with a smirk: 'The cocks began to crow long ago. Why is your building only just finished?' Lu Pan had no answer, but thought to himself: 'This beautiful, high, pointed pagoda. My miserable temple, which took so long to build, is nothing compared to that.' He was depressed at losing face, but later he worked it out and discovered that he had been cheated. He rushed off to the pagoda in a towering rage and gave it several kicks, so that it leaned ever afterwards.

82. *The Water Mother*

MANY years ago, so many, in fact, that people have forgotten her name, there lived a poor woman. No one else lived in the house but an old mother-in-law and a little daughter. Because the woman was dutiful she was always obedient to her mother-in-law, and always was kind to her daughter. But the old woman hated her, and said she was lazy. One day she said to her daughter-in-law: 'All the water we use in the house is brought by water-carriers. That is too extravagant. From now on you can carry the water, or you won't get anything to eat.'

The poor woman had to do as she was told, and every day, as well as feeding the pigs and the dogs, cooking the food, and mending the clothes, she had to do this hard work. As soon as it was light she went to fetch water from the distant well, and if she had not brought enough, she had to return two, or even three times. No woman is strong enough for such work, but even if she lacked the strength she had to go, because otherwise she received no food and a beating into the bargain.

One day she could no longer endure this slavery. She put down her pail by the well, and seating herself on the edge, she felt her aching and burning little feet, and said: 'Oh Heaven, how wretched I am! The live-long day I have to work, and at the end of it I don't even get enough to eat. Death were better than such a life,' and as the thought of suicide passed through her mind, she got up to throw herself into the well.

Suddenly an old white-haired woman appeared who motioned her back, saying: 'Why do you want to die?' The woman was terrified, not knowing where the old crone had come from, but when she saw the kindly, good-natured expression on her face, she lost her fear and told her all her troubles.

'That's nothing,' said the old woman, and pulling out a little wand, she continued: 'I will give you a treasure. All you need do when you get up in the morning is to strike the pail with this rod, and it will be filled with water at once, but beware of striking it twice and don't tell anyone else about it.'

The poor woman did not believe that such things existed, but the old woman gave it to her so carefully that she began to doubt, and eventually decided to have a try. Thanking her benefactress, she returned home, and when she secretly tapped the pail it filled with water in an instant. Now she was very happy, because she no longer had to fetch the water; but she took care to hide the wand and to let no one see it.

Everything went well, till one day the mother-in-law became suspicious. She knew her daughter-in-law had to fetch water several times a day so as to fill the pail, but for a long time she had not seen her walking, though the pail was always full. This roused her suspicions, and she secretly watched her daughter-in-law till she discovered that, instead of fetching water herself, she tapped the pail with a strange stick. She waited until the woman was not watching, and stole the wand, and

233

being ignorant of its magic powers, she beat the pail again and again.

Once, twice, thrice . . . in a flash the water poured out of the pail and covered the house, and all the houses in the whole village. All the rich fields became one big lake.

When the poor woman saw what had happened she could do nothing, for the old woman had not told her how to escape, and she sat down and died. The water is still flowing out of the pail and it has formed a large new spring.

Later the people built a temple in her honour, and called her the Water Mother.

83. *The Kitchen God*

WHEN on earth the Kitchen God was a miserably poor mason, who was fated to remain poor all his life; and therefore the harder he worked the worse off he became, until at last he had to separate from his wife and marry her again to other people.

One day he was engaged to do some work by the man who had married his former wife. The mason had no idea who she was, but his wife still used to think about him, and since it was not possible to call to him, she thought she would help him in a secret manner. He was still very poor, but her family was fairly rich, and she baked some seal cakes, in each of which she hid a piece of money. When the mason took his leave she sent him these as a gift for the journey without mentioning a word about the money. He, however, being destined never to have money, naturally was not able to keep these unexpected riches. On his way home he went into a small tea-house to rest, where another customer saw his basket full of cakes and asked to be given one to taste. The mason handed him one, and the other man found the money inside. He talked the mason round, and eventually persuaded him to sell them for a small sum. The mason was born under an unlucky star and thought he was doing a good bit of business by getting some money for the cakes, but in this way he wasted everything that his wife had given him out of love.

Later he discovered that his wife had sent him cakes filled with money, all of which he had given away, and he thought to himself: 'I am fated to live my life in poverty, what is the point of continuing?' And he took his own life. But the Ruler of Heaven took pity on his miserable existence and appointed him God of the Kitchen in recognition of the probity.

84. *Minister Li assists the Water-spirit*

ON the west bank of the lake, near the village of a thousand springs at Ch'üan-chou, there is a tiny temple to the goddess Kuan-yin. In front of it stretches the lake, behind it lie the fields, and it is quite separated from other houses. Far from the noisy highway, it is an ideal place for study, and Li, a prominent scholar, had chosen it for his place of abode, thinking it particularly suited for reading and teaching. But in course of time many people had been drowned in the lake, and at dusk and during the night it became very lively, until eventually the spirits tried to entice men into the water even in broad daylight. The ghosts of the drowned have to find substitutes before they can leave the site of their accident, and when Li saw people dashing madly into the lake, he knew that they had been bewitched by the spirits, and to save them he loudly called out a warning. In this way he prevented the water-spirits securing a substitute, and naturally they hated him for his interference and looked upon him as their bitter enemy.

235

Li had a few pupils who used to come in the morning and return home at night, leaving Li alone to work. Then the water-spirits, who were angry with him, appeared outside his window as shadows and tried to terrify him by uttering strange sounds. But Li was very brave and refused to be intimidated, and if the ghosts made too much noise, he shouted at them to be quiet till they realized that they were powerless against him.

But one of the female spirits was particularly savage and used to remain behind after all the others had departed. Li knew her and planned to give her a lesson. One evening when she came again she waited outside the window till he had finished reading an essay, and then asked him for a light. Li told her to put in her arm and take it, but when she did so he wrote the character 'Fire' on her hand. The spirit gave a shriek and tried to withdraw her arm, but she was unable to do so.

Do you know why she could not do so? The reason was that Li was destined to become a Minister and therefore his handwriting in red ink possessed great power. When he wrote the word 'Fire,' fire appeared and burnt the hand of the ghost.

'Please, sir, I promise never to disturb you again. Please wipe the character off my hand,' she begged Li, who took a piece of paper and scraped off the sign. The spirit fled, but several nights later it reappeared and behaved in the most exemplary manner, hardly daring to make a sound. 'Master,' she said, 'I am always looking for a person to take my place, and this time you prevented me. Have pity on me! If I cannot find a substitute, I must remain for ever in the water. Save me!' 'Do you want to be born again?' asked Li. 'Fortunately, you have not harmed anyone and I can find you a place. In such and such a village a new Buddha has just been made; you can go and live in that.'

236

The spirit thanked Li, and its soul went off to take up its post in the image of the Buddha. The next day it was rumoured in the village that the new Buddha was possessed, and from that time it performed countless miracles. Superstitious people came from far and near to say their prayers and burn their incense before it.

Many years later Li passed the State examinations and was appointed Minister, after which he begged for leave to visit the graves of his ancestors. It is a great day for a town when a Minister visits it, and I need not tell you that he brought a large retinue with him. One day, on his way home from a visit, he passed by a temple in which a great fair was taking place in honour of the god. The crowd was so great that his chair-bearers could not get through the throng, and even on foot he could scarcely make any progress.

At this point he recognized the temple in which he had confined the water-spirit, and he pushed his way through the throng to see what was happening. He saw before him a beautiful new temple in which thousands of incense-sticks were being burnt by people who hoped to influence the god in their favour. Li went to the entrance of the temple, and pointing at the image with his finger, he said: 'Water-spirit! Have you still found no peace?' And from then on the god performed no more miracles.

85. *Tung Po-hua sells Thunder*

AT midday, on the festival on the fifth day of the fifth month according to the Chinese calendar, the members of the Kuo family in Ch'üan-chou exhibit in the guest-hall for all to see the old pictures they have inherited from their ancestors. On the day of the exhibition the guests

237

are also invited to dinner and to see various entertainments, and at the same time a bowl is brought out, which is full of water formed by polishing the old family stone. The water is carried off in a few minutes by the visitors, who consider it as a real treasure. People say that water collected on the fifth day of the fifth month is able to cure all ills, and naturally everyone wants to procure some. The stone is said to be a thunder-stone, and the pictures that are exhibited at the same time represent wind, thunder, clouds and rain. After the festival the pictures are rolled up again and the stone is put away. They are both connected with Tung Po-hua, the story of whose connection with the Kuo family I will now relate.

The Immortal Tung was really a man named Tung Po-hua, who lived during the Ming Dynasty. As his mother loved eating pigs' liver, he used to buy some for her early every morning in the market. At the same time, a son of the Kuo family, who was also very filial, lived in the East Street in Ch'üan-chou, and every morning he used to go to market to buy pigs' chops, his father's favourite food. The two boys met there every day and soon became fast friends.

Young Kuo was an official in the district administration and was also owner of a wine-shop, in which he and Tung used to drink together after they became friends. If Tung had no money, he had his debts written down on account, but as he never paid it, the wine-shop was brought to the verge of collapse. Tung was very worried about this, and he advised Kuo to give up the wine business and fill his casks instead with oranges, which would eventually earn him a handsome profit. He gave no reason for this advice, but he was already a magician though not yet an Immortal. Mr. Kuo had complete confidence in him, and in accordance with his advice filled all his casks with the fruit. That year there was a terrible outbreak of plague in Ch'üan-chou, the only cure for which was oranges. Kuo could now sell his supply at threefold the price, and since even after all the oranges were sold he could still get money for the juice, he ended by becoming a rich man.

One day, Tung arrived to say good-bye to Kuo. An Immortal had appeared to him in a dream and made an appointment to meet him on such and such a day at the new bridge to escort him to the Immortals. It was a sad wrench to take leave of his life-long friend, but he gave his old mother into Kuo's care and departed.

At the stated time, Tung Po-hua was waiting for the Immortal at the bridge. He soon arrived, and, pointing at the swift flowing river, he ordered Tung to leap in. Without a moment's hesitation, Tung did as he was told, and to his surprise, before he touched the water, he found himself in a peaceful landscape, and by his side was walking the Immortal.

His guide led him on until they found themselves face to face with a tiger, towards which Tung was told to walk. He fearlessly advanced, and when he was quite close the tiger bared its teeth, shot out its claws, and swallowed him. But strange to relate, he suddenly found himself in a beautiful green forest, with the Immortal beside him.

They went on again till they arrived at a huge, blazing furnace. At the Immortal's command, Tung sprang into the flames and found himself in a marvellous palace in another world. He felt he must have shaken the dust of the world off his feet and now be in the land of the Blest, for everything was unspeakably beautiful. He thought with sorrow of his old white-haired mother, who was now living with his friend, and he regretted no longer being able to serve her. He had never thanked her enough for the love she had lavished on him. It occurred to him also that two thousand years ago Liu An had ascended to Heaven with his whole family, and he repented not having asked the Immortal before his departure to allow his mother to accompany him. It would have been so pleasant. But while he was lost in thoughts of home, the Immortal appeared before him with a stern look on his face: 'You have not lost your earthly heart,' he said. 'You must return to the world,' and while he was speaking, the beautiful house vanished and Tung found himself in the midst of savage mountains. He was wandering in the trackless waste when the Immortal reappeared and said: 'This place is many thousand miles from your home. If you want to return, you only need go towards the East and you cannot miss the way. This stone I give you in place of journey money. If you have no money, call out "I sell thunder," and if anyone wants to buy it, write the word on his hand with the stone and then close it. Later, if the man wants to hear thunder, he only needs to open his hand and terrific peals will occur. In this way, you can earn money for your journey,' and with these words the Immortal was gone.

Tung followed the instructions of the Immortal and went towards the East, with the thunder-stone in his hand. He travelled by day and slept by night. He traversed great distances and passed through many important towns, and whenever he had no money he called out: 'I sell thunder!' And after one person had bought some, everyone thought it a great joke and wanted to have a copper's worth themselves. In this way, he found it easy to get money for his long journey.

Many months passed before he finally reached Ch'üan-chou. Mother and son met again with delight, and his friendship with Kuo was closer than before. If he wanted to, he used to pull out his stone and sell thunder, and everyone, particularly children, gladly bought it. On one occasion, the Magistrate of Ch'üan-chou, Hsiung Shang-ch'u, was holding court, and before his arrival Tung had been selling great quantities of thunder, which the purchasers had taken into the session in their hands.

240

Without any bad intention, these people opened their hands and the halls rocked with peals of thunder. When the bystanders began to laugh, other people, who still had some thunder, thought it funny to let theirs loose, and the claps never ceased. The Magistrate was very surprised that there should be thunder with a blue sky and a beaming sun, and seeing that the crowd was laughing, he sent two people to investigate. When they reported that a man was standing outside the Yamen selling thunder, the Magistrate accused Tung of rebellion and sorcery, and cast him into prison.

It was terrible for Tung to be sitting in prison, but fortunately his friend Kuo was an official, and he took the responsibility for the affair. One day, as the Magistrate was escorting guests to the gate, Tung said cautiously to Kuo: 'Magistrate Hsiung will soon meet with a misfortune. Please don't accompany him on a circuit.' 'As an official, I can't avoid going,' said Kuo. Tung Po-hua made no further objections, but gave him a pill against all dangers, and insisted on Kuo's swallowing it in his presence. Soon after, Kuo fell ill, and grew worse from day to day.

At this time there was revolt in the province and the Magistrate led the troops in person against the rebels. But his forces were too weak and he was taken prisoner and killed. Kuo had been saved by his friend Tung, because the pill he had given him had made him too ill to lead his men into battle.

Tung Po-hua was so attached to his friend that when he was in prison he gave him his pictures of the wind, the thunder, the rain and the clouds, and also the thunder-stone of the Immortal. Soon after, he died. To this day, though, on the fifth day of the fifth month the descendants of Kuo exhibit the pictures and stone of Tung Po-hua.

86. *How the Eighteen Lohans became Immortal*

THERE were once eighteen robbers, who were always thieving, burning houses, and murdering people. One day, their booty was so large that it was too heavy to carry away, and so they stole a cow from a rich man's stable and tied all the stolen goods on to its back. They drove the animal for about two miles, but then it stopped and refused to move another step, and, although in their rage they beat it with an iron club, it still refused to obey. The robbers had perforce to change their tone and beg the animal to advance, but suddenly it began to speak, saying: 'It is quite useless to use force. In my former life I only wore one sleeve that belonged to you, and by carrying your burdens for two miles I am quite adequately punished.' The robbers looked at each other in terror, and said: 'In that case, what sort of punishment shall we have in the next life for all our crimes?' They returned home, and piece by piece gave back the things they had stolen, and day by day they became better, helping mankind with all their might. After their death, the people whom they had aided put up images of them, which they worshipped, and later everyone began to worship the Eighteen Lohans in temples.

87. *The Wang-liang*

THE Wang-liang spirits are said to be very big, with bodies covered with hair. If they see a human being, they eat him. They live in the midst of hills and cool valleys, so we seldom see them. Some people say that if you see one of them coming towards you, you must hold a stake in front of you, with one point straight

242

against your breast and the other directed towards the Wang-liang. This makes it feel very uncomfortable; but unless you know this way of preventing its approach, you are sure to be eaten up.

There was once a young fellow named A San, who suddenly met one of these spirits at night. He quickly took a bamboo pole and placed one end against his breast and the other towards the spirit, who became very upset and begged to be set free. But A San replied: 'I have no intention of letting you go until you give me something.' The spirit quickly pulled off a boot and offered it to A San, but knowing that the boot was a coffin, he refused to take it. Then the spirit asked him: 'What do you want?' And A San answered: 'I want the straw hat you are wearing on your head,' for A San knew it was a treasure, which makes its wearer invisible. Much against its will, the ghost was forced to surrender it, and A San set the ghost free and went joyfully home.

From now on, A San wore his cap the whole day. One day he stole some things from a fruit-stall as he was passing by, but unfortunately a Wang-liang saw him and took his cap away, which made him visible to the shopkeepers, who beat him hard before allowing him to run away.

Another man, named A Lin, also caught a Wang-liang with a bamboo stick. He demanded the skin on its face, and despite the pain, the poor ghost had to strip it off and give it to him. This skin is like a mask, and whoever puts it on is invisible, like the wearer of the cap. A Lin now let the Wang-liang go, but one night he met another, whose cap he also took with the well-known trick.

A Lin was delighted with his two treasures, and he also became a thief. He first ordered his wife to steal silver. She put the cap on her head and went into the house of a rich man, but just as she was going to take the money, the man's daughter, who was sleeping in the room, began to cough, and thinking she had been seen, the woman ran away. A Lin asked his wife why she had stolen nothing, and she told him about the girl coughing, but A Lin said: 'What a fool you are; no one can see you. You are too cowardly. This time I will go.' And he took the cap and went into the rich man's house, where he stole a lot of valuable jewellery and silver, which he carried back to his house. In this way, he soon became rich, though he still wore his dirty old clothes to lull his neighbours' suspicion.

Every two or three months he stole something. All the rich families lost money and valuables, but no one could catch the thief. One day he hung up the cap on a beam by the fire, but his wife, who was short-sighted, mistook it for rice-straw and shoved it into the fire as fuel. A Lin was furious with her, but luckily he still possessed the mask, for although he had stolen so much silver, he lost most of it again gambling.

One day, when he again gambled away all his money, he laid the mask on the table as security, but none of his friends were willing to lend him money on the filthy white thing. Then A Lin said to them: 'You must not undervalue this thing. It is a treasure, which makes its wearer invisible,' and when they tried it on and found that A Lin had not lied, they were willing to accept it as a pledge. But A Lin's luck did not turn, and after losing all his money the mask passed into another man's hands.

88. *Mother and Child*

A THOUSAND years ago, during the Sung Dynasty, the poet Su Tung-p'o lost the favour of the court and was banished to Hui-chou. In those days, the province of Kuangtung was considered a land of barbarians, and, therefore, when Su left the court after his disgrace, he was alone except for his secondary wife Chao Yün. Su was deeply attached to this woman, who remained true to him on his disgrace, and who was willing to accompany him to the south. There was a beautiful lake at Hui-chou, on the shores of which Su used to wander all day long in company of Chao Yün, composing poems and verses, which show how much he admired it. A son was born to him, but before it was one year old, Chao Yün, Su's beloved, died. With many tears, he buried her on a small hill on the farther side of the West Lake, and now lived alone and deserted with his child that was not yet one year old. Su was afraid that the poor little thing would soon die, because babies cannot live without a mother to care for them; but strangely enough every night, when he was quietly sleeping, he saw his adored Chao Yün coming to nurse her child, dripping with water as if she had crossed over the lake, and in this way the little orphan was able to live. Su Tung-p'o realized that his wife was unable to forget her child, but he did not understand why her whole body was always wet. Later he realized that, her grave being on the other side of the lake, she would have to cross over the water every night, and with the idea of preventing her getting wet, he had a dam constructed between the two banks. But who would have thought it? When the dam was ready, his wife did not appear that night, nor any of the following nights, and the child, who no longer had anyone to care for him, soon followed his mother into the grave. I have heard that the reason why the wife could not cross over the dam was that when a bridge is built it receives a bridge god, who does not allow any spirits to cross over. As the dam was built by Su Tung-p'o, it is called to-day Su's Dam.

89. *Why men are so Bad*

A LONG time ago somewhere or other died a man and a dog. One of the Immortals happened to be passing, and he decided to bring them to life again. He first examined the man, whose heart he found had vanished; but the dog's heart was still in its place. So he took out the dog's heart and gave it to the man; and made a heart out of earth for the dog. Then he said a few spells and they both came to life again. The dog raised its head and wagged its tail in gratitude. The man, however, not only did not thank him, but even cursed him.

90. *Why are there Cripples on Earth?*

AFTER P'an Ku, the Creator, had made Heaven and Earth, plants and animals sprang up everywhere, but there were still no men. P'an Ku considered it a grave defect that there was no reasoning being who could perfect and employ other living things, which at the moment were stupid and without knowledge of any kind. He set to work, and for one whole day fashioned men and women out of clay. When they became dry, they were impregnated by the vital forces of Yin and Yang from Heaven and Earth, and became men. P'an Ku had made a large supply, which were already half-baked by the rays of the sun, when suddenly dark clouds appeared in the North-West, and obscured the whole sky. Fearing lest all his labour should be wasted, the god brushed all the figures into a heap and carried them into the house with an iron fork; but before he had got them all inside, there was a terrific storm and some of the men were spoilt, which is the reason why now there are lame, blind, deaf, and other ill people on earth.

246

91. *Why does the Cock eat the Millipede?*

FORMERLY the cock had a pair of beautiful horns on his head; but at that time there was a dragon, who was prevented from ascending to Heaven by his lack of a pair of horns, and so he offered the millipede as guarantor and borrowed the horns from the cock. When the millipede came for the horns, he said to the cock: 'When you want your horns back, you must call out at dawn, "Give me back my horns," and they will be returned at once. You needn't worry.' The cock knew how difficult it was to ascend to Heaven, and, reassured by the good security, he lent his horns without any more trouble. He also thought he would ask the dragon how things were in Heaven, when he returned; and if it was very beautiful, he might think of going there himself one day. Next morning, at break of day, the cock called out loudly, 'Give me back my horns,' but although he repeated it over ten times, there was no sign either of the dragon or the horns. The cock went off and complained to the millipede, who quietened him, saying: 'If he has not returned them this morning, he will certainly do so to-morrow; at latest the next day. Just be a little patient, and you will certainly get them back.'

The cock waited several days, but although he called out every morning, 'Give me back my horns,' they never reappeared. He was extremely annoyed at this and ordered all his descendants to eat the millipede at sight, but he has not yet given up hope of getting his horns. He ordered his children always to call out at break of day, 'Give me back my horns,' because he hopes that the dragon will hear him.

92. *The Rat and the Ox*

THERE was once a half-god living among men—I forget exactly at what time—who wanted to find twelve animals for the Zodiac in order to name the years. He had already placed the dragon, the snake, the tiger and the hare, when the rat and the ox began to quarrel about which was the bigger. Naturally the body and the appearance of the ox was much larger, and when it heard the claims of the rat, it shook its horns and shouted out: 'Everyone knows that I, the ox, am big and immeasurably strong. How can a rat that only weighs a few pounds dare to compete with me? I call it ridiculous!' The sly cunning rat merely laughed coldly at the boasts of the ox, and said: 'Everyone is conceited about their own size and capabilities. That is no standard. We must bend to the judgment of the majority. It is true that I am only a poor little rat, but I will measure myself with you to-day.' Fearing that the battle of words between the ox and the rat would develop into a serious quarrel, the half-god quickly interrupted: 'Naturally a rat is not as big as an ox. But, since he won't believe it, we must trust to the decision of the crowd. That is the justest way to decide. I suggest that you think the matter over and then go out and hear the people's verdict.' The ox agreed at once to the suggestion of the half-god, for he thought that his victory was assured.

The rat, however, pretended to be in despair, and lay on a chair sunk in gloom and depression. 'Of course we can go round,' he said, 'but I must be a little bigger before I can appear before the people.'

Seeing the rat so disheartened, the ox thought that, whatever happened, the rat would be much smaller, and agreed to its doubling its size. He himself did not trouble, because he was still one hundred times bigger than the rat. When the rat had grown, they went out into the town. 'Look! Never before have I seen such a big rat. It really is incredibly big!' From the moment they left the house until their return they heard on all sides exclamations of wonder at the size of the rat; but no one looked at the ox, because people see oxen every day, whereas they had never seen such a large rat before.

The stupid ox had fallen into the rat's trap, but it did not realize that it had been tricked, but merely thought the people had no eyes. As it lost, it had no dignity left, and had to resign the first place to the rat, and from that time the rat became the first animal in the Zodiac.

93. *Whence comes the Ox?*

IN ancient times man had a hard life and was never able to get enough to eat. Sometimes he ate every third day, sometimes only every fifth or sixth day, and he was always hungry, although he worked day and night. Really he was to be pitied.

The Heavenly Emperor was sorry for men, who laboured ceaselessly without getting enough to eat, and he ordered his subject, the Ox—that is the Ox Star in the sky—to go down to Earth and say to the people: 'If you men are energetic, you can have one meal every three days.'

The ox, however, misunderstood his orders; he went quickly down to Earth and announced to the people: 'The Heavenly Emperor says you shall have three meals a day and not starve any more.' When he returned to Heaven and made his report, he was punished for his mistake by being sent down to Earth to help men at the plough. 'I told you to tell them,' said the Emperor, 'that they should have one meal every three days, but you have now given them three meals every one day. Just think of it; men have only two hands and two

249

feet, how can they prepare three meals a day? It is all your fault, and you must answer for it. You must go down to Earth and help men plough, so that they can really get three meals a day.'

The ox, therefore, went down to Earth and helped man in agriculture. The oxen that are now on the earth originally came from Heaven.

94. *The Titsang P'usa and the Ox*

IN former times there were no oxen on earth and man had to plough the fields with his own power, which was very tiring. The kind-hearted Titsang P'usa was sorry for them, and one day he said to Yü huang ti: 'Mankind has such a hard time tilling the fields. Couldn't we send down the ox from Heaven to help him plough?' Yü-huang ti considered it for a moment and then said: 'No! Men on the earth are not kind-hearted. So long as the ox is young and strong and can help them at their work they will treat it well; but when it is worn out and too weak to plough, they will kill it, to eat its flesh and use its hide.' But Titsang P'usa broke in, saying: 'Men are really not so bad. I will be guarantor for them. If they kill the ox, eat its flesh and strip off its skin, I will go down to Hell,' and seeing how earnest he was, Yü-huang ti granted his request.

At first men treated the ox very well, because it was so strong and could plough so well; but the moment it became old, they slaughtered it, ate its flesh, and skinned it, and although the ox wept bitter tears before its death, men paid no attention to its prayers.

Yü-huang ti was enraged by this news and banished Titsang P'usa to Hell, where in punishment he had to keep his eyes perpetually closed, except on the thirtieth day of the seventh month. For this reason men on the earth light incense in honour of Titsang P'usa on that day.

95. *Pocket Crabs*

WE are told that in the old days all animals could speak just the same as men. But they were always betraying the secrets of Heaven, for which the God in Heaven punished them with dumbness. In those days the crab was still round.

One day a cow was secretly eating rice in a field when a red crab caught it and began to shout: 'The cow is stealing rice! The cow is stealing rice!' The cow crossly told the crab to mind its own business, but the crab took no notice, and merely shouted louder. This enraged the cow to such a pitch that she lifted up her foot and stamped on it. The poor crab was squashed flat, and one still sees the mark of a cow's hoof on the shell of a crab.

96. *Where does Rice come from?*

LONG, long ago man had no rice with which to still the pangs of hunger, but had to live from fruits and the flesh of wild beasts. It is true that the rice plant was there, but at this time the ears were quite empty, and naturally no food could be extracted from them.

One day the goddess Kuan Yin saw how difficult men's life was and how they were always hungry; her compassionate heart was touched and she decided to help them. One evening she secretly slipped down to the fields and pressed her breast with one hand until her milk flowed into the ears of rice. She squeezed until there was no more left, but all the ears were not yet filled, so she pressed once more with all her might and a mixture of blood and milk came out. Now her task was finished and she returned home contented.

From that time the ears were filled and man had rice to eat. The white grains are those that were formed out of her milk, and the ruddy red ones are those that were formed out of her milk and blood mixed.

97. *The Dog and the Rice*

AFTER the deluge, when the plains had dried up, mankind came down from the hill-tops; but there was very little to eat, because the old things had all been spoilt and new ones had not yet appeared. Man was very worried about this, though for the moment he lived by hunting. Then the people saw a dog creeping out of a flooded field, on whose tail several long yellow seeds were hanging. These they planted in the drained fields, and when they came up and produced rice crops they had something to eat. For this they were very grateful to the dog, and always, before beginning to eat rice, they gave a little to the dog; and for this reason, too, at the first meal after the new rice harvest, we give the dog its share.

98. *Why do Crops no longer come flying into the House?*

IN former times, when rice was ripe, the corn fell out of the ears of its own accord and rolled into the store-houses; and if one did not shut the door fast, but only drew the bolt, it even opened the door in the depths of the night. Every year it was the same, man had no trouble with the harvest and the granaries were always overflowing.

252

Later there was a lazy-bones who fastened up his door during harvest-time and went to sleep, so that the corn had to call and shout for ages, before he got up to let it in. One evening the corn was again banging on the door for more than half an hour without anyone getting up. It became bored of waiting and shouted out: 'You never open the door. I have been waiting too long, it's impossible, I . . .' This woke the man up and he grumbled sleepily: 'You never arrive at a reasonable hour, why do you always come when I am fast asleep? Go away now and come back earlier to-morrow evening.' The corn nearly burst with rage when it heard this, and replied: 'If you are so fond of sleep, sleep on. You won't let me in to-day; from now on you can come to the field yourself, reap me, thresh me, and beat me a hundred times; otherwise I won't come.'

From that time the corn no longer went to the granary of its own accord, but man had to reap it with a sickle, and thresh with a flail, and even then it had to be carried into the house in a basket.

99. *Flies and Ants*

IN former times there were neither ants nor flies. These two pests were created by the Lord of the Earth and the goddess Kuan Yin.

One day the god went over to Kuan Yin's for a gossip, and he saw that in the gallery in which her throne was placed everything was clean and white and there was not even a speck of dirt. This made him jealous, and in order to tease her he rolled some balls of paper, mumbled some magic formulas, and threw them on to her head. They changed at once into flies, which flew around in the house and covered everything with filth, till even the body of the goddess became soiled and stank. The goddess was furious with him, and after

253

long consideration she thought of a marvellous plan of revenge.

The next day she went over to pay a casual call on the Lord of the Earth, whom she found quietly resting in the shadow of a tree. He was feeling very contented, but Kuan Yin secretly squeezed ants out of earth, one after the other, and set them loose on his couch. Having nothing better to do, the ants crawled all over him and caused the most terrible itching. The god could not complain, because he had started the whole thing, but had to bear it in silence. From this time there were flies and ants in the world to plague men.

100. *The Cinnamon in the Moon*

ON a clear night, when not the softest breeze is stirring the heavens, one can see some shadows in the moon, shivering to and fro like the branches of a tree. They are the shadows of the cinnamon in the moon.

I have heard that in former times this tree did not exist; instead there were fields of lovely flowers in which bewitching Immortals used to play. All of them, except Wu Kang, who guarded the Dragon, were women and maidens. Wu Kang was so lazy that he often allowed the dragon to run away, while he amused himself and drank wine.

One day he went past Mount K'un Lun on his way back from the seas with the dragon. He met a large number of his friends there, and soon he was tossing down cup after cup of wine, composing poems, and throwing dice. He drank till he was completely tipsy, and even at sunset no idea of returning entered his head. During the night he felt gayer and gayer, and when he found some other Immortals playing chess he joined them with a shout of joy. The others all advised him to return home, but Wu Kang paid not the slightest

attention and insisted on joining their game. The
gamblers were loath to have such a poor devil as a player,
because they were playing for marvellous treasures, but
Wu Kang proudly struck his chest and said: 'I have a
dragon pearl. I will wager that.'

A few moves later the jewel was already lost, but he
thought to himself that, since he could not drive the
dragon home without it, he might as well continue the
game and stake the dragon itself. But once again luck
was against him and he lost the dragon too. Now he
had nothing more and had to crawl home shamefacedly.

The Immortals were furious when they learnt of the
loss, and immediately sowed a pearl in the earth, out of
which grew a tall cinnamon tree. They gave Wu Kang
an axe and told him to hack off the branches; if he
could manage to do this before the branches grew again,
they would forgive him. He was very strong and easily
cut off all the branches; but as soon as he had done so
new ones sprouted out of the wounds and became stronger
and bigger than before. If he was ever lazy now the
tree would grow so strongly that it would completely
cover the moon, and therefore he never dared to rest
for a moment. He is there to this day, and his beard
has grown down to his waist. Day and night he cuts
off the branches, and the trembling shadows are the
branches falling down.

101. *The Discovery of Salt*

ONCE a peasant, who was working in the fields, saw a
phoenix perched on a heap of earth by the seashore.
A second later it vanished, but the peasant recalled that
a phoenix only rests on the site of buried treasure. In a
great state of excitement he began to turn up the earth,
and after digging for a while he thought no more of other
treasures, but rushed home with a piece of earth as quickly

as he could, hoping at last to have made his fortune. But then it occurred to him that people who don't declare treasures to the Emperor are punished with death, and if anyone heard about his discovery and reported it, his life would be in the gravest danger. Next morning, therefore, he went to the Emperor and said: 'Your Majesty, yesterday while at work in the fields I saw a phoenix seated on a mound by the sea. I dug something up and now I present it to Your Majesty.' The Emperor looked and looked, but he could see nothing strange about it, and it had a horrible salt taste into the bargain. He became angry and said: 'You dog, you wanted to play a joke on me. You will be executed,' and without delay the unfortunate peasant was beheaded.

This happened during the wet season when the rain streams down from heaven, and naturally the piece of earth also became damp. The moisture ran off it drop by drop, and one day, as the imperial cook was going past with the Emperor's dinner, a few drops fell into the food. The cook knew he would get into terrible trouble if the Emperor discovered it, but there was no time to cook any more.

At the first bite the Emperor realized that the taste was incomparably stronger and better than that of his ordinary fare. 'What did you put in the food to make it taste so good?' he asked the cook. 'Your servant would not dare to put anything into your food,' answered the cook, trembling in all his limbs, 'but a few drops fell into it from the piece of earth the peasant brought you some time ago.'

The Emperor now began to wonder whether the piece of earth was really a treasure after all and, sending for a cup of the liquid, he poured it over his food, which tasted much spicier than before.

Later, many pieces were dug out of the mound, and when the moisture off them was dried in the sun it turned into salt.

The Emperor honoured the poor peasant who had formerly brought him the salt by appointing his son a high official and giving him great riches. Now the old peasant could sleep peacefully in his grave.

102. *Why is the Carrot Red Inside?*

MU-LIEN was a good, intelligent man, but his mother was very bad. She was a scold and lazy, and did nothing in the house. She thought and talked of nothing but food, and she killed many animals, whose bones and hairs were heaped up year by year in the garden, till they were almost as high as an artificial mountain. Mu-lien often reproached her, but instead of listening to him she cursed him for interfering. He was pained by her behaviour and wept many tears, but he did not know what to do.

One day she became very ill, and said sadly to her son: 'I am going to die now, and my soul will be banished to Hell by the God of Heaven to suffer punishment for all the living things I killed,' and she passed away before she had finished speaking. Mu-lien wept bitterly and then made arrangements for her burial. He invited many famous Buddhist and Taoist priests to read masses day and night in order that his mother might be spared a portion of her punishment. In this way he used up his whole fortune, but his mother's guilt was so deep that there was no means of saving her. Mu-lien, however, became a monk and retreated into the mountains to perfect himself.

Later he became a Buddha and went down to Hell to save his mother, who had suffered such dreadful punishment that her term was already finished. Mu-lien took her up in his arms and ran and ran until he was too tired to go another step.

R

It was late in the spring and tender carrots were sprouting in the fields. Mu-lien lay down to rest by the roadside, but his mother's character was still the same, and, having suffered the pangs of starvation in Hell, she could not resist the temptation of pulling up a carrot and eating it. Mu-lien knew that, according to the Buddhist canon, his mother had committed a grievous sin, and he knew that he would not be able to rescue her again if the Lord of Heaven heard of it. In spite of the pain, he cut off one of his fingers and stuck it into the hole where the carrot had been. Later the finger turned into a real carrot, but the inside is now red as blood, because it was the finger of Mu-lien.

103. *The Origin of Snow*

AT New Year every family bakes New Year cakes. There is often a fall of snow at this time, but formerly flour used to fall instead. The hearts of the Immortals were touched when they saw that mankind had to suffer the pangs of hunger at New Year, and they threw down flour, which the poor people collected and made into cakes.

For several winters the plan worked very well, but soon desires were awakened in men's breasts, and they became lazier than ever. They were always demanding more flour so as to work less. Finally, they began to quarrel over it and steal it from each other, which led to bloody fights and many cruelties. The rich were even worse, for they engaged labourers and collected great hordes of flour.

The Immortals were angered by the evil behaviour of mankind, and they ordered the snow-god to send a fall of cold snow to cleanse the hearts of the wicked.

104. *The Origin of the Glow-worm*

THERE was once a peasant whose wife suddenly died, leaving behind an only child called Ying Hu. The next year the peasant married a new wife, who was very cruel to her stepson and made him do all the work alone. One day she gave him one hundred coppers and sent him out to buy oil. But the street market was twenty miles away from their home, the road to which passed through mountains and waste land.

After a hard journey of six hours, Ying Hu at last reached the market, but when he felt in his pocket the hundred coppers were gone. He was in a terrible state, since he knew his step-mother would never forgive him. With tears streaming down his face, he begged the gods to have pity on him, and then he returned the way he had come to look for the money. The poor child searched till dark all through the mountains, but there was nothing to be seen. Finally he set off home, trembling with fear, but on the way a terrible storm sprang up which soaked him to the skin, and he slipped in the mud and fell into a stream.

He screamed for help, but no one heard his cries, for the whole neighbourhood was fast asleep. The poor child was drowned in the river, and after his death he became an insect, which flies around with a lantern in one hand seeking for the money that it once lost. In memory of Ying Hu, from whom it was formed, it was called the Ying Hu insect. But in time it became known as the Ying Huo insect, or the Glow-worm.

105. *The Origin of Opium-smoking*

THERE was once a man named Wang Ta, who had married a very ugly woman with a face covered with pock marks. Wang Ta could not bear her, and was always cursing her and threatening to throw her out. The woman never replied to his curses, for she loved her husband, but in time, when she saw there was nothing to be done about her ugliness, she fell ill. Even then Wang Ta paid no attention to her, but when she felt death was near she said to him: 'All my life you have treated me badly, but after my death you will realize how much I loved you,' and as she stopped speaking, she died. Wang Ta thought no more about her last words.

About a week later a cowherd came running up to Wang Ta and said to him: 'Very strange! There is a small plant growing on your wife's grave!' Wang was very astonished and went off at once with the boy to the burial-place. There he really found a little plant which had just put forth a beautiful snow-white flower. In the middle of the bloom was a small round fruit as large as an ear of rice. Wang Ta went home slowly, deep in thought, and rather worried by what he had seen.

That evening he could find no rest; he thought and thought of how brutal he had been to his wife, and then he thought of her last words, and finally of the little plant on her grave. He felt regrets and began to reproach himself for treating her so badly. What could he do if she had turned into a plant to injure him? He lay awake half the night, turning the matter over in his mind, and only towards midnight did he glide into the land of dreams.

From now on the picture of his wife often appeared before his eyes, and not only did he fail to sleep at night, but even during the day he found no peace. Finally he fell ill, and although he sent for the most famous doctors, none of them could cure him, and his illness grew daily worse, till he was on the verge of death. Now Wang Ta had no wife and no daughter to care for him; he lay quite alone on his bed and groaned in anguish. Then one evening he had a dream. His wife appeared to him and said: 'The little plant by my grave is formed from my soul. No doctor can cure your present illness, only the flower can help you. To-morrow go to my grave, scratch the skin of the fruit with a knife, peal it off a little, and then let the juice run out. Let this become hard, and then stick it in a pipe and light it. If you breathe it in for a long, long while, you will gradually become well.' At this Wang Ta awoke and sat up in bed.

The next morning he got up and did everything his wife had told him, and scarcely had he breathed in the smoke when he felt much better, and finally his disease completely disappeared.

From now on Wang Ta smoked every day, but if he did not smoke he felt ill at once, just as if he was going to die, and his body felt weak and slack. Then he believed in the final words of his wife. And this miraculous balm was the dangerous, destructive opium which so many people smoke now.

106. *The Donkey in Kweichow*

THERE are no donkeys in Kweichow. Once a man brought one up the river on a cargo-boat, but on his arrival he saw that it could not be used in the high mountains and set it loose. A tiger saw it, and was terrified by the enormous beast, which he thought must be a god. He hid in a wood to observe it. After a while he approached a little nearer, but the donkey pretended not to notice anything. The next day the donkey brayed, and the tiger ran away in a terrible fright, thinking that the donkey was going to bite him. He was still afraid when he went up and looked at it again, but it did not seem to have many tricks and gradually he became used to the braying. He went nearer and nearer, now in front, and now behind, but did not yet touch it. Day by day he became braver, until at last he gave it a push. At this the donkey could no longer contain its anger and lashed out with its leg, much to the delight of the tiger, who now knew that the donkey had no other means of defence. He leapt on to its back, tore out its neck, and ate it up.

A donkey looks so big, one thinks that it must be very strong; and brays so loud that it must be very powerful. As long as it did not display its powers, the savage tiger did not dare to attack it and eat it up; but when it displayed them, its doom was sealed.

107. *Money makes Cares*

CH'EN PO-SHIH was a famous rich man in Ch'üan-chou about one hundred years ago. He had so much money that he was always busy investing it, lending it, and getting in and paying out taxes, and from morning to night he never had a moment's peace. He had no time to eat and he never had dinner till late at night. His wife pitied him for all the worries he had, and kept on saying to him: 'Look after yourself and don't slave yourself to death.' And Ch'en Po-shih agreed with her, but he did not know how to avoid his work.

His neighbour, Li the Fourth, was as poor as a church mouse. As a labourer, he only earned three hundred cash a day, but that, with the one hundred and eighty cash that his wife managed to gain through her energy and thrift, was sufficient to keep them alive. Li was an industrious man, and it was usually evening before he stopped work. Then he went home, gave his wife the money he had earned, and worried about nothing else. If he was in a good humour, he sang songs to a flute or a mandoline, and that was his only amusement.

The sound of his playing and singing was borne across to the house of Ch'en Po-shih, but Ch'en was too busy to notice the strains of the mandoline or the flute, or even to hear the carefree talk of his two neighbours. He was going through his bills with his debtors or tenants, and till far into the night he had no time for food. His wife, however, was saddened by the gay sounds. After the people had gone, and Ch'en was eating his evening meal, the sound was still to be heard, and his wife said to him: 'Listen, Li sounds so happy, although he is so poor. We are so rich, and yet we are never happy.'

'Have you never heard the proverb, "The penniless man has plenty of time"?' asked Mr. Ch'en. 'He can be gay, because he is poor. It is quite easy to make him quiet. We need only give him some money.' 'If you do that he will be happier still,' answered Mrs. Ch'en. 'Wait till to-morrow,' said her husband. 'If you still hear him singing I will admit myself in the wrong.'

Next morning, Ch'en sent a servant to ask Li to come to his house. Li did not dare to refuse and appeared at once. 'How have you been getting on lately?' asked Ch'en. 'Oh, sir, we have been neighbours for so long, you must know what I do. Working for other people, one has no time to wonder whether one is well or badly off,' answered Li. 'Exactly,' said Ch'en. 'I thought you would never earn much as a labourer, and since, as old neighbours, we more or less belong together, I have thought of something for you. I will give you five hundred pieces of silver, which you can use to start a promising business. You can take the money with you, you needn't come back later and discuss it,' and with these words, he handed Li the five hundred pieces of silver.

Never having dreamt of such an offer, it was some time before Li could stammer out: 'Many thanks for your kindness.' Then he took the money and rushed home in a wild state of excitement, to tell his wife all that happened. Now he no longer went to work.

The power of gold is really uncanny. After Li had received the money, he did nothing but wonder how he could use it to the best advantage, but he could never find a completely satisfactory solution. In the evening, he arrived one hour late for dinner, which he gulped down quickly, and naturally he had no time for singing or playing; on the contrary, he groaned and sighed, and tossed about on his bed all night without getting a wink of sleep.

Ch'en and his wife had listened very carefully that night to hear what neighbour Li did, but there was no sound of music. 'Was I right?' Ch'en asked his wife, and his wife smilingly admitted he had won his bet.

For two nights Li could get no sleep. On the morning of the third day, he was so exhausted that he could hardly stand or sit, but just sleepily rolled about in bed. Suddenly the God of Luck appeared before him and said: 'Money makes cares. Think of that and bother no more about it.' Li understood at once, and leaping out of bed, he hurried over to Ch'en's house and returned the money just as he had received it. 'Well, Li,' asked Ch'en, 'have you got any plans?' 'No, I have no plans,' answered Li. 'I am here to-day to give you back your money, and to thank you for your kindness,' and placing the money in Ch'en's hand, he left the house.

Li felt as though a weight had been taken off his heart. He went home and slept the whole night through. The next day he went out to work, and in the evening the sound of his singing and playing was carried over to Ch'en's house.

A few years later, Ch'en himself became poor, but the singing and playing of Li still continued.

108. *The Mirror*

WANG the Third was a stupid man. Moreover, he had married a wife. One day his wife wanted him to buy her a wooden comb, and being afraid that he would forget it, she pointed at the narrow moon crescent in the sky and said: 'Buy me a wooden comb, but it must be just like the moon in the sky.'

A few days later, the moon shone full and round in the sky. Wang the Third remembered what his wife had told him, and, as his purchase was to be as round as the moon, he bought a round mirror and took it home. But the moment his wife saw it, she stamped on the ground, fled back to her parents' house, and said to her mother: 'My husband has taken a concubine.' The mother-in-law looked into the mirror and said with a sigh: 'If only he had chosen a young woman; why did he take such a hideous old hag?' Later they brought the case before the District Judge, but when he saw the mirror he said: 'How dare you people, when you have a quarrel, dress up just like me? It's unbelievable.'

109. *Fool robs Fool*

A POOR foolish man by chance became possessed of one hundred dollars. He hunted everywhere in his house for a place to conceal the money, but could find nothing suitable. For a long time he was puzzled, but at last he decided that the wall offered the only possible hiding-place. He was afraid that even that was unsafe, because someone might see traces of it, but at last he had a brain-wave: he stuck up a notice on the wall at the place where the money was hidden: 'There is no money buried here,' it said. 'Passers-by needn't bother to break it open.'

The next morning the money was gone, stolen by some rascal in the neighbourhood. But the thief did not feel quite at ease, being afraid other people might notice something, and so as to avoid all suspicion, he also stuck a notice on his door: 'I, Chang San, am an honest man. I have not stolen Wang San's money.'

110. *The Fool meets his End*

A-HO'S son was called A-po. Although he was twenty years old, he sat the whole day doing nothing. His wife saw their neighbour earning money with his business, and filled with envy, she said to her husband: 'Why don't you do the same? Look! Our neighbour is making a fortune with his business.' 'Other people have money,' said A-po, 'but I have none and cannot open a business.'

His wife, therefore, gave him some money and said: 'If you buy something, buy things that don't go bad too quickly.' A-po rushed off to the market and bought a basket of mussels. On the way home he heard the mussels calling 'ho-ho,' and he thought it strange that they knew his father's name. Hardly able to believe it, he put the basket down, but the mussels continued to behave in the same way. This made him very angry and he flung them all into a stream by the roadside. It soon occurred to him, however, that he had paid good money for them and that he oughtn't to throw his money into a stream. Regretting his hasty action, he took off his clothes and searched in the water for the mussels, but in spite of searching for a long time he could only retrieve a few, and in the meantime a beggar saw him in the water and stole his clothes. A-po chased him, without success though.

Now he was naked, but he saw a crowd approaching

266

with a coffin, on top of which lay a red cloth. A-po ran up and pulled off the cloth to wrap himself up in, but the coffin-bearers gave chase, and as A-po stumbled they caught him and gave him a good beating. When he reached home his wife said to him: 'You did business to-day? Why have you come back empty-handed?' A-po told her what had happened to him, and she said: 'If you meet a funeral, you must say to the people, "My sympathy!" On no account must you steal the covering.'

Another day a neighbour celebrated a marriage, and A-po ran over and said: 'My sympathy.' The people beat him black and blue, and he had to creep home. His wife said: 'You must say "Congratulations!"' Two days later he saw a house on fire. Everyone was helping to put it out, but A-po stood by and roared with laughter. When the fire was out, the people beat A-po and he ran home. 'You must help people to quench the fire,' his wife said to him.

One day A-po saw a smith forging iron. The fire was very fierce, so A-po took a jug of water and put it out. The smith was furious and beat A-po, who rushed home and complained to his wife, who explained to him: 'You ought to have helped him do his work.'

The next day A-po saw two cowherds fighting. He ran up and thrashed them so hard that they wept. Their fathers came up, and seeing A-po laughing they beat him, until blood poured out of his nose. 'You ought to have separated them,' said his wife, 'and advised them not to fight.'

A few months later A-po saw two bulls fighting under a tree. He began to laugh, and pulling them apart he said, 'You must not beat each other,' but the bulls, being very excited, butted him, and tore out his stomach, so that he died.

III. *The Deluded Thief*

THERE was once a man who lived by catching frogs. He lived a wretched, lonely life without a wife or children, but he needed so little that he did not spend all his gains and gradually he collected a small store.

A thief heard that he had a little money and wanted to steal it from him. One night, when the fisherman was asleep, the thief bored a hole in the wall; but just as he had finished, he heard a voice from the bed say: 'Ah! There you are. I thought you would come soon.' The thief jumped back a few paces in terror and heard the voice continue: 'Now you are running away; I knew that also.' The thief wondered how the man could know everything when he was fast asleep, and hesitatingly walked away and sat down on a large stone to puzzle the matter out. Then he heard again: 'Now you are sitting on a large stone.' The thief realized that there was something wrong and scratched his head and stroked his chin in bewilderment, but again he heard the voice say: 'Now you are touching your head and stroking your throat.' The thief was overcome by terror, but as he ran away he heard further: 'Don't run away. Don't run away. Come to my hook.' The thief thought that he was being pursued and fled home as fast as he could run.

The next morning, on awaking, the fisherman saw the hole in the wall. He knew a thief must have been there, but when he looked through his things he could find nothing missing. It had so happened that he had dreamed of catching frogs during the night, and his experiences and words could be applied so well to a thief that the latter thought the fisherman knew everything and ran away.

112. *The Foolish Man*

THERE was once a rich man who was returning home after collecting money on his bills. On the way he met a very respectable-looking merchant. They entered into conversation, and the merchant said: 'You must be careful here, if you have any money with you, there are so many thieves.' 'I am not afraid of them,' said the rich man. 'No one knows where I hide my money.' 'In a few days I must bring a large sum of money with me on this road,' said the merchant. 'Can you advise me where to hide it?' 'My plan is very safe,' the rich man said. 'I stick the notes in the false heel of my shoe.' No sooner had his fellow-traveller heard this, than he appeared in his true colours and, pulling out a weapon, said calmly to the rich man: 'Now give me the money you have in the false heel.' The rich man now realized that he had unwisely given away his secret, and handed over the money to the clever robber.

113. *The Silly Son-in-Law buys Clothes*

HIS clothes were all torn, he said; he must buy some new ones. His wife told him to go and look for some himself, but he must be careful to have them of thick material which was not transparent. He mumbled 'Yes,' and went out.

In the market he could find nothing but transparent materials, and eventually he decided not to buy any clothes, but to have a suit made of thick yellow paper which no one could see through. The salesman asked him why he wanted such clothes—ordinarily they were used for clothing funeral figures—but the silly fellow said his wife had told him to get them; so the tradesman took the money and went off laughing to himself.

When the clothes were ready the simpleton put them on. Everyone stared at such a strange sight, but he strutted along as proud as a king. On his way home it began to rain, and there was no house and no tree to afford him shelter. He hurried along through the rain, but his running strained the paper clothes, which soon burst, and as he had neither umbrella nor straw hat, the rain soaked him through and the paper fell off piece by piece, so that by the time that he reached home he was quite naked. Everyone that saw him fled into their house, and his wife blushed with shame and was furious.

He accused her of giving him bad advice, and as he was such a fool she gave him back his old ragged clothes and wept the whole evening.

114. *A Fool marries his Daughter*

A FOOL one day arrived at the town gate with some bamboo poles, but the poles being long and the gate low, he could not get them through. At this moment a clever man went by, who found a solution of the problem. He climbed on to the wall and pulled the poles over. The fool passed through the gate, and in wonder at the solution he could not hide his admiration for the man. They found each other charming, and both having children they arranged a match between them. The fool returned home to tell his wife, who asked him how old the stranger's son was. 'Exactly two years old,' said the fool. The woman counted on her fingers and then said angrily: 'Our daughter is one, he is two, exactly twice as old. When, therefore, our daughter is twenty, he will be forty. She has got to marry an old man. That won't do at all!'

They began to quarrel, until their neighbour, an old mother of nearly thirty, came over and asked: 'What are you fighting about?' And the wife of the fool told her the whole story. Then the neighbour said: 'But next year your daughter is also two years old, and then she will be as old as the boy.'

115. *The Three Foolish Servants*

IN a village of several hundred inhabitants there lived a rich man, who was over fifty years old. He had three servants, who were named after their peculiarities. The first was called 'Precision'; he brought tea when guests came. The second was called 'Mean-well'; he made the purchases. The third was called 'Slowcoach'; he always took the child out to play.

One day 'Slowcoach' took the child out as usual, and they went to a lotus pond. The boy wanted to pick a lotus, but he slipped and fell into the water. Being a dullard by nature, 'Slowcoach' went slowly home and reported the matter; but meanwhile two hours had elapsed and the rich man's child was long drowned. The father was very angry with 'Slowcoach,' and kicked him out of the house.

He ordered 'Mean-well' to buy a little coffin for the child. 'Mean-well' ran off to the nearest undertaker and bought an enormous coffin, and then he bought a smaller one, which he put inside and carried them home, because it was cheaper to buy two coffins at once and his master later on could use the big one. But when his master saw them he asked angrily: 'I told you to buy a small one. Why have you bought this enormous thing? You stupid fool! Get out,' and he chucked him out. Two of the servants were gone now and only 'Precision' remained.

Some time after, the old man went round with 'Precision' to collect his rents. When he had collected everything he set off home.

On the way he arrived at a river, which he had to cross, but the ferry had just left and he had to wait for the next. 'Precision,' though, was impatient and said: 'I will carry you over, master,' and he took his master on his back and entered the water. The rich man said to him: 'The two others did everything wrong, so I had to throw them out. Now there is only you left. You are so good that I really must give you a wife on my return.' When 'Precision' heard that he was to receive a reward, from habit he stretched out his arms and made a bow down to the ground without thinking of anything else. But the rich man was let go; and, falling into the water, he was drowned.

116. *Hsü Wen-ch'ang shames a Girl*

ONE day a man came to visit Hsü Wen-ch'ang and complained that his daughter used to stand the whole day in the doorway in spite of all his protests. 'What can you suggest?' he asked Hsü, who told him that it would only cost three coppers to cure the girl of her bad habits. The father was enchanted and straightway gave Hsü the three coppers, with which he bought a copper's worth of bean-curd and two coppers' worth of soya-bean oil. He took these in his hands, and just as he was passing the girl's door he stuck out his belly and his trousers fell down. He called out to the girl: 'Hey! I have got both my hands full and I have lost my trousers. Please, young lady, tie them up again.' Blushing as red as a peony, the girl fled into the house and never again stood in the doorway.

(*Note.*—Hsü Wen-ch'ang was a famous painter and scholar of the Ming Dynasty. Now he is the hero of many tales.)

117. *Hsü revenges himself on a Monk*

ONE day Hsü went to a temple, the abbot of which enjoyed a great reputation. When he saw the ill-famed Hsü, he not only refused to receive him, but even began to curse him, and Hsü returned home in a rage.

Six months later, when his cousin's mother died, the family engaged the abbot and twenty monks to say masses. Hsü was also there, and at the sight of his enemy, the abbot, seated on a platform in the matshed, reading masses, he swore to have his revenge. In the evening he slipped into his aunt's room, where he washed his hands, covered them with paint and powder, and put on a few rings and bracelets. Then he returned to the platform where the mass was being read and made a hole in the mat just behind the abbot's chair. The abbot looked round and, seeing a girl's hand, he imagined that she wanted to flirt with him, and he felt for her with one hand, while he carried on the mass with the other. But Hsü caught hold of his hand, pulled it through the hole, and tied it fast to the leg of the platform; for the abbot, who was reading mass, could not defend himself.

Hsü now ran back, took off the rings, washed the paint and powder off his hands, and went back to the platform to talk with the monks. He handed a pipe to the abbot, who, with only one hand, naturally could not take it. 'What made you put your hand outside?' asked Hsü. 'Now I understand why my niece, who was looking on, suddenly came weeping into my room. You were trying to flirt with her,' and calling out to the people not to let the abbot go, he went into the town to make a complaint. The abbot was simply furious, but his only hope was to ask someone to arrange matters, and when many hours later Hsü returned, go-betweens arranged with him that the whole ten days' mass should be said free, to which arrangement the abbot had to give his consent.

118. *Hsü Wen-ch'ang has a Millstone carried*

ONE day a servant brought a letter to Hsü, and as he entered he said rudely: 'My master said you were to come quickly.' Hsü read the letter without saying a word and then replied: 'Your master also asks for the loan of a millstone. He said in the letter that you were to take it with you.' The servant had to do as he was told and lugged along the stone, until he was bathed in sweat. When his master saw him he asked in surprise what he was bringing. 'Hsü said you wanted to borrow this,' explained the servant. Then the man knew that his servant must have offended Hsü and he told him to carry the millstone back again.

119. *Hsü beats a Monk*

ONE day Hsü was going to town from the country, but it grew dark before he arrived and he looked for a temple to sleep in. When the monks saw that his clothes were not clean they treated him as their inferior, but when a rich merchant appeared they treated him with obsequious politeness. Hsü Wen-ch'ang became very cross and asked the monks: 'Why do you treat me badly and the other man well?' 'Don't you know the reason, my man?' replied the monk. 'The law of the Buddha says: "Bad treatment is good treatment and good treatment bad."' Hsü's only retort was to give the monk a few punches in the face. In a

274

fury the monk asked him what he meant by it. 'Don't you know, master monk?' he said. 'With us scholars beating is not beating and not beating is beating,' and the monk was at a loss for a reply.

120. *The Stone Mason falls into the Trap*

ONE day Hsü Wen-ch'ang was travelling on the same ship as two stone masons, who were saying to each other that Hsü was a rascal. This annoyed Hsü, who made up his mind to play a trick on them. As he was leaving the ship, he said to one of them: 'I have got a job for you. Can you do it?' The stone mason gladly went along with him, and they went on until they reached a house in front of which was lying a large stone. Pointing at it, Hsü said: 'Please break this stone up into four pieces. Do it quickly so that I can give you the money.' But while he was working, a man came out of the house and cursed him for ruining his stone, ending up by giving him a beating, and it was not until the mason had told him the whole story that he realized that the man who had employed him to break the stone was the famous Hsü Wen-ch'ang.

121. *Hsü Wen-ch'ang swindles Two Men of Ten Strings of Cash*

ONE day a schoolmaster threw an old pumpkin rind into his neighbour's yard just as Hsü was going by. Hsü ran up to him in a very excited state and said: 'Sir, something terrible has happened. The old excellency next door insists on lodging a complaint against you.' 'But why?' asked the schoolmaster. 'Because you hit and wounded his son with a pumpkin,' answered Hsü. 'What can I do? Please help me,' begged the poor man. Hsü thought the matter over and then said: 'Give him five strings blood money and he will be content,' and with a heavy heart the teacher handed over the money.

Then Hsü ran round to the old scholar and said: 'Excellency! Something terrible has happened. The teacher next door insists on complaining. He heard that you slandered him for throwing pumpkins into the courtyard.' 'Oh, dear! Oh, dear! What can I do?' said the old man. 'The only thing,' said Hsü, 'is to give him five strings of cash,' and the man handed over the money and agreed on a meeting day. Hsü also informed the schoolmaster, and on the appointed day they both met.

Hsü said: 'The money is now paid, we don't need to talk about the matter any more,' and since both thought he was talking of their money, Hsü got away with the ten strings.

122. *Hsü Wen-ch'ang kills his Wife*

A MONK once insulted Hsü, who swore to have his revenge. Near by the temple there lived a warrior, and Hsü bided his time until his daughter was standing at the window waiting for her father, and then relieved nature in front of her clad in the monk's clothes and hat. The girl complained to her father, who soon after quarrelled with the monk and killed him. The murdered man's soul now hated Hsü, who one night clearly saw his wife in the arms of a monk. He grasped his knife and slew them both; but looking more carefully, he saw that there was no monk and that he had killed his wife without reason. He was put in prison for many years for this crime.

123. *Ma Tanpi wins Two Pigs*

ONE day, one of Ma Tanpi's uncles, who lived a long way away from him, was in the best of spirits: he was putting the two little pigs he had raised into a basket to carry them off to market. His wife, who was gladly helping him, had just returned to the kitchen, and her husband was just leaving the pig-sty with the basket in his hand when Ma Tanpi went by, still only half awake.

The uncle was an amiable man; he was not very old and dearly loved a joke. His greatest pleasure was joking with nice little children, and when he saw the half-dressed Ma Tanpi coming, he could not resist having a joke with him. 'Heh! Ma Tanpi,' he called out gaily, 'where are you off to so early? Come here for a moment, I want to make a bet with you.' 'Bet ? What bet do you want?' answered Ma Tanpi, without stopping, and turned his head in a bored manner towards his uncle, rubbing his eyes with his hands, just as small children do when they wake.

'I will explain,' said the uncle, who was standing by the pigs. 'I am going to stay here on the steps and not move. If you can think of a way of enticing me down the steps, I will give you the two little pigs that are ready-packed for sale at the Southern Horse Market; the two grey-white piglets will then belong to you,' and he pointed at the two animals in the basket and looked at him temptingly.

'Really?' said Ma Tanpi, when he understood what his uncle was talking about, and swung round as quickly as if he had been stung. 'You wouldn't play a trick on a child, would you, Uncle?' 'Quick, Uncle, the pillars of the verandah are broken, the roof tiles will hit you. Come down quickly,' shouted Ma Tanpi with a very worried expression, just as a gust of wind blew the door shut with a bang, and he jumped off the steps himself.

'Ha! ha! you can't deceive me in such a silly manner,' laughed the uncle.

'Oh! what a pity. I have used up all my ideas and now I can't think of anything else. I was sure you would be deceived. Now I have lost the bet. Oh, dear!' Ma Tanpi plainly showed his deep disappointment and, taking his head in his hands, he shook it. 'Ah! Ha! Ma Tanpi. Don't imagine you can trick your old uncle so easily. But, truth to tell, no one could persuade me to leave these steps, so you need not be downhearted,' the old man said, full of pride and conceit.

'Of course, I couldn't entice you downstairs, Uncle. But if you came down, I could easily get you up again,' said Ma Tanpi casually. 'Could you really?' said the uncle, and came down the steps. 'Ha! Ha! Uncle. I managed to get you off the steps after all. Ha! Ha! that was my real trick. I am a lucky boy to go out in the morning and win two pigs.'

124. *Pao San buys Pots*

PAO was coming out of the town laden with goods, which he felt too tired to carry, though he could think of no means of getting rid of his burden. While he was wondering what to do, a pedlar came by with a great load of earthenware pots, and Pao San asked him: 'Are your goods for sale?' 'What do you suppose?' answered the man. 'Why should they not be for sale?' 'How much do you charge?' 'I ask so and so much per piece.' 'If I were to buy your goods,' answered Pao San, 'I would not buy them in your way; I would weigh them and buy them by the pound. Would that suit you?' The potter laughed to himself, and thinking that the man must be a little wrong in the head, he agreed at once. Pao San then said to him: 'Bring them to my house and we will talk about the matter there,'

278

and he added all his things to the man's load, who carried them home for him. When he arrived home, he carried the things into the house and then came out again and said to the potter: 'I should like to buy four ounces, please cut me off a few bits,' and the pedlar had to go away angry and disappointed.

125. *A Tale about Ma Ch'ao-chu*

MA, who was a native of a village in the district Weng-yüan, was a man who could weave spells very well. There are many stories about him, which I heard when I was a child, and now I will tell you one of them.

Ma Ch'ao-chu wanted to go every day to the theatre in the capital, but his native town was several hundred miles away. You would think it was impossible for him to go there and back in one day, but in spite of that he went every day and afterwards was able to repeat the texts he had heard in the theatre by heart, and tell his relations all that had happened without a single mistake. A friend of his was incredulous of his story, and one night he watched what he did. About the second watch, ten o'clock in the evening, Ma got up, dressed, and mounted a hobby-horse. Then he waved his whip, and the horse sprang into the air like a dragon or a tiger, and in a flash was out of sight. Just before dawn he returned, got off his horse, and lay down to sleep on his bed, but the hobby-horse stood in the room with thick beads of sweat running down its body. This really caused the friend to wonder at Ma's power.

The next evening, when Ma was leaving for the capital, the friend wanted to join him. 'But how can you come with me?' asked Ma. 'Can't you take me on your horse?' the friend implored Ma. 'Who told you I rode?' asked Ma. 'I saw you myself last night,' explained the friend. Seeing the friend knew his secret,

Ma feared that, if he refused him and his secret was betrayed, his power would be destroyed. He therefore agreed to take him, but warned him, saying: 'If you open your eyes to have a look you will be certain to fall off the horse.' He waited until the friend agreed to this condition, and then pulled him on to the horse and got on himself. 'Close your eyes,' he shouted, and they sped away like the wind. It was icy cold in the air and the friend clasped Ma in terror. About fifteen minutes later Ma shouted, 'Open your eyes,' and the horse stopped at once. When the friend looked round he found himself surrounded by blazing lights in the middle of the busy town of Canton with its innumerable houses. Then he went through a street, where he marvelled at the beautiful things and teeming life, to the theatre. There he saw and heard things such as he had never seen or heard before, and his delight was boundless. At the end of the night they got on to the hobby-horse again to return home; but this time the friend was more courageous, and, being very curious, he just opened one eye. But before he knew it he fell off the horse, and turning round and round in the air, he finally landed in a far-away district where he was almost banged to bits. He had to beg his way home, which took him more than a month.

126. *The Unsuccessful Suicide*

THERE was once a ten-year-old child. He had been through the preparatory school, but his father did not have enough money to send him to the middle school; instead he decided to apprentice him to a shop. He made many enquiries and eventually sent him to a tea-house to learn the entertainment trade.

The boy, however, was a greedy and badly behaved

child. He was delighted to find the tea-house filled with cakes and pastries that could be eaten, and every day he took some away with him, until the proprietor caught him in the act and threw him out. His father was furious when his son came home, and after punishing him severely, he looked round for another opening. He decided at last to send him to a grocery store; but the son had not reformed, and when he saw the fruit in the shop he ate as much as he could, until after ten days he was again dismissed. Seeing how incorrigible his son was, the father made arrangements to send him as apprentice to a chemist, because there would be nothing for him to eat in it. The son was very relieved when he discovered there was nothing edible in the chemist shop, and nothing occurred for over six months.

On the day of the Mid Autumn Festival the proprietor bought a duck and two bottles of wine. One bottle was red and the other white. Just as the duck was nicely roasted a man appeared and invited him to visit a sick man; for in addition to his chemist business he was also a doctor. Fearing, though, that his pupil would eat the duck and drink the wine, he said to him: 'I must now visit one of my patients. Don't dare touch this duck or I will kill you'; then he pointed to the bottles of wine and added: 'These bottles don't contain wine, but red and white poison. Be careful not to drink any because you would die of it.'

The boy knew that his master had lied to him, and at once gobbled up the duck and swallowed the wine. His master was furious when he came back and saw what he had done, but the boy met him with a long face and said: 'I had to go out for a moment and the cat ate the duck. I was very frightened because you had sworn to kill me if I did it. I thought it therefore better to take my own life, and drank the bottle of white poison, but finding I did not die, I swallowed the red one as well. I don't know why I am not dead yet; perhaps the

poison was too weak.' The master could not scold him,
but had to laugh in spite of his anger.

127. *The Doctor in Hell*

A THIEF, a rake, and a doctor were once seized by
Oxhead and Horseface at the same moment and carried
down to appear before the seat of judgment in the
Underworld. Yen-lo-wang first called up the thief,
whom he asked: 'What did you do in the world?'
The thief answered: 'When I saw that people who had
put out their clothes to dry on a pole had not taken them
in by sunset, I removed them for them.' 'That was a
good deed. I will give you a few more years of life as
a reward,' said the Judge.

Then the Judge sent for the rake and asked him:
'What did you do in the Upper World?' And the rake
replied: 'When I saw that by midnight many people
had found no place to sleep I let them come into my
house.' 'That is still better. You also may live a few
more years on Earth,' rejoined Yen-lo-wang.

Meanwhile the doctor was thinking to himself: 'If
deeds like those of the thief and the rake are considered
praiseworthy here, mine are far better,' and he went
before Yen-lo-wang, who asked him: 'What did you do
on Earth?' The doctor replied: 'If I saw anyone ill
or in pain I helped them and they were all cured.' When
he heard this, Yen-lo-wang banged his fist on the table
and shouted angrily: 'Now I know why no souls have
appeared before me in the last few days. You held
them all up,' and without further delay he ordered
Oxhead and Horseface to cast him into the Seventeenth
Hell. The poor doctor could scarcely bear the torment
and screamed ceaselessly, but suddenly he heard someone
crying out in the next Hell. Greatly surprised, he

282

thought to himself: 'I have suffered such injustice, is there really someone worse treated than I?' And he called out: 'Brother, excuse my asking, but why are you sitting in the Eighteenth Hell?' The reply came: 'I was a teacher in the Upper World and the King of Hell accused me of teaching mankind false learning, and as punishment for corrupting them I was thrown into Hell.'

128. *An Ideal Marriage*

THERE was once a hunchback, who was not yet married although he had reached the proper age; and there was also a girl with a harelip, who was sixteen years old and not yet engaged. The go-betweens of the two parties met together and took great trouble to arrange a match, which would only succeed if neither knew of the other's failings. One of them, therefore, said to the man: 'You see, it isn't easy to find a bride for a hunchback. I have been fortunate enough to discover one, but you must not talk about the matter.' Then the other said to the girl: 'You see, it isn't easy to find a husband for a girl with a harelip. I have found one, but you must not talk about it,' and both parties agreed to be silent.

But the go-betweens had still another plan to prevent quarrels and complaints in the future. They gave the two parties a lecture and said: 'Marriage is a serious matter; it is best if the two partners meet once before, and then there can be no heartbreak later.' One man told the girl to look at her bridegroom through a crack in the wall and the other told the hunchback to take a cauldron on his back and walk past outside. As he went by, the go-between said to the girl, 'It's the one carrying the cauldron' (play on words: Lo Kuo, hunchback, and Lo Kuo, carry cauldron), and another said to the man,

283

pointing to the crack in the wall, 'It's the one with the crack, with the crack' (play on Huo Tzu, harelip, and Huo Tzu, crack in wall). The couple were quite contented at each other's appearance and arranged the marriage at once. But on the evening after the ceremony the hunchback saw for the first time that his wife had a harelip and he was very angry; and his wife nearly fainted when she saw that her husband had a humpback. They both rushed off to complain to the go-betweens, but one excused himself, saying: 'Didn't I tell you that she had a harelip? I never tried to deceive you,' and the other said: 'I told you he had a humpback, and now you see he has one,' and the couple had nothing further to say. But the go-betweens said to each other: 'They were destined by Heaven to marry; the matter had nothing to do with us.'

129. *The Greedy Schoolmaster*

IN the village of Eastbrook there was a greedy scholar who kept a private school with thirty or forty pupils. At first the children did not know that he was so grasping; but as he always stole their lunch, they took good care when they brought food with them to hide it well, so that the teacher could not see it.

On the seventeenth day of the eighth month, one pupil brought a large mooncake from home—the kind that is eaten at the Mid Autumn Festival, on August 15th—but not wanting the teacher to see it, he went in by the back door. Unfortunately, the teacher happened to be standing at the back door, and when he saw the boy was very agitated, he knew that he had something to conceal. Realizing that the boy must have a cake hidden in his case, he formed a plan to get it out of him. 'Come into my room,' he said, 'I will tell you a story,' and the

284

boy, being very fond of stories, willingly went with him. Then the teacher said: 'What have you got in your case?' 'Nothing—nothing—books,' said the boy, and trembled so violently that the teacher knew he must have a mooncake. His mouth began to water, and he said happily: 'Put your mooncake on the table. When I have finished the story, you can take it away again.'

Then he took a knife out of his pocket and cut the cake into six pieces. 'I will now tell you the tale of how Ch'in Shih-huang-ti destroyed the six kingdoms,' he said. 'The six pieces of cake are the six kingdoms, and my mouth is the Emperor Shih-huang-ti. First he destroyed the Han Kingdom,' and so saying, he shoved the first bit of cake into his mouth and gobbled it up, and then taking all the other bits, he continued: 'After the destruction of Han, the other five states Chao, Wei, Ch'u, Yen, Chi were all destroyed,' and in telling this story of Ch'in Shih-huang-ti he ate up the whole cake.

But he noticed some crumbs still lying on the table, and these he explained were the Huns. 'After Shih-huang-ti had destroyed the six kingdoms,' he said, 'North China was continually attacked by the Huns. The Emperor sent out General Meng T'ien with 100,000 soldiers, who swept them all away,' and using his fingers as soldiers, he swept the crumbs off the table and crammed them into his mouth: 'After Meng T'ien had dispersed the Huns, and Shih-huang-ti destroyed the six Kingdoms, the Empire was united. Finish!' 'But where is my cake?' asked the pupil. 'That was destroyed by Ch'in Shih-huang-ti,' explained the teacher.

130. *The Clever Thief*

THERE was once an old man who, although not exactly a millionaire, was at any rate comfortably off. He had one son, who was as worthless as he could be.

The Clever Thief

He sat about the whole day drinking tea and wine, and was always to be found at the places of amusement. His chief fault, though, was this: he was a thief. If he made any money, it went in a moment, and in the night he went to the houses of the rich and stole clothes and jewellery, which he sold for money to spend. At first people could not believe that the son of such a rich man could be a thief, but so many cases occurred that they no longer had any doubts.

His father scolded him, saying: 'Why do you never do anything right? Why do you want to be a thief?' 'I can do nothing about it,' answered the son, 'I was born a thief. If I don't steal anything for some time, I feel quite unwell. Then I must go out and steal, and apart from having some money to spend, I feel very much better.' The father was in despair when his son paid no attention to his advice, and he wondered if it would be the wisest course to beat him to death. It seemed, however, too cruel to kill his only son, and he went off to a temple to ask the advice of an old monk. This monk was a clever man, and he suggested that the son should steal salt vegetables from the temple. If he came, he would be caught, taken to the police station, and punished for his misdeeds. They could ask the police to keep him in prison for several months, which would perhaps make him mend his ways.

The father went home and said to his son: 'I know that you are a clever thief. Please steal the salt vegetables from the temple this evening.' The son agreed at once and went to the temple, but on climbing on to the roof he saw four bad monks standing by the vegetable pot with sticks in their hands. The thief then went into the kitchen and shook the frame in which the crockery hung to create a diversion. Hearing the clatter, and thinking that the thief wanted to steal the crockery, the monks rushed into the kitchen to catch him. But he slipped away, picked up the salt vegetables out of the pot, and ran home long before the monks discovered what had happened.

The father was horrified when his son brought back the spoil, and the next day he returned to the monk, who said to him: 'Yesterday, the novices were careless and let him get away. Tell him to steal the staff out of my hand to-day and we will certainly catch him.' The father went home and told this to his son, who said: 'That's quite easy. I am always stealing sticks.' Then he went off, climbed on to the temple roof, and looked through the window, where he saw the old monk sitting on the edge of the bed with the staff in his hand ready to lash out at the slightest sound. The thief climbed down again and scratched a hole in the wall behind the bed. Then he went to the outer door and called out: 'Monk, old Monk! You are requested to send six monks to celebrate mass at the Wang house.' The monk smelt business when he heard this and, dropping his staff, he went to open the gate. But he went slowly and the thief quickly, so that when he opened the door there was no one to be seen. Realizing that it was a trick of the thief, he hurried back to his room, but the rascal had already climbed through the hole and stolen the staff.

The father nearly fainted when he saw the staff, and the next day he went again to the old monk, who was crestfallen at the failure of his plans. 'This evening make him steal me; then I am certain to get a chance of capturing him,' he said. The father went home and told this to his son, who made no objection, but waited till it was dark. Then he climbed on to the roof and looked through the window, where he saw the monk again sitting on his bed. He called out again at the outer door: 'Monk, old monk! You are requested to send six monks to say mass at the Wang house,' and then he quickly ran back to the hole in the wall, which had not yet been repaired. When the monk heard the noise at the outer door, he knew that it was another of the rascal's plans, and he thought to himself: 'He is certainly waiting now by the hole. If I climb out, I will be able to catch him,' and he scrambled through the wall. But outside, the thief was holding a sack in front of the hole, and the monk dropped straight into it and was carried home by the thief.

The father was flabbergasted when his son arrived with the monk in a sack, and the two old men stood gaping at each other not knowing what to say or do.

1 3 1. *The Calendar-seller and his Wife*

A mixed-goods tradesman had daily losses, and after selling his stock he had no money left to buy new ones, and there was nothing left but to shut up his shop. He was quite desperate, until suddenly his wife produced any number of goods, with which he began a prosperous new business. This put him in the best of humours, and he asked his wife where she had got the things from. 'One after the other I took your things away and stored them,' she said. All the neighbours praised the clever wife.

Next door lived a calendar-seller, whose business went from bad to worse, until he decided to retire. He also had a wife, who took the wife of the mixed-goods man as a pattern. Every year she removed a few calendars. These she now produced, but who could buy old calendars?

1 3 2. *Chao K'uang-yin (No. 1)*

IN his youth Chao K'uang-yin (who later became the first Emperor of the Sung Dynasty) was good for nothing and the terror of his village. One year there was a terrible drought and all the crops were burnt up. The people beseeched the gods to send them rain, but not even a drop of dew appeared.

Chao was a passionate gambler. If he won, he went off with the money; if he lost, he never paid a cent. In this way he gained his living, but naturally during the drought no one wanted to gamble, and he was in a bad way. He became more and more quick-tempered and depressed, but one evening a new plan occurred to him, which, if successful, would enable him to live a little longer. He went to the headman of the village and said: 'If you give me one hundred strings of cash, I will beg the gods to send rain.' The headman was a little sceptical of his being able to do this, but he called together the inhabitants and consulted them as to whether he should pay the money or not. 'What do you need for the sacrifice?' he asked Chao K'uang-yin. 'Nothing really,' he replied, 'just make a circle of fire, and put a table in the middle for me to stand on.' The village elders and the peasants were surprised at this request, but in view of the desperate plight that the village would be in if no rain fell, they agreed to provide the things. When the fire was burning, Chao got on to the table and called out: 'When is rain coming?' He himself never expected anything to happen, but, having a golden tongue and jade words, the Wind Count and the Rain Master, without hesitating, sent a storm of rain at once.

Chao K'uang-yin (No. 2)

ONCE, in the vicinity of Mount Hua Shan, Chao saw two Taoists playing chess. He sighed when he saw one of them make a false move, and afterwards the same man asked him whether he played. Chao asked: 'What is your noble name?' 'Lü,' answered the man. Chao saw that he was only a moderate player and wanted to display his prowess and win. Mr. Lü agreed and said: 'If I lose, I will give you ten thousand ounces of silver.' 'Good; if I lose, I will give you this mountain,' said Chao, pointing at Hua Shan. Chao, however, lost and Lü retired into the mountain to perfect himself. They say that Mount Hua Shan remains tax-free to this day because it was ceded to the Taoist Lü. And do you know who this Lü was? He was Lü Tung-pin of the eight Immortals.

133. *Chu Yuan-chang*

CHU YUAN-CHANG was once cowherd for a rich man who treated him very well. He had a maid-servant who once, when Chu was asleep, saw a gold snake and a shining bright light come out of his nose and then disappear again. She knew by this time that he was no ordinary man, but was destined to gain high honours, and she begged Chu to make her his wife. For some reason Chu found her agreeable and promised secretly to marry her. Later, when Chu was a monk, all the other monks loved him for his diligence. On the first and fifteenth of every month the temple was swept out by the young monks, and Chu swept it particularly clean without help from anyone else. His companions found this suspicious, and next time that it was his turn to do the sweeping several monks followed him and hid themselves to see what he did. They saw him go into the temple, shut the door, and say to the gods with a growl, 'Hurry up and come down'; and all the big and little gods stepped down to the floor, and Chu got on to the altars and without any trouble brushed away the dirt. When he had finished he told the gods to climb up again, and they all returned to their places. All the monks were very surprised and realized that he had a golden tongue and jade words and that he would become Emperor. Later, when rebellions broke out, he became a soldier and eventually gained the whole empire.

134. *Drinking Poems*

SU TUNG-P'O, Huang Shangku, and Foyin were close friends. It is true that Foyin was a monk, but he was also a glutton. One day Su Tung-p'o and Huang Shangku arranged to dine together on a boat without Foyin. Foyin, however, discovered their plan and hid in the boat to wait for them. They soon arrived with some wine, and after rowing about for a bit, they sat down to the repast. They had only been eating for a short while when Su Tung-p'o said: 'It is meaningless to eat like this. We must compose some poems,' and with Huang's approval, he stated the rules: 'In the first line the word "rend" must be used; in the second line the word "appear," and in the third and fourth the word "Yes."' Huang made the first verse:

> The scurrying clouds are rent,
> The gleaming moon appears.
> Yes ! Where is the sky ?
> Yes! Where is the sky ?

Then they drank a cup of wine and Su Tung-p'o recited:

> The twining weeds are rent,
> The darting fishes appear.
> Yes! They are in their element.
> Yes! They are in their element.

At this, Foyin could no longer bear his confinement and called out:

> The planks of the ship are rent,
> The Foyin appears.
> Yes! How can man be hidden!
> Yes! How can man be hidden!

And then he came out and the wine-cups passed round gaily.

135. *The Vainglorious Poets*

THERE were once two men living in a distant mountain village, in which there were no educated people; they, therefore, became very conceited about their talents, as the proverb says: 'If there is no tiger in the mountains, the ape becomes king.' They were together the whole day, and being the same age, they swore blood brother-hood. One day, Chia said boastingly to Yi: 'There is no one in the village that can compare with us in learning. Let us go into the world and compete with Su Tung-p'o.' Yi agreed at once: 'A brilliant suggestion,' he said. 'Let's set off without delay and match our poetry with Su Tung-p'o's.' They wandered along arm in arm, alternately praising each other's genius, and boasting of their own, until they saw a tree, about which they decided to compose a poem to display their talents. Chia said: 'From far I see a tree,' and Yi continued: 'From near I see two trunks,' and on their arrival at the tree they found that it really did have two trunks. Full of joy and pride, they marvelled at their own brilliance, and they went on, until they saw a white goose in a field. Chia was again inspired and declaimed: 'By the roadside stood a goose,' and Yi added: 'With a long neck; it eats much corn.' And seizing hold of

292

the bird, they found that its neck was really full of corn. Weeping with delight, Chia said: 'Brother! In antiquity Yen Hui's great talents prevented his growing old; he died at thirty-two. We are already such supreme poets that I fear we will also die young. The thought of it makes me weep.' Yi wiped away his tears and said: 'I was just thinking the same.' And becoming more and more depressed at the idea of their early demise, they began to howl out loud. A manure-carrier passed by at this moment and asked in astonishment what they were weeping about. The two friends told him what marvellous poems they could compose, and how they wanted to compete with Su Tung-p'o, and about the tree and the goose, and finally that they were afraid of dying young. The manure-carrier burst out laughing at this: 'I can compose casual verses ten times better than yours. You needn't worry about dying young; I am more likely to die of laughing.' The two poets said angrily: 'If you are so good, continue our poem about the goose.' Without a moment's hesitation, the manure-carrier said: 'Plum blossom falls bit by bit—into the water, and on the wind it floats away.' Chia and Yi were very ashamed and did not know what to do, but the manure-carrier admonished them, saying: 'Formerly I was as conceited as you about my poems and I competed with Su Tung-p'o; but I lost, and was condemned to carry manure buckets for three years. If you go on and match yourselves with the immortal poet, it is quite possible that he will force you to eat dung.' The two friends returned home in a chastened mood and never dared to boast again.

136. *The 15th of January*

IN the last years of the Mongol Dynasty the whole country was filled with unrest and rebellion, and all true patriots wanted to drive out the usurpers. There were signs that soldiers were being collected, but at this time, when loyalty and devotion to the ruler were so deeply engrained in the people, these movements received little popular support, and, therefore, never had much success.

Chu Yuan-chang, the future Emperor, also failed to make much headway to begin with. But at that time there was an outbreak of plague, in which innumerable people died, and against which no medicine or charm was effective. At last Chu managed to discover a remedy, and he went round selling it, dressed up as a Taoist, and everyone that bought it was cured, which spread his fame over the whole country. Shortly afterwards, he went round again selling medicine, and when people asked him why he sold medicine when no one was ill, he replied: 'Soon there will be another plague, perhaps even worse than last time,' which frightened people so much that they bought up all he had. Chu told them that the medicine was not the same as last time; they must open it and drink it on the 15th of January, before the illness broke out. Naturally, the people did as they were told, because they believed in him as in a god, and when he had sold all his medicine he returned to his troops.

The 15th of January arrived, and everyone that had bought the medicine opened the packet, but instead of medicine they found a red slip with the words: 'This evening, January 15th, the Mongols must be driven out. You must gather together and exterminate them.' Everyone hated the cruel Mongols, and now scales fell from their eyes and they seized their weapons. Chu Yuan-chang had his troops in readiness, he joined with the people, and together they drove out the Mongols.

137. *Women*

AFTER he was married, Chang the Third no longer wanted to go to work. He sat at home the whole day and played with his wife. He gazed endlessly at her beautiful face, and the longer he looked the less he wanted to go out. Finally he gave up his job and remained night and day with his wife. He went on in this way for six months, and then for a year; but even the largest fortune is soon exhausted if one does nothing, and Chang had merely lived on his earnings. In two years all his wife's jewels, the chairs, the tables, the linen, the clothes, in fact everything they had, was pawned or sold, and they were left without a penny.

His wife was really unusually beautiful, but she thought to herself: 'Since his marriage my husband has never left the house. Day and night he sits around doing nothing but eat. In a short while we shall no longer have the wherewithal to live.' So she upbraided him, saying: 'You really can't stay at home all day. All men must go to work.' But Chang saw her beauty, and he thought anxiously: 'If I went out another man could come and make love to her.' And instead of listening to her words he remained at home, preferring to eat the most miserable food.

But one day their poverty became unbearable. They could no longer live if he did not work. Finally, one morning, he said good-bye to his wife and decided to go to a village. On his way he met a fine-looking man of about fifty years, who said to him: 'Which is the way to such and such a village?' Chang answered: 'I am going there myself, so we can go together.' During their walk Chang told the stranger his story: 'I am so unhappy at leaving my wife,' he said. 'But I must look for work to enable us to live.' The stranger replied: 'The simplest thing is to bottle up your wife. I will

give you the bottle, and every day, when you leave, you
will only need to look at your wife and blow into the
bottle, and she will vanish inside at once. As you can
always take it with you, you will never lose your wife.
I must now take another road, so farewell.' Then he
handed Chang a large three-inch bottle from his bag
and disappeared. Chang dropped the bottle into his
bag, noting what the man had said, and set off gaily
for the village. The next day he tried the gift. As
his wife was combing her hair before the mirror he
secretly blew into the bottle. The woman saw reflected
how her husband blew into a bottle, but then she lost
consciousness and woke up to find herself inside the
bottle. Chang put the bottle in his pocket and went
off to his work in the village. He was quite contented,
for now no other man could flirt with his wife. In the
evening he tipped up the bottle and his beautiful wife
stood before him as before.

One day, however, he was forced to leave his wife at
home to do the washing. He begged her not to leave
the house when the washing was finished, and then set
off to the village, forgetting to take the bottle with him.

After her husband's departure the wife went down to
the river to wash the clothes. While she was rinsing
a shirt she suddenly felt a long, hard thing between her
fingers. She took it out and looked at it carefully. 'It's
a bottle,' she said to herself. 'Every morning my
husband blows into it and I vanish inside. Why has he
forgotten it to-day?' While she was pondering over
the matter, a handsome young man passed by on the
other bank. She looked up at him, and without thinking
what she was doing blew into the bottle, whereupon the
young man disappeared. When she had finished the
washing she replaced the bottle in her husband's clothes.

When the man arrived home he immediately asked
for the bottle he had left behind, and his wife handed
it to him without a word. The next day when he went

out he blew into the bottle as usual, and his wife disappeared, and again he flattered himself that she was safe from the caresses of other men inside the bottle.

That evening on his return he tipped up the bottle, but this time two people appeared, his wife and a handsome young man. He was very surprised and said to himself: 'How strange! I thought my wife was quite safe shut up in the bottle, but now she has got a man with her! How odd it is! And how impossible it is to keep a beautiful wife to oneself.'

NOTES

1. From: Shan-tung min-chien chuan-shuo, vol. i. pp. 37-60. Provenience: Prov. Shantung, Chang-ch'iu.

2. From: Lin Lan: San-ko yüan-wang, pp. 70-80.   Provenience: Prov. Kuangtung, P'an-yü.

3. From: Min-su, No. 15, pp. 42-48. Provenience: Prov. Kuang-tung, Weng-yüan.

4. From: Sun Chia-hsün: Wa-wa-shih, pp. 107-119. Provenience: Kiangsu, Kuan-yün.

5. From: Lin Lan: Huan-hsin-hou, pp. 94-97. Provenience: Central China.

6. From: Lin Lan: San-ko yüan-wang, pp. 4-10. Provenience: Chêkiang, Nan-t'ien.

7. From: Sun Chia-hsün: Wa-wa-shih, p. 135. Provenience: Kiangsu, Kuan-yün.

8. From: Lin Lan: Yün-chung-ti mu-ch'in, pp. 14-20. Provenience: Kiangsu, Kuan-yün.

9. From: Lin Lan: Kui-ko-ko, pp. 1-13. Provenience: Central China.

10. From: Lin Lan: Huan-hsin-hou, p. 53. Provenience: Kiangsu, Kuan-yün.

11. From: Lin Lan: Tung-hsien mai-lei, pp. 46-48. Provenience: Kuangtung, Weng-yüan.

12. From: Sun Chia-hsün: Wa-wa-shih, pp. 149-159. Provenience: Kiangsu, Kuan-yün.

13. From: Min-su, No. 31, pp. 7-12. Provenience: Kuangtung.

14. From: Min-chien, vol. ii. Nos. 10-11, pp. 332-334. Provenience: Chêkiang, Chü-hsien.

15. From: Lin Lan: Huan-hsin-hou, pp. 39-43. Provenience: Southern China?

16. From: Lin Lan: Sha-lung, pp. 80-81. Provenience: Fukien, Ch'üan-chou.

17. From: Lin Lan: Huan-hsin-hou, pp. 49-52. Provenience: Central China.

18. From: Lin Lan: Chin-t'ien-chi, pp. 1-10. Provenience: Chêkiang, Hang-chou.

19. From: Tung-hsien mai-lei, pp. 51-53. Provenience: Kuangtung, Hai-men.

20. From: Lin Lan: Chin-t'ien-chi, pp. 65-69. Provenience: Chêkiang, P'u-chiang.

21. From: Min-chien, vol. i. No. 12, pp. 100-103. Provenience: Chêkiang, Shao-hsing.

Notes

No.

22. From: Min-chien, vol. ii. No. 6, pp. 1-5. Provenience: Chêkiang, Hsiao-shan.

23. From: Lin Lan: Huan-hsin-hou, pp. 9-12. Provenience: uncertain.

24. From: Lin Lan: Tu-chiao hai-tse, pp. 61-65. Provenience: Kiangsu, Kuan-yün.

25. From: Lin Lan: Kui-ko-ko, pp. 18-21. Provenience: Central China.

26. From: Lin Lan: Kui-ko-ko, pp. 31-33. Provenience: Central China.

27. From: Lin Lan: Chin-t'ien-chi, pp. 83-95. Provenience: Central China.

28. From: Lin Lan: Sha-lung, pp. 60-67. Provenience: Fukien, Ch'üan-chou.

29. From: Lin Lan: Sha-lung, pp. 100-105. Provenience: Kuang-tung, Chao-ch'ing.

30. From: Min-chien, vol. i. No. 4, pp. 46-51. Provenience: Chêkiang, Hang-chou.

31. From: Collection of Mr. Ts'ao Sung-yeh, vol. vi. pp. 37*b*-39*b* of his manuscript, now in the Ethnogr. Mus., Berlin. Provenience: Chêkiang, Yung-k'ang.

32. From: Lin Lan: Hui-ta-wang, pp. 97-100. Provenience: Chêkiang, Hsin-shih.

33. From: Lin Lan: Tung-hsien mai-lei, pp. 92-95. Provenience: uncertain.

34. From: Lin Lan: Hui-ta-wang, pp. 105-117. Provenience: Kiangsu, Sung-chiang.

35. From: Lin Lan: Chin-t'ien-chi, pp. 99-107. Provenience: Kiangsu, Ju'kao.

36. From: Min-chien, vol. i. No. 10, pp. 45-49. Provenience: Kuangtung.

37. From: Lin Lan: San-ko yüan-wang, pp. 41-46. Provenience: Chêkiang, Chin-hua.

38. From: Lin Lan: Ts'ai-hua-lang, pp. 36-40. Provenience: Chêkiang, Feng-hua.

39. From: Lin Lan: Ts'ai-hua-lang, pp. 31-35. Provenience: Chêkiang, Feng-hua.

40. From: Lin Lan: San-chiang-chün, pp. 63-64. Provenience: Chêkiang.

41. From: Lin Lan: San-chiang-chün, pp. 98-102. Provenience: Central China.

42. From: Lin Lan: San-chiang-chün, pp. 106-108. Provenience: Central China.

43. From: Lin Lan: Chin-t'ien-chi, pp. 45-51. Provenience: Kuangtung, San-yüan.

44. From: Lin Lan: San-ko yüan-wang, pp. 115-116. Provenience: Chêkiang, Hsiang-shan.

300

No.

45. From: Ch'ing-shui: T'ai-yang ho yüeh-liang, pp. 33-36. Provenience: Kuangtung, Weng-yüan.
46. From: Lin Lan: Sha-lung, p. 99. Provenience: Fukien, Changchou.
47. From: Lin Lan: Min-chien chuan-shuo, vol. ii. pp. 39-43. Provenience: Central China?
48. From: Liu Ta-po: Ku-shih-ti tan-tse, pp. 113-115. Provenience: Chêkiang, Shao-hsing.
49. From: Lin Lan: Hui-ta-wang, pp. 31-35. Provenience: Central China.
50. From: Lin Lan: Min-chien chuan-shuo, vol. i. pp. 97-100. Provenience: uncertain.
51. From: Lin Lan: Lü Tung-pin-ti ku-shih, pp. 84-88. Provenience: uncertain.
52. From: Lin Lan: Niao-ti ku-shih, pp. 82-87. Provenience: Hupei, Wu-ch'ang.
53. From: Shan-tung min-chien chuan-shuo, vol. i. pp. 24-25. Provenience: Shantung, Yang-hsin.
54. From: Lin Lan: Yün-chung-ti mu-ch'in, pp. 71-73. Provenience: uncertain.
55. From: Lin Lan: Tu-chiao hai-tse, pp. 92-96. Provenience: Kiangsu, Kuan-yün.
56. From: Min-su, No. 13/14, pp. 8-9. Provenience: Fukien, Ching-ting.
57. From: Lin Lan: Min-chien chuan-shuo, vol. ii. pp. 95-97. Provenience: An-hui, Hsüan-ch'eng.
58. From: Lin Lan: Min-chien chuan-shuo, vol. i. pp. 94-96. Provenience: Kiangsu, K'un-ming.
59. From: Collection of Mr. Ts'ao Sung-yeh, vol. ii. Provenience: Chêkiang, T'ang-ch'i.
60. From: Lin Lan: Tu-chiao hai-tse, pp. 74-78. Provenience: Kiangsu, Kuan-yün.
61. From: Lin Lan: Min-chien chuan-shuo, vol. ii, pp. 44-52. Provenience: Central China.
62. From: Min-chien, vol. ii. No. 3, pp. 53-58. Provenience: Chêkiang, Hsiao-shan.
63. From: Min-chien, vol. ii. No. 1, pp. 33-34. Provenience: Kuangtung, Chieh-yang.
64. From: Min-chien, vol. i. No. 6, pp. 4-11. Provenience: Chêkiang, Hang-chou.
65. From: Lin Lan: Chin-t'ien-chi, pp. 53-57. Provenience: Kuangtung, Ch'ao-chou.
66. From: Lin Lan: Huan-hsin-hou, pp. 78-82. Provenience: Central China.
67. From: Lin Lan: Chin-t'ien-chi, pp. 71-74. Provenience: Chêkiang, P'u-chiang.

No.

68. From: Lin Lan: Chin-t'ien-chi, pp. 19-31. Provenience: Kiang-su, Yün-t'ai-shan.

69. From: Lin Lan: Kua-wang, pp. 59-61. Provenience: un-certain.

70. From: Lin Lan: Huan-hsin-hou, pp. 4-8. Provenience: Southern China?

71. From: Ch'ing-shui: T'ai-yang ho yüeh-liang, pp. 21-23. Pro-venience: Kuangtung.

72. From: Ch'ing-shui: T'ai-yang ho yüeh-liang, pp. 17-18. Pro-venience: Kuangtung, Weng-yüan.

73. From: Lin Lan: Huan-hsin-hou, pp. 45-48. Provenience: Chêkiang, Feng-hua.

74. From: Ch'ing-shui: Hai-lung-wang-ti nü-erh, pp. 73-74. Pro-venience: Kuangtung, Weng-yüan.

75. From: Min-su, No. 78, p. 65. Provenience: Fukien, Fu-chou.

76. From: Ch'ing-shui: Hai-lung-wang-ti nü-erh, pp. 75-78. Pro-venience: Kuangtung, Weng-yüan.

77. From: id., pp. 84-85. Provenience: Kuangtung, Weng-yüan.

78. From: Lin Lan: Min-chien chuan-shuo, vol. ii. pp. 25-26. Provenience: Shantung, Ch'ü-fou.

79. From: Lin Lan: Min-chien chuan-shuo, vol. ii. pp. 70-71. Provenience: Central China.

80. From: Lin Lan: Kui-ko-ko, pp. 38-45. Provenience: Kiangsu, Kuan-yün.

81. From: Lin Lan: Lü Tung-pin-ti ku-shih, pp. 80-83. Provenience: uncertain.

82. From: Min-su, No. 11/12, pp. 48-51. Provenience: Kiangsu, Nanking?

83. From: Lin Lan: Min-chien chuan-shuo, vol. ii. pp. 90-92. Provenience: Central China?

84. From: Wu Ts'ao-ting: Ch'üan-chou min-chien chuan-shuo, vol. i. pp. 24-29. Provenience: Fukien, Ch'üan-chou.

85. From: Wu Ts'ao-ting: Ch'üan-chou min-chien chuan-shuo, vol. iii. pp. 1-8. Provenience: Fukien, Ch'üan-chou.

86. From: Collection of Mr. Ts'ao Sung-yeh, vol. vi. pp. 30-31. Provenience: Chêkiang, I-wu.

87. From: Min-chien, vol. ii. No. 7, pp. 5-7. Provenience: Chêkiang, Shao-hsing.

88. From: Lin Lan: Sha-lung, pp. 36-39. Provenience: Kuangtung, Hui-chou.

89. From: Min-su, No. 75, p. 39. Provenience: Chêkiang, Shao-hsing.

90. From: Lin Lan: Min-chien chuan-shuo, vol. i. pp. 7-8. Pro-venience: Hopei, An-p'ing.

91. From: Lin Lan: Min-chien chuan-shuo, vol. i. pp. 43-44. Provenience: Central China.

No.

92. From: Lin Lan: Hsiang-se-shu, pp. 96-100. Provenience: Fukien.

93. From: Ch'ing-shui: T'ai-yang ho yüeh-liang, pp. 15-16. Provenience: Kuangtung, Weng-yüan.

94. From: Lin Lan: Kuai-hsiung-ti, pp. 7-8. Provenience: Kiangsu, Sung-chiang.

95. From: Lin Lan: Hsiang-se-shu, pp. 83-84. Provenience: Kuangtung.

96. From: Ch'ing-shui: T'ai-yang ho yüeh-liang, p. 28. Provenience: Kuangtung, Weng-yüan.

97. From: Lin Lan: Hsiang-se-shu, pp. 77-78. Provenience: Ssech'uan, Sui-ning.

98. From: Ch'ing-shui: T'ai-yang ho yüeh-liang, pp. 24-25. Provenience: Kuangtung, Weng-yüan.

99. From: id., pp. 26-27. Provenience: Kuangtung, Weng-yüan.

100. From: Lin Lan: Hsiang-se-shu, pp. 18-20. Provenience: uncertain.

101. From: Min-chien, vol. i. No. 12, pp. 71-73. Provenience: Chêkiang, Shao-hsing.

102. From: Lin Lan: Hsiang-se-shu, pp. 3-5. Provenience: uncertain.

103. From: Min-chien, vol. i. No. 12, pp. 70-71. Provenience: Kiangsu, Sung-chiang.

104. From: Min-chien, vol. ii. No. 9, pp. 206-207. Provenience: Chêkiang, Hang-chou.

105. From: Min-su, No. 13/14, pp. 35-37. Provenience: Kangtung, Lien-ch'eng.

106. From: Liu Tsung-yüan hsien-sheng-chi. Provenience: uncertain. From the eighth century.

107. From: Wu Ts'ao-ting: Ch'üan-chou min-chien chuan-shuo, vol. i. pp. 84-89. Provenience: Fukien, Ch'üan-chou.

108. From: Lou Tse-k'uang: Ch'iao-nü ho kai-niang, pp. 88-89. Provenience: Chêkiang, P'ing-hu.

109. From: Lin Lan: Hsin-tse-hsü, pp. 125-126. Provenience: uncertain.

110. From: Ch'iu Yü-lin: I-jen yü chiao-jen ku-shih, vol. i. pp. 97-99. Provenience: Kuangtung, Ch'ao-chou.

111. From: Lin Lan: Ch'iung Hsiu-t'ai, pp. 130-132. Provenience: Kuangtung, Weng-yüan.

112. From: told in Hopei, Peiping, to me.

113. From: Ch'ing-shui: Hai-lung-wang-ti nü-erh, pp. 113-114. Provenience: Kuangtung, Weng-yüan.

114. From: Ch'iu Yü-lin: I-jen yü chiao-jen ku-shih, vol. i. p. 51. Provenience: Kuangtung, Ch'ao-chou.

115. From: id., vol. i. pp. 104-105. Provenience: Kuangtung, Ch'ao-chou.

116. From: Lin Lan: Hsü Wen-ch'ang ku-shih, pp. 1-2. Provenience: Chêkiang, Shao-hsing.

No.

117. From: id., pp. 17-18. Provenience: Chêkiang?
118. From: id., p. 73. Provenience: Chêkiang?
119. From: id., pp. 20-21. Provenience: Chêkiang?
120. From: id., p. 77. Provenience: Chêkiang.
121. From: id., pp. 143-145. Provenience: Honan, K'ai-feng.
122. From: id., pp. 156-157. Provenience: Chêkiang.
123. From: Lu Chia-mu: Ma Tan-pi-ti ku-shih, pp. 7-10. Provenience: Chêkiang, Tung-yang.
124. From: Lin Lan: Min-chien ch'ü-shih hsin-chi, vol. iii. pp. 49-50. Provenience: uncertain.
125. From: Min-su, No. 75, pp. 34-35. Provenience: Kuangtung, Weng-yüan.
126. From: Lin Lan: San-erh-hsi, pp. 11-13. Provenience: Central China.
127. From: id., pp. 131-133. Provenience: Central China.
128. From: Lin Lan: Min-chien ch'ü-shih hsin-chi, vol. ii. pp. 170-172. Provenience: Central China.
129. From: Ch'iu Yü-lin: I-jen yü chiao-jen ku-shih, vol. i. pp. 57-58. Provenience: Kuangtung, Ch'ao-chou.
130. From: Lin Lan: San-erh-hsi, pp. 22-26. Provenience: Central China?
131. From: Ch'iu Yü-lin: I-jen yü chiao-jen ku-shih, vol. i. p. 48. Provenience: Kuangtung, Ch'ao-chou.
132. From: Lin Lan: Chu Yüan-chang-ti ku-shih, pp. 57-58 and 59-60. Provenience: uncertain.
133. From: id., pp. 4-5. Provenience: uncertain.
134. From: Lin Lan: Wen-jen-ti ku-shih, pp. 19-20. Provenience: uncertain.
135. From: Lin Lan: Ch'iung Hsiu-ts'ai, pp. 151-154. Provenience: Central China.
136. From: Min-su, No. 37, pp. 24-25. Provenience: Kuangtung, Lu-an.
137. From: Min-chien, vol. i. No. 8, pp. 76-79. Provenience: Chêkiang, Shao-hsing.

Note.—For careful scientific examination of these and 3000 other Chinese modern folk tales, see my 'Typen chinesischer Volksmärchen' (Types of Chinese Folk Tales) in: *Folklore Fellow Communications*, Helsinki, 1937.

Printed in the USA
CPSIA information can be obtained
at www.ICGtesting.com
LVHW010852120224
771452LV00038B/656